The Time-Life Gardener's Guide

PERENNIALS

A

BOOK

TIME® **LIFE BOOKS**

Other Publications:

MYSTERIES OF THE UNKNOWN
TIME FRAME
FIX IT YOURSELF
FITNESS, HEALTH & NUTRITION
SUCCESSFUL PARENTING
HEALTHY HOME COOKING
UNDERSTANDING COMPUTERS
LIBRARY OF NATIONS
THE ENCHANTED WORLD
THE KODAK LIBRARY OF CREATIVE PHOTOGRAPHY
GREAT MEALS IN MINUTES
THE CIVIL WAR
PLANET EARTH
COLLECTOR'S LIBRARY OF THE CIVIL WAR
THE EPIC OF FLIGHT
THE GOOD COOK
WORLD WAR II
HOME REPAIR AND IMPROVEMENT
THE OLD WEST

For information on and a full description of any of
the Time-Life Books series listed above, please call 1-800-621-7026
or write:

Reader Information
Time-Life Customer Service
P.O. Box C-32068
Richmond, Virginia 23261-2068

This book is one of a series of guides to good gardening.

The Time-Life Gardener's Guide

PERENNIALS

TIME-LIFE BOOKS, ALEXANDRIA, VIRGINIA

CONTENTS

1
GARDENING UNLIMITED

2
THE GENTLE ART OF NURTURING

3
PROPAGATING YOUR OWN PLANTS

Perennials are the mainstays of gardens everywhere, and among the most rewarding of plants to grow. They bloom in various seasons—some of them in all seasons provided the climate is warm enough—and they live practically forever. They are enormously varied; they come in all the colors known to horticulturists, and in all sizes and shapes—tall and spiky, short and sprawling, middle-sized and rounded. They are adaptable enough for the amateur to plant and care for, and diverse enough for the hobbyist and the expert to experiment with.

This volume tells how to grow them. The first three chapters explain how to plan and plant a garden with perennials, how to maintain them and how to propagate them. Following is a chapter that defines the zones where perennials flourish, with tips on maintenance and troubleshooting. Finally, there is a dictionary that describes more than 180 perennials and the conditions in which they grow best.

MAKING THE MOST OF NATURE

DICTIONARY OF PERENNIALS

1
GARDENING UNLIMITED

Perennials are arguably the most rewarding sorts of plants a gardener can cultivate. They are long-lived, reappearing uncoaxed year after year; some hardy peony roots have been known to retain their vigor for more than a century. They are wonderfully varied in their foliage, and the flowers offer a broad palette of colors from declarative primaries to subtle pastels. And perennials are marvelously versatile. Many will thrive in the hottest, sunniest spot in your garden; others do well brightening a cool, shady corner. A number are downright theatrical, with broad, saucer-sized blooms. Some produce delicate mists of pink and lavender and light yellow. A majority are highly complementary; combined in a garden plot they show each other off and take turns sending out waves of color through a growing season that lasts from early spring to late fall.

In the following section of this volume, you will find a wide variety of ways that perennials can lend color and beauty to virtually every part of the landscape around your house. You might start with a single showy bloomer, to highlight a doorway, adorn a mailbox or provide a splash of brightness under a tree. For other limited spaces, you can use small groups of perennials in pots or planters. For somewhat larger areas and for damp ones that need help with drainage, you can create compact rock gardens with perennials. And some perennials, you will discover, produce such splendid foliage that, set out in masses, they create the illusion of a billowing green sea. You will even find that a special breed of perennials, the ornamental grasses, allows you to have a garden that endures and attracts the eye all winter. Most important, the following pages show in detail how you can make plans and select plants for the three classic perennial beds that, first created by the flower-loving English, have become standard in America and elsewhere: formal borders, dramatic island beds and intimate cottage gardens. No garden you might plant could be more graceful than these—nor, given the virtually unlimited material offered by the hundreds of species of perennials, will any afford a greater measure of creative excitement.

DEPENDABLE DAYLILIES FOR ANY SPOT IN THE YARD

A broad band of 'Mary Todd' daylilies brightens the base of a white picket fence. Each bloom lasts only a day—hence the name—but fresh new flowers appear day after day for three weeks or more. The daylily is one of the quickest plants to take hold in a garden.

A gardener starting modestly with a simple accent to brighten a yard might well choose a daylily. This hardy plant flourishes in sun or shade, in light or heavy soil, in dry or boggy conditions and in a wide range of climates. Dozens of species are commercially available, and many of them blithely survive the long, cold winters of Maine and Minnesota; others shrug off the heat of Florida's summers. Daylilies are more resistant to pests and diseases than most other garden plants. They are easy to plant *(opposite),* and after they are established, they need little care—not even watering, unless a persistent drought sets in.

Almost without fail, daylilies flower lavishly; a single stalk produces a dozen or more blooms in the course of a season. And there are varieties that bloom in different seasons, so you can use them for color at almost any time; spring-flowering daylilies will give way to ones that blossom in the summer, and these will be succeeded in turn by ones that bloom in the fall. The flowers come in a broad range of colors, including subtle shades of red, yellow, orange, peach, pink and lavender. But even when it is not in bloom, the plant is attractive because its foliage remains a rich green until the advent of winter.

Being so hardy and versatile, daylilies can be used in any part of a garden—as a band of color in front of a line of shrubs or trees, as a border alongside a brick terrace or as a highlight for a small area such as a turning in a walkway or the base of a lamppost. You can start with a single plant.

1 To prepare the ground for planting a clump of daylilies, shave off turf with a flat-bladed spade. Next, dig a hole deep enough and wide enough to accommodate the plant's root ball; shovel the soil into a bucket and reserve. Using a trowel, enrich the reserved soil by mixing in 1 part composted cow manure to 3 parts of soil. Pour some of this mixture from the bucket into the bottom of the hole.

2 With one hand, hold the plant steady near the base of the stalks; with the other, secure the root ball (so the weight of the soil won't tear the roots from the stem). Set the clump of daylilies in the hole. Make sure the plant sits at the same depth in the ground as it did at the nursery; the stem will be paler below the soil line. If it sits too high, take it out and deepen the hole; if too low, raise the level beneath the plant by adding amended soil from the bucket. Use the trowel to fill the hole around the root ball with reserved amended soil.

3 Once the root ball is firmly in place, tramp down lightly around the plant to firm up the soil and ensure that there are no large air pockets around the roots; they need to be fully in contact with the soil to draw nutrients from it. Irrigate the plant thoroughly but gently with a watering can. □

BRIGHT ACCENTS
IN SHADY LOCATIONS

Pale pink astilbes, with feathery, delicate blossoms and handsome foliage, provide a textural accent in a shady area at the edge of a lawn. When the blooms are gone, the brown seed heads of the spikes can be picked for dried arrangements.

P erennials are surprisingly adaptable. Although most of them thrive in full sun, some flourish in shade *(see box below).* With their combination of colorful flowers and lush foliage, they make wonderful accents in a garden that has light to medium shade.

Light shade lasts for two or three hours between 10 a.m. and 6 p.m. in the summer; medium shade lasts for four or five hours. The shade need not be constant. If you have tall deciduous trees that cast lacy patterns of shadow on and off throughout the course of the day, or a slatted fence or a hedge that filters the afternoon sun, you have light to medium shade.

Walls provide shade, too—but some walls are better at doing so than others. A wall that faces east is preferable to one that faces west; in facing east it allows the plants sun in the morning and shades them in the afternoon, when the sun is hottest. A wall that faces west will cancel out the benefits of the shade it gives in the morning; not only does it leave the plants exposed to afternoon sun but redoubles the heat by absorbing the rays of the sun and reflecting them back upon the plants.

Shade-loving plants not only require respite from the heat of the sun, they also have certain other requirements. They need rich soil with plenty of humus. Most of them need fertilizing in spring, when their buds are forming, and once or twice again in summer, as the plants continue growing. And all of them need plenty of moisture. Water them well and often, and mulch them to help the soil remain moist.

SOME PERENNIALS FOR SHADE

Astilbe	Goatsbeard
Barrenwort	Hosta
Bergenia	Houttuynia
Bethlehem sage	Lenten rose
Bleeding heart	Primrose
Coralbells	Saxifrage
Columbine	Siberian bugloss
Gentian	Solomon's-seal

1 To plant perennials in a shady spot, set them in position first—still in their pots. Consult the Dictionary of Perennials *(pages 90-148)* for proper spacing. With a trowel, dig a hole for each plant, making the hole slightly larger than the pot. Amend the soil by combining 3 parts soil with 1 part humus, compost or other enrichment, and partially refill the hole.

2 Turn the pot upside down, stabilizing the plant between your index and middle fingers. Knock on the bottom of the pot to loosen the plant, and lift off the pot. Check the root ball. If you find encircling roots, loosen them with your fingers if you can; if they are tightly bound, cut them apart with a knife *(page 41)*.

3 Turn the plant right side up and set it in its hole, placing it at the same depth as it was in its pot. Using your hands, press the soil down firmly around the base of the plant. When you have finished, water all of your plants thoroughly. □

TURNING THE SOIL
FOR LONG-LIVED PLANTS

*Tall purple delphiniums lend a special elegance
to the luxuriant and colorful perennial border
above. To grow well and blossom profusely,
delphiniums require a meticulously prepared bed
with nutrient-rich loamy soil that drains well
without becoming either too wet or too dry.*

Because perennials by definition grow year after year and their roots remain in the ground for many seasons, they must be started in soil that has good consistency and a proper chemical balance. One way to ensure rich, deep soil in a new bed is a procedure called double digging *(below and opposite)*.

The dug-up soil should be examined for quality and consistency—and amended, if necessary. The ideal soil is a medium-textured blend of clay, sand and silt called loam, which holds both moisture and the nutrients plants feed on. When you pick up loam in your hands, it forms large clods, but they break easily into smaller chunks.

Less desirable is sandy soil, which is so loose it retains neither moisture nor nutrients. Such soil can, however, be improved by adding humus—partly decomposed organic matter such as fallen leaves—which helps bind the sand particles together. At the other extreme is clay—soil that becomes a sticky mass when wet and stony-hard when dry. But clay can be broken up and made usable with additions of humus or compost, with straw, sand and peat moss.

After you have determined the kind of soil you have, the next task is to measure its pH level—that is, its acid-alkaline balance. Gather soil samples from all corners of the bed and from the center, and combine them in a clean container. You can analyze the mixture yourself with a pH test kit or send it to an agricultural extension service for analysis. Slightly acid soil—pH 6.5 on a scale of 0 to 14—is best for most perennials. If the soil is too acid (say pH 4.5), mix in ground limestone. If it is too alkaline, add acid organic matter—compost or cow manure, or small amounts of sulfur mixed with peat moss.

It is best to double-dig a perennial bed in the fall, so that winter snow and rain can help break down the chemical and organic substances you have added, making the soil ideal for spring planting.

DOUBLE DIGGING

Double digging entails making a series of narrow trenches and refilling one with soil from another. A layer of topsoil is removed from the first trench *(far right)*, amended and set aside. The subsoil in that trench is then broken up and amended. Topsoil from the second trench *(center)* is transferred to the first trench and amended. Digging, transferring and amending continue in this fashion until finally the topsoil set aside from the first trench is used to fill the last trench *(large arrow)*. The operation may have any number of trenches, but in each step the subsoil stays in its own trench and the topsoil moves to another.

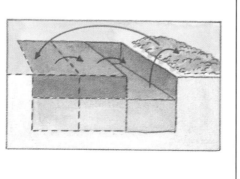

1 To begin making a new perennial bed, first remove any sod with a flat-bladed spade. Dig out a spade's depth of soil to make a trench about 2 feet wide and as long as you want the new bed to be. Put the removed earth in a wheelbarrow or on a tarpaulin, removing weeds, roots and large stones as you work. Into the earth in the wheelbarrow mix the compost, peat moss, lime or other amendments that soil tests indicate.

2 With a garden fork, turn over the subsoil in the bottom of the trench to the depth of the fork; break up all clods thoroughly. Work the same organic matter and chemicals into this layer of soil as you did into the first layer you removed.

3 Remove a spade's depth of topsoil from your second trench and transfer it to the first trench. Again, amend the soil with the necessary organic and chemical additives. Then turn over and break up the subsoil in the second trench and in successive trenches, as described above.

4 Continue digging up, transferring and amending soil from one trench to another. When the entire bed has been turned over, break up any remaining clods and rake the surface smooth. □

13

THE PERENNIAL BORDER—
MAINSTAY OF THE GARDEN

Outlining a broad strip of sunlit lawn, two perennial borders form a fluid design by mixing and matching heights and textures as well as colors —among them mounds of purple verbena, carpets of pinks and spires of white salvia.

The most eye-catching area of any garden may well be the perennial border—the flowering plants that run in a broad swath along a fence, a wall, a pathway, the edge of the lawn, the property line; in fact, the line demarcating any boundary.

The following pages show how to plan and lay out a perennial border. The plan shown on pages 16-17 uses a combination of flowers that will bloom at the height of summer and make a spectacular display of colors: yellows, purples, blues and a few splashes of white and orange for accent. With only graph and tracing papers, colored pencils, a ruler and the Dictionary of Perennials *(pages 90-148)* for tools, you can follow the same technique to fashion a border of any combination of colors and textures. If you want bold colors, for instance, you can plant coreopsis for yellow, bellflower for blue, bee balm for red, phlox for an assertive pink, candytuft for standout white. If pastels are more to your liking you can use foxglove for yellow, astilbe for peach, lamb's-ears for silvery foliage.

Choose an area that has good drainage, light and space. An unshaded southern or southeastern exposure is ideal because most perennials like lots of sun. A site measuring 4 feet by 12 feet is appropriate; that is enough space to allow you to mass plants for effective displays of color, but not so large as to be unmanageable.

1 Measure the dimensions of your perennial border with a yardstick or a measuring tape. If the bed is to be placed against a wood fence, a thick hedge or, as here, a low stone wall, allow room for a 1-foot gap between the rear of the border and the backdrop to ensure air circulation for the plants and room for you to go in for weeding and other maintenance chores.

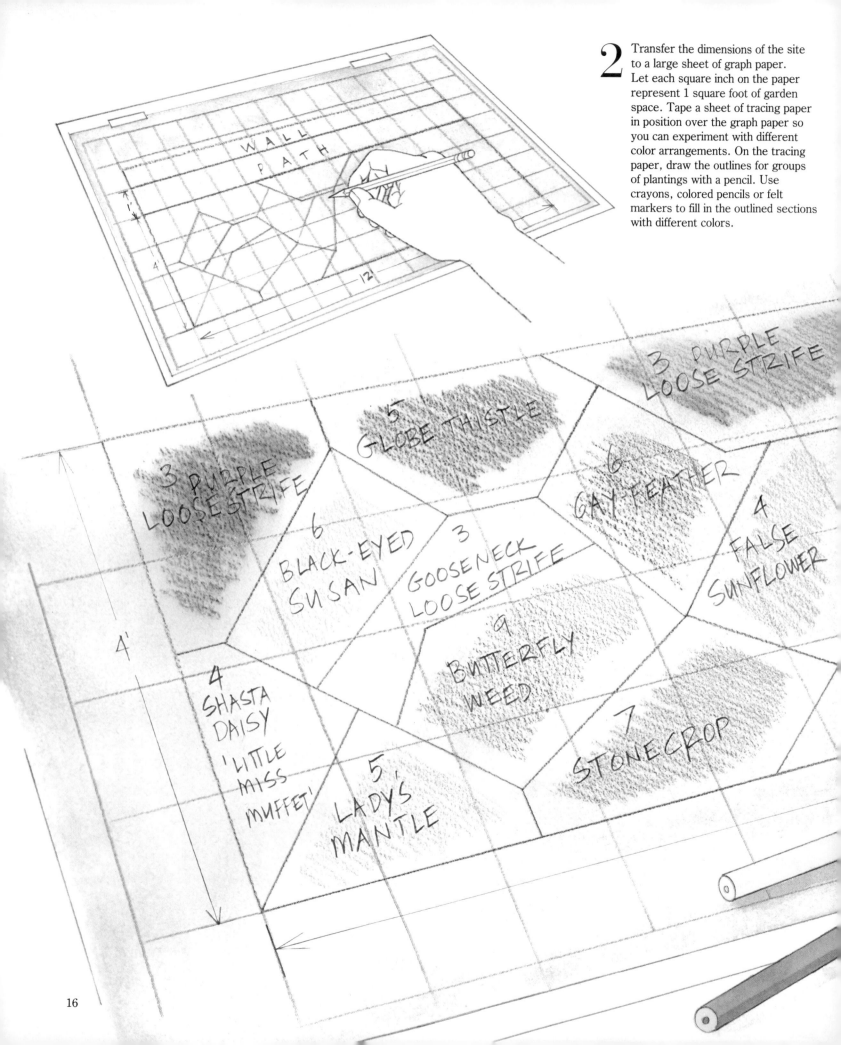

2 Transfer the dimensions of the site to a large sheet of graph paper. Let each square inch on the paper represent 1 square foot of garden space. Tape a sheet of tracing paper in position over the graph paper so you can experiment with different color arrangements. On the tracing paper, draw the outlines for groups of plantings with a pencil. Use crayons, colored pencils or felt markers to fill in the outlined sections with different colors.

WALL
PATH

3 PURPLE LOOSE STRIFE

5 GLOBE THISTLE

3 PURPLE LOOSE STRIFE

6 GAY FEATHER

6 BLACK-EYED SUSAN

3 GOOSENECK LOOSE STRIFE

4 FALSE SUNFLOWER

9 BUTTERFLY WEED

4 SHASTA DAISY 'LITTLE MISS MUFFET'

5 LADY'S MANTLE

7 STONECROP

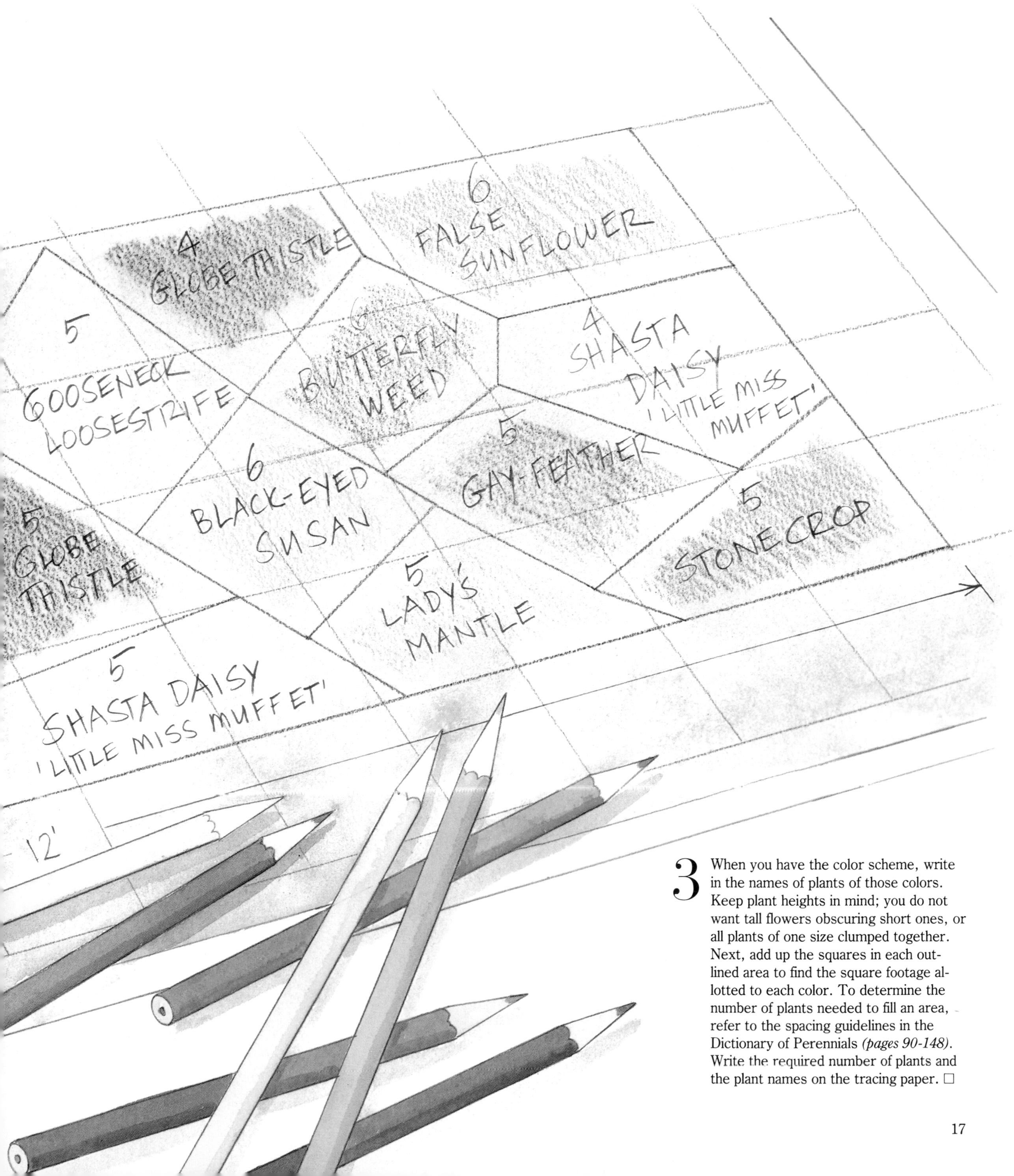

6 FALSE SUNFLOWER

4 GLOBE THISTLE

5 GOOSENECK LOOSESTRIFE

6 BUTTERFLY WEED

4 SHASTA DAISY 'LITTLE MISS MUFFET'

6 BLACK-EYED SUSAN

5 GAY-FEATHER

5 GLOBE THISTLE

5 STONECROP

5 LADY'S MANTLE

5 SHASTA DAISY 'LITTLE MISS MUFFET'

12'

3 When you have the color scheme, write in the names of plants of those colors. Keep plant heights in mind; you do not want tall flowers obscuring short ones, or all plants of one size clumped together. Next, add up the squares in each outlined area to find the square footage allotted to each color. To determine the number of plants needed to fill an area, refer to the spacing guidelines in the Dictionary of Perennials *(pages 90-148)*. Write the required number of plants and the plant names on the tracing paper. □

17

TRANSFERRING A PLAN
FROM PAPER TO GARDEN

Once the graph-paper design for a border of perennials has been completed *(pages 14-17),* it needs to be duplicated in the actual garden plot—and tested to make certain that it will in fact work out. The first step is to mark the border-to-be with lines corresponding to the divisions drawn on the plan, as shown in the drawing at upper right. The second step is to assemble the plants that have been bought or collected and set them out in their allotted spaces *(bottom, opposite page).* During the second step, the eye may catch problems not evident on the paper plan.

For example, are there too few of some species in evidence? Perennials look best when planted in groups of three, five, six and even more. Four plants grouped together tend to form a square and look boxy. Fewer than three and the group will not be large enough to notice.

Another problem may be overcrowding. On an average, each perennial needs a square foot of garden space to get its share of light, air and nutrients, and there should be a few inches of extra room between plant groups because some groups will grow larger than their neighbors. This is also the time to decide about the border's overall plant density. Putting in a maximum number of plants will make a border look lush the first season —but will necessitate thinning in two or three years, when the grown plants begin to crowd each other. Less dense planting may give a thin look at first, but healthy perennials will fill the gaps in a couple of seasons.

The best time to plant a perennial border in most regions is April or May, before the weather becomes punishingly warm. Early-spring planting also gives perennials time to put down roots before blooming season. A border can also be set out in the autumn, however, as long as it is done early enough for the plants to establish themselves before the onset of winter.

Yellow yarrow and purple loosestrife, planted in clusters large enough to make the most of their colorful blooms, emerge from a bank of lavender cupid's-dart in a casual-seeming but carefully planned perennial border.

1 Before starting to transfer your design from graph paper *(pages 16-17)* to garden plot, write the names of the plants you intend to use with indelible ink on small white plant stakes. Over the already prepared ground, use extra stakes and lengths of string to lay a simple grid that corresponds to heavy lines on the plan. Then, with the strings as guidelines, sketch in the various planting areas with sprinkled handfuls of bone meal or sand as shown above. Insert the marked stakes in the appropriate areas, indicating where the plant groups belong.

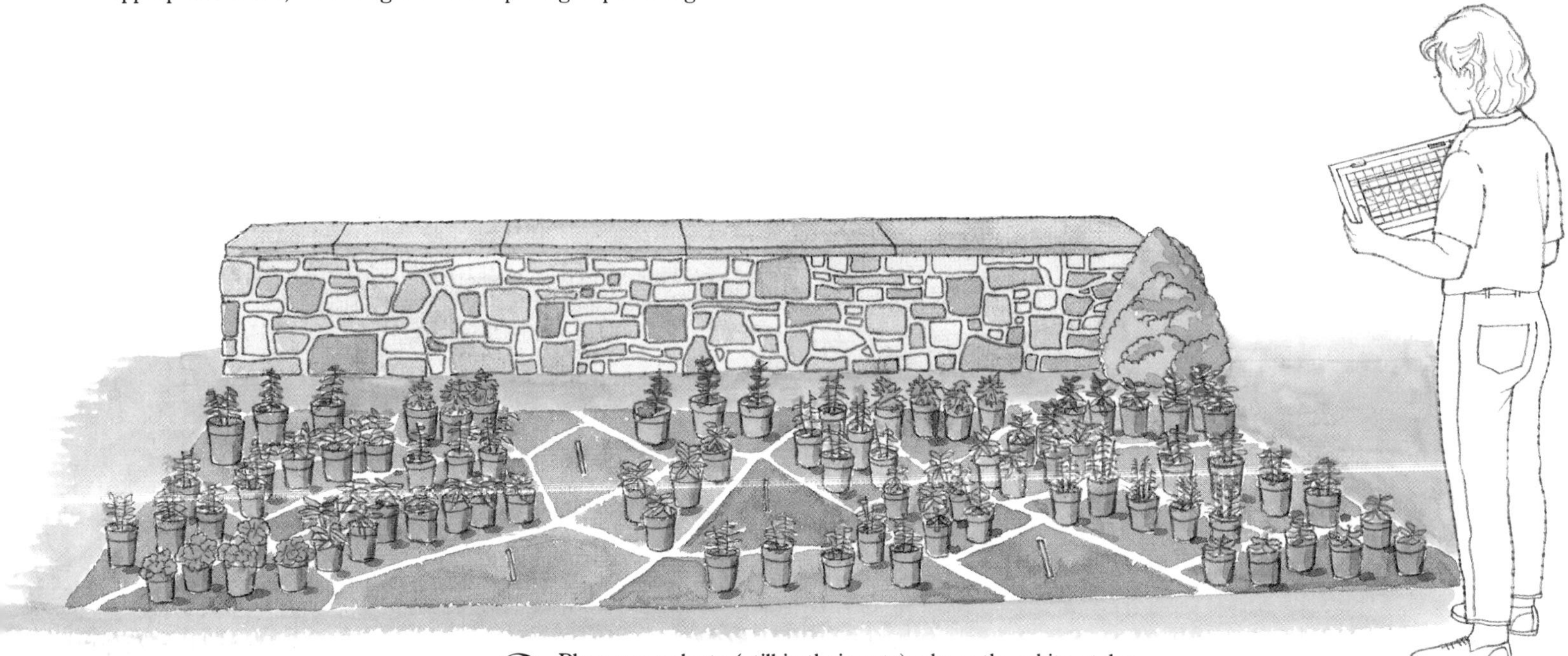

2 Place your plants (still in their pots) where the white stakes indicate; then stand back and study the design before doing any planting. Any overcrowded areas should quickly become evident, as should places where there are too few plants of any given sort. You should also check to be sure that the various species are located where you will want them to remain. Later transplanting should be avoided if possible. No perennial is improved by being moved, and some, such as peonies and gas plants, suffer if they are disturbed. □

AN ISLAND BED FOR SHOWING OFF PERENNIALS

Few spots in a garden make a more spectacular showplace for bright-blooming perennials than an island bed—that is, a garden standing alone on a broad swath of lawn—which can be viewed and appreciated from different vantage points.

An island bed can be oval or rectangular, or it can flow in curves that follow the contours of the land. It can be small or large. But within the bed, the plants must be carefully chosen and placed for height. As a rule of thumb, the tallest plants should grow about half as tall as the plot is wide—4 feet tall, for example, in an island bed that is 8 feet across. In general, tall plants should go in the center, shorter ones at the outer edges—but not so rigidly as to produce a conical effect. The rippling contours of tall and short plants interspersed will provide interest.

Among the most dramatic of plants for an island bed are peonies, which produce magnificent flowers in a broad range of colors and grow tall enough to show to advantage. The best time to plant them is in the fall, after the roots have been divided *(page 62)*. Like most perennials, they require well-prepared soil and plenty of light. But peonies make some special demands *(opposite)*. Each plant has one or more "eyes," sometimes called growth buds, the pinkish protrusions that grow on the crown. For the plant to bloom, the eyes need below-freezing temperatures for at least six weeks. They should be planted from just below the surface (in the south) to 2 inches below the surface (in the north); the soil insulates the roots, and in a warm climate, too thick a layer of soil will prevent the necessary chilling.

The fuchsia-colored blooms and rounded shape of a peony plant make it stand out in an island bed of white and yellow iris, cream-colored lupines and yellow-centered white asters.

A GUIDE TO PLANT HEIGHTS

Fifteen perennials that would make a handsome island garden are shown and named below, with taller and shorter species interspersed so they provide hills and valleys in the flower bed.

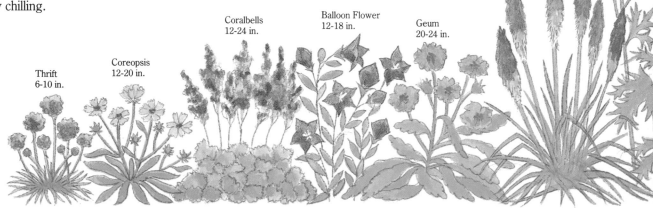

Thrift
6-10 in.

Coreopsis
12-20 in.

Coralbells
12-24 in.

Balloon Flower
12-18 in.

Geum
20-24 in.

Red-hot Poker
2-4 ft.

Delphinium
4-6 ft.

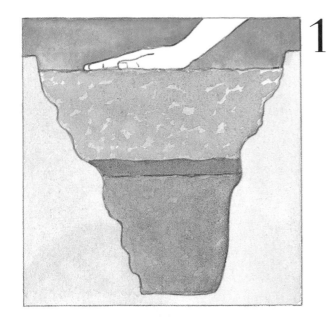

1 To plant a peony, first dig a hole 18 to 20 inches deep and 20 inches wide. Fill the hole to within 8 inches of the top with a mixture of composted cow manure and garden soil. Add a 1-inch layer of plain soil (to separate the peony roots from direct contact with the manure, which would burn them) and then a 6-inch layer of soil mixed with about four trowelfuls of bone meal. Firm with your hand. Allow 3 feet between holes; peonies grow large and need room.

2 Place the peony root on the top soil layer so that the eyes, or buds *(inset),* are below the surface of the ground—immediately below the surface if you live in the south, where winters are mild; up to 2 inches if you live in the north. Add or remove soil to get the depth correct. Spread the roots evenly over the soil. Fill the hole with more soil, tamp it down and water it. □

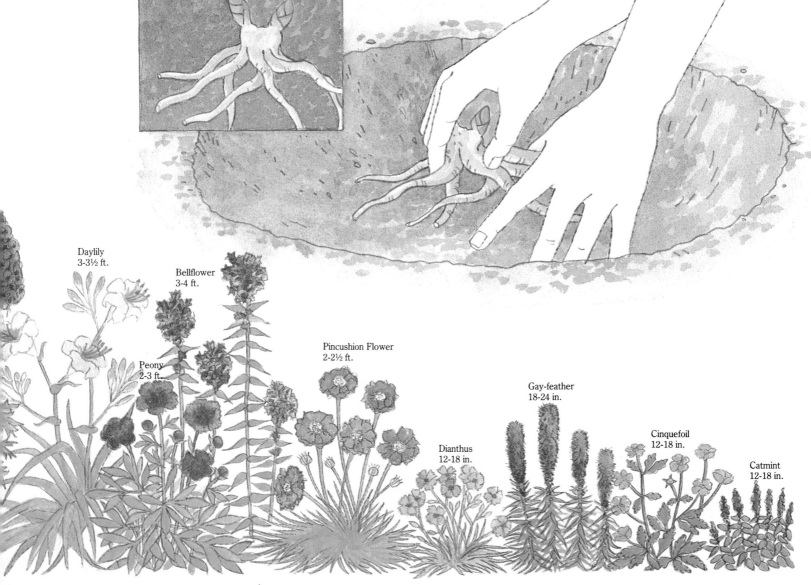

Daylily
3-3½ ft.

Bellflower
3-4 ft.

Peony
2-3 ft.

Pincushion Flower
2-2½ ft.

Dianthus
12-18 in.

Gay-feather
18-24 in.

Cinquefoil
12-18 in.

Catmint
12-18 in.

MAINTAINING A COTTAGE GARDEN: THREE CLASSIC TECHNIQUES

Against the base of a stone wall, a combination of phlox, bee balm, sunflower, false sunflower, bellflower, globe thistle and countless other perennials blooms in profusion and seeming spontaneity.

The English were the first to make an art of growing what they call cottage gardens—banks of perennials massed together in a profusion of seemingly random varieties. The name is wonderfully appropriate. Like cozy British village houses, cottage gardens are informal, rambling, homey and full of delightful half-hidden crannies. They are the opposite of grand—and thus suit perfectly any modest country house, vacation home or suburban backyard.

Planting and nurturing a cottage garden of course takes more planning and care than the casual-looking result suggests. Tall perennials should be planted so that they do not obscure lower-growing ones; give the same thought to laying out a cottage garden that you would to a perennial border *(page 14)*. The plants should be chosen with an eye to colors that show each other off to best advantage; two strong-hued bloomers put next to each other may clash. And to make sure the garden remains colorful through the growing season, select perennials that bloom at different times. By mixing plants that flower early and late, you can have a cottage garden ablaze with color from early spring until the first frost. Consult the Dictionary of Perennials *(pages 90-148)* for plant colors and flowering times.

Once the garden is planted, you can dramatically increase the number and size of your flowers by employing techniques known as deadheading, pinching and disbudding *(opposite and following pages)*. Paradoxically, all involve pruning; cutting back most plants forces them to put fresh energy into producing more blooms or bigger ones. That is because the goal of any plant is to produce seed. The flower is merely a carrier for the seeds. Once the plant has bloomed, its yearly cycle is completed. But if you prevent some of the flowers from going to seed by judicious pinching or snipping, most plants will try again—and will help make your cottage garden more richly colorful through more of the growing season.

DEADHEADING FADED BLOOMS

Removing flowers that are past their prime spurs some plants to flower again. Snip well down the stem, taking off the entire flower head. This technique, called deadheading, works well for delphiniums, asters, balloon flowers, lupines and columbines. Some perennials bloom only once no matter what you do; even so, deadheading is useful—it makes the garden neater and channels the plants' energy into developing their root systems.

PINCHING STEM TIPS

Another way to encourage some perennials to produce more flowers is to remove emergent stem tips just above the top leaves. They can be pinched off with the fingers. Pinching forces the plants to send out three or four stems where only one existed before, and each new growth will generate blooms. The stems will be shorter, which will make the plants bushier. The flowers will be smaller, but there will be more of them. Pinching off works well with plants that can develop numerous stems and buds, and look attractive when bushy. Chrysanthemums can be pinched two or three times, up until the flower buds develop in July.

NIPPING PERENNIALS IN THE BUD

On spider and football chrysanthemums, peonies, delphiniums and some other perennials, buds generally grow in groups, a large central bud surrounded by side buds. If you want a few large, showy flowers—rather than more numerous blooms—you can employ a process called disbudding. Cut the side buds as shown here, letting the plant throw all its energy into growing a masterpiece. Gardeners growing specimen plants for flower shows often use this technique, but it can also be useful in a cottage garden—especially in a secluded corner where a bright show of oversized blooms will catch the eye better than crowds of smaller flowers. □

DECORATIVE GREENERY UNDER A SHADY TREE

Areas under trees need not be bare and cheerless. Some perennials, those that have thick water-storing roots, thrive in partial shade and can convert such areas into rich banks of dappled greenery. Not all shade-tolerant perennials produce large, splashy blooms; some have flowers that are rather small and delicate. What shade-tolerant perennials offer in abundance is luxuriant and varied foliage. A few have leaves almost as large and shiny as dinner plates; others grow lacy, fernlike fronds. Colors range from subtle silvery greens to mossy velvets to deep, woodsy hues. Some sport stripes and spots; a number put on rich autumnal golds in the fall.

Before setting out any shade plants, it is best to determine whether the intended area is suitable. The overhanging tree should not be a maple or any other sort that sends out dense networks of small roots, which make planting difficult and soak up most of the available moisture and nutrients. Deep-tap-rooted trees such as oak, hickory, tulip poplar and ash can be planted under, but avoid black walnut—its leaves and nuts contain toxins. Also, the shade should not be too deep. Even vigorous shade growers such as heart-leaved bergenia, Bethlehem sage, Lenten roses and hostas need some sun in the morning and again in late afternoon. If necessary, trim some lower branches to let in more light *(box, opposite)*. Once you have put the plants in the ground, make sure that they get extra water and some general-purpose fertilizer to compensate for the food and moisture leached away by the tree.

Red epimedium, yellow globeflower and leafy hosta adorn the gnarled roots of a mature beech tree.

1 Before planting perennials near the base of a tree, plunge a spade into the soil in two or three places. If probing reveals workable soil between large roots, you can put in some plants. If the spade is stopped by dense meshes of small roots, the ground is unsuitable for perennials.

REMOVING A TREE LIMB NEATLY

To avoid tearing bark, make a first cut on the underside of a limb about 12 inches from the trunk, then a second cut above it, an inch or two farther out; the limb will then break off of its own weight. Cut the remaining stub off close to the trunk.

2 Begin planting by locating a space between large roots. Dig a hole with a sturdy trowel or a small spade. You may need to cut through a few stray smaller roots. Line the hole with 2 inches of light, mildly acid soil containing a good deal of humus. Remove the perennial from its pot and place it in the hole. Fill the hole with more of the soil mixture, firm the soil with your hands and water the plant well. □

THE SCREE GARDEN— A BED OF STONES FOR EASY DRAINAGE

Many choice perennials will not flourish in an area where the soil is perpetually damp. But there is an easy way to reclaim an ill-drained plot—a scree garden, so called because its layers of stone chips resemble a real scree, one of those collections of loose broken rocks deposited by erosion at the foot of mountain slopes.

A scree garden is a small, man-made rock garden specially constructed to drain efficiently. It can have much of the variety and beauty of a full-fledged rock garden, and offer the same welcome contrast to regular beds and borders. And with its many drainage layers, it will form an excellent habitat not only for the more or less standard perennials that like a semidry environment, but also for more exotic ones: rock-clinging Alpines in cooler regions, interesting desert-adapted plants with thick water-retentive leaves in warmer zones. A list of scree-loving plants appears in the box on the opposite page.

A scree garden will look its best if it simulates nature, sloping like a real scree and seeming to emerge from a rock outcrop. If your yard has some large rocks in place, situate the scree garden around them. Locating the garden where it will get some shade is also a good idea; a stony scree can get hot. It is also important when planting a scree garden to choose species that are compatible with the predominant stone being used in the underlayers and on the surface. Lime-loving plants grow best around limestone; perennials favoring acid soils do better with acid sandstone. For a neutral environment, neither acid nor alkaline, try granite. If you live in the Northwest, where the climate is moist, you might need to add more stone chips and sand; in the Southwest, where it is arid, you might need to add more peat moss.

Appearing to flow naturally from a stone outcropping, a scree garden blooms with shrubs and perennials that need well-drained soil, which the scree garden provides.

1 To make a scree garden, dig out your area to a depth of 2 feet. Shovel in a drainage layer of large chips and coarse gravel 6 inches deep. Add a 1-inch layer of straw. Fill the excavation to within 1 inch of the top with mixed stone and soil. The mixture should include loam, compost or leaf mold, peat moss, stone chips, sand and some slow-release fertilizer in proportions that depend on climate. After letting the main stone-loam layer settle for a week to 10 days, spread on a 1-inch covering layer of stone chips (diagram).

2 Make holes with a trowel in the top stone layer for the plants you have chosen, such as the sedums shown below. Water them well for several days. □

PLANTS FOR A SCREE GARDEN

Alchemilla	Pussy-toes
Basket-of-gold	Rock Soapwort
Candytuft	Sea Pink
Crested Iris	Sedum
Ground Pink	Wormwood
Missouri Primrose	Yarrow

A MINIATURE GARDEN
WITH POTTED PERENNIALS

*Tall purple salvia, arching yellow coreopsis
and low-growing artemisia make a sculptural
display in a rounded terra-cotta pot.*

Perennials thrive in containers of all sorts and sizes—old stone sinks, wooden barrels, antique kettles, land-locked rowboats and, as shown here, terra-cotta pots. The container itself may add color to a terrace or any other paved area. A pair of planters, one on each side, can frame a doorway handsomely. Perennials in pots or tubs fit in the odd corners of a garden, providing accents and expanding the growing space. And by mixing the proper amendments with the earth, you can turn a planter into a special environment suitable for growing species that could not survive in regular garden soil.

Different materials have different virtues and drawbacks. Terra-cotta, being made of earth, blends naturally with any garden setting. The only disadvantages are that unglazed pots are porous and lose moisture rapidly, so you may have to water the plants in them very frequently, and the pots are susceptible to cracking in the winter. Wooden planters provide good insulation and are durable if you treat the wood with a sealant to discourage boring insects. Do not use creosote, however; its fumes will harm plants. Metal containers also work well, as long as they are protected with rustproof paint.

Whatever container you use, make certain there is a drainage hole somewhere in the bottom of the vessel. Excess moisture must be able to escape freely or the plants will become waterlogged and die. If the container has no hole, drill one. For earthenware, stone and concrete vessels, use a masonry bit at slow speed; for wood, a spade bit.

If the container has previously held plants, scrub it well with a disinfectant to remove any traces of disease and insects, and rinse well. When choosing perennials, be sure that the plants you combine all have similar soil, light and moisture requirements.

PLANTERS IN MANY STYLES

The size and style of the planter you choose will depend on the space you want to fill and the ambience of your garden. Large containers possess the advantage of retaining moisture and needing less watering. But large planters may be too heavy to move; small ones can be shifted about and brought indoors for the winter. As for mood, a formal French-inspired garden might call for the sort of elegant wooden Versailles box shown at right, or a pedestaled urn. For a more rustic setting, you might use a squat earthenware pot *(far right)* or even an old stone sink. Real stone vessels have become rare, but good substitutes are made of powdered stone mixed with cement.

1 Set a broken piece of clay pot, concave side down, over the drainage hole in the center of the pot so that the hole will not become clogged with soil.

2 Set more potsherds in the bottom of the planter until you have a layer about 3 inches deep. Add another drainage level, of coarse gravel, completely covering the bits of broken pot to prevent them from shifting. Then pour in soil mixture, leaving about 4 inches of space at the top to accommodate the plants. If the soil mixture is very dry, water it and wait a day before planting so that the moisture will be evenly distributed.

3 Work out the design you want by setting the plants on the surface of the soil while they are still in the pots in which you bought them. Here a plant with a tall stalk provides height in the center; lower-growing plants with variegated foliage stand around it, and a plant with tendrils is placed so that it will drape gracefully over the sides.

4 With your hand or a trowel, make a hole in the soil large enough for the center plant. Check the hole's size by placing the potted plant in it. Remove the perennial from its pot. If the roots are matted, gently loosen them with your fingers or a knife. Set the center plant in its hole and then follow the same procedure for the remaining plants, working from the center of the planter toward the rim.

5 Once the perennials are all planted in the container, firm up the soil with your hands. Water the plants well but with a gentle stream; do not flood the container. If the container is light enough to be moved, place it in the shade for a few days while the plants adjust to the stress of transplanting. If the container is too heavy to move, shield the plants from direct sunlight for a few days with a sheet of cheesecloth. □

ORNAMENTAL GRASSES — PLANTS WITH YEAR-ROUND INTEREST

An assortment of ornamental grasses, their heads tossing in a breeze, lend a wild, natural look to a seashore garden. The foliage changes color with the seasons, but the grasses give form to the landscape all year.

Grasses, many gardeners have discovered, are not just for lawns. There are scores of ornamental varieties that, planted in gardens and left uncut, provide a sort of wild, windblown beauty. The blades come in subtle shades of blue-green and gold and tan; the flowers draw on an exotic palette of coppery pinks, lavenders and yellows. Grasses also grow to any height your design may require, from 12-inch pygmies to giants 12 feet tall. Best of all, ornamental grasses give a garden life and color in winter; when most other plants have withered and died, grasses assume warm shades of tan and brown, and many remain plumed with their feathery, varicolored seedpods, looking like dried bouquets.

Many decorative grasses are perennials, and they demand only minimal care. You just have to cut them back to about 6 inches each spring, to remove last year's dry blades and promote vigorous new growth. A sprinkling of all-purpose granular fertilizer also helps, as does some watering during dry spells. Virtually the only problem presented by grasses, and then only by some species, is creeping—invading the territory of other nearby plants. You can control this tendency to spread by planting in plastic pots—the sort that saplings and shrubs are often sold in will do fine. Remove the container's bottom *(opposite)* and sink it with a clump of grass in the ground.

1 Remove the bottom of a 10-gallon plastic pot with a sharp knife. Where you will plant the grass, dig a hole as large as the container. Amend the removed soil.

2 Set the container in the hole so that the rim is a full inch above the ground, as extra protection against spreading. Fill the pot or can with enough soil to position the clump of grass at ground level. Finish filling the hole with soil, tamp it down gently and water the grass well. □

2
THE GENTLE ART
OF NURTURING

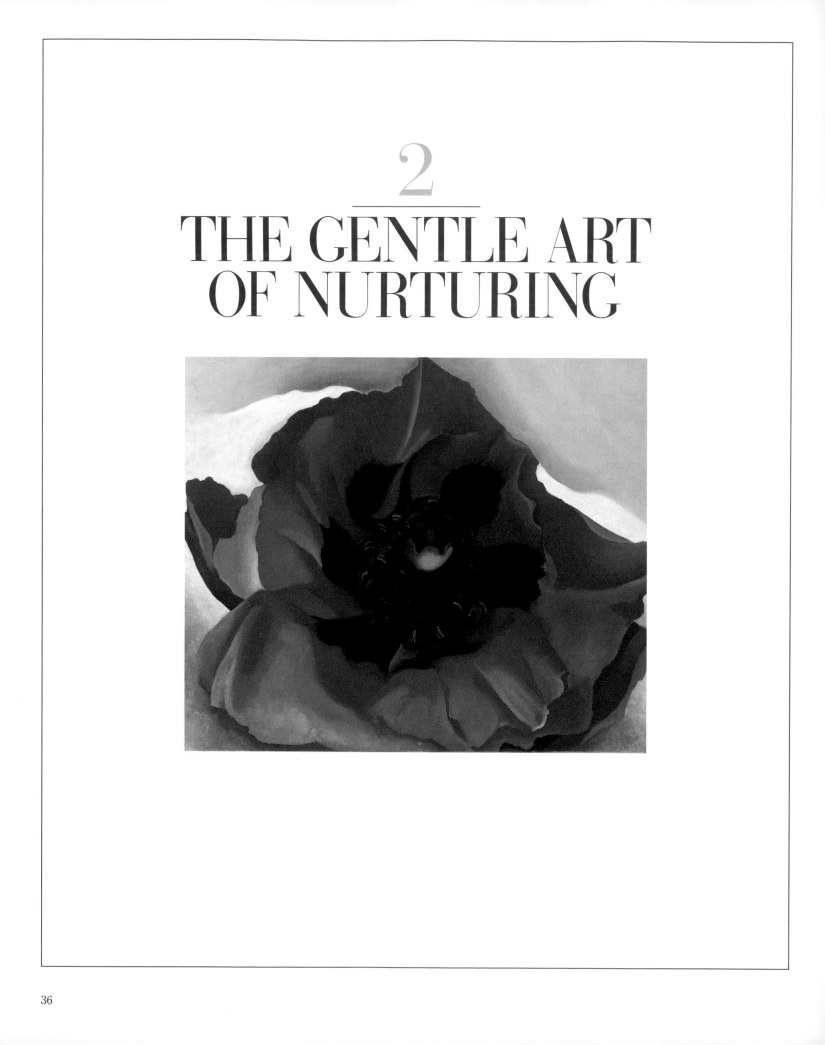

Perennials as a rule are not temperamental plants, and few demand any fussy care. In fact, many varieties, once planted in nourishing soil, display an almost disconcerting abundance of rude health, growing upward and outward with increasing exuberance each season. But perennials do require a gardener's attention periodically, in part because many of them grow with such surprising vigor. A number of the old tried-and-true favorites—delphiniums, hollyhocks and peonies, for example—become so tall that they need supports to keep their long stems from bending under the weight of their extravagant blooms. The best (and least conspicuous) ways to stake these and other lofty plants are shown in the following section of this volume. You will also find directions for doing some other tasks, most of them called for because perennials retain their vigor year after year. There are ways, for example, to reclaim a neglected perennial bed and nurse it back to health. As for new plants, they need to be put in the ground with special care from the start—because, unlike annuals, they will stay there for many seasons. For the same reason, perennial beds require some tidying up and renewing of the soil, especially in the spring, to keep them fresh and comfortable for their long-term tenants. The last task of the year is winterizing. Done as outlined here, it should keep your perennials alive through the cold, dormant months and help get them ready to burst upward with renewed energy when spring returns.

RESTORING AN ABANDONED FLOWER BED

A well-tended bed of black-eyed Susans and bright pink phlox makes a handsome display in front of a Victorian veranda. These flowers are so hardy that they can be brought back from near extinction by dividing and transplanting.

A neglected perennial bed is a sad sight to behold. Crowded by weeds and grass, plants become embroiled in exhausting competition for breathing room and nutrients. Some plants actually force themselves half out of the ground to escape overcrowding; then, with the roots exposed, they are likely to die. Others are so weakened by the struggle to survive that they scarcely bloom. Undoing the ravages of neglect takes hard work. First, look for clues to the original design of the bed. Was it organized around certain colors, textures, fragrances? Identify and label plants that are in bloom; without flowers, it's hard to tell a purple from a yellow iris. Make sketches or record seasonal changes with a camera. Decide what to keep and what to discard. Some plants, such as bee balm and aster, grow new shoots on their outer edges and develop bare centers as they mature. They can be restored to health by a process called root division *(opposite)*. Use a spade to redefine the bed's edges. Remove all weeds. Check for invasive plants such as daylily and phlox, which may have overrun their neighbors; divide these and transplant them.

Test the soil and add lime or sulfur if needed. Work organic matter around plants, or dig up plants and set them aside while you amend the soil.

1 To rejuvenate a plant that has died in the center as it has grown outward, use a sharp, narrow spade to dig a hole in the center of the clump. Remove any dead or woody sections. With a trowel, work amended soil—4 parts soil to 1 part organic matter—into the hole to the depth of the spade.

2 Slice a small division from the outside of the clump with the spade, taking care to injure as few roots as possible. Set the division in the hole at the center of the clump. Make sure that the crown—the place where roots and stems join—sits at the same depth as in the plant's previous location. Firm up the soil around the plant with your hands. Water well. □

CONTAINER-GROWN PLANTS— CHOOSING WISELY, PLANTING WELL

The quickest way to get perennials started in a garden is to buy them, container grown, from a nursery. But a careful check is necessary to make sure that the plants are healthy. The leaves should have fresh, uniform color; obvious blemishes indicate trouble with pests or disease. Buds, if present, should be tight; any flowers that have bloomed should be bright and crisp-looking. Stems should be straight; droopy stems may indicate overcrowding or lack of light. Tall plants are not necessarily desirable; they may have sent up spindly stems to reach the sunlight in a crowded greenhouse. It is better to select plants with several shorter but more vigorous shoots.

It is also better to buy in the early spring. Nurseries still have the largest selection then—and spring is the right time to put most potted perennials into the ground. The sun and earth are not too hot, and early planting allows the new arrivals several weeks to adjust after the transition from pot to flower bed before they bloom. If perennials are to be transplanted in the summer, choose a day that is cool, even drizzly. The plants should be watered liberally and shaded for some days afterward.

Spring is best for another reason: a perennial may have been in its container about a year before being sold and its roots may already be crowded. The plant may be root-bound—the ends of the roots twining around one another and beginning to form a tight knot. No harm will have been done as long as numerous small, pale, healthy-looking feeder roots are still visible. And there is an easy cure for the problems presented by bound roots; separating them *(right)* will ensure that the perennial is planted properly and will help its chances for a long, healthy life.

Ranks of clearly labeled perennials, their foliage crisp and their flowers bright-hued and healthy-looking, stand in a clean and neatly organized nursery—ready for transplanting to a garden.

1 A plant with a dense root ball will not come out of its container easily. To loosen it, first try striking the bottom of the container several times with the palm of your hand. If that does not work, run a knife around the inside of the pot *(right)*. Then turn the container upside down and gently slide out the plant.

2 Cut the root ball vertically partway up with a knife or the blade of a trowel. If you find that the pot contains a clump combining several plants, divide them and plant them separately. You get more plants, and each will grow more vigorously, since the root systems will not have to compete for nutrients.

3 Gently pull the two halves apart and loosen the plant's roots. This will encourage the roots, once they are in the ground, to grow outward in all directions.

4 Dig a hole at least half again as wide as the root ball and somewhat deeper. If the soil is very dry, soak the hole with water before planting. Mix the soil you have removed with some organic matter—humus or compost—and also add a few spoonfuls of a phosphate fertilizer. Put some of this soil mixture in the hole—enough so that when you plant the root ball its top is level with the ground. Add soil until the hole is filled. Water well. □

PUTTING BARE-ROOT PERENNIALS INTO THE GROUND

Many gardeners order perennials from mail-order nurseries—and for good reason. Selections are much wider than at local suppliers, and prices are often lower. In addition, mail-order nurseries offer the latest and most interesting varieties that are hard to find anywhere else.

Mail-order plants are usually shipped in a dormant state with bare roots or with a small soil plug attached to the roots. Dormant plants may look dead; do not be put off if they look spindly, even sticklike.

Most nurseries plan shipments so that the plants arrive at the beginning of the best planting season for your area. Plant them as soon as possible; bare-root plants dry out quickly and should never be left exposed to sun or wind.

If weather or other reasons prevent you from planting immediately, keep the plants in their original wrappings until the moment you are ready to put them in the ground. Provided they haven't produced new green growth, bare-root perennials will survive in these wrappings in a cool, dark place (35° to 45° F) for up to two weeks. If further delay is unavoidable, transplant them to a pot and keep them in a well-sheltered place or in a cold frame *(page 72)*.

Read the instructions that come with the plant to see if organic matter should be added before the soil is put back in the hole. The instructions will also tell you how deep to plant. The placement of the crown—the area where the roots and stems meet—is crucial. Hosta *(right)* does best when the crown is 1 or 2 inches below the soil surface, but depth varies with other species. The plant has spent millennia evolving, and if planted at an unfamiliar level will spend so much energy trying to adapt that it will not thrive.

Four varieties of hosta—(from bottom) blue 'Halcyon,' violet-flowered 'Aureo-marginata,' deeply ribbed 'Gold Standard' and 'Golden Tiara' with its heart-shaped leaves—share a shady bed. These hostas are most easily obtained by mail order and are shipped bare-rooted.

1 Using a trowel, dig a hole 10 to 12 inches deep and wide —enough room for the fully extended roots. Add organic matter to the removed soil if needed. When you are ready to begin planting, unwrap the plant. Save the identifying marker. Check for dryness, damage or disease; cut off any unhealthy roots with a pruner or scissors. Then trim excessively long roots so they will fit in the hole without bending or curling.

2 With soil you have previously removed, build a cone in the bottom of the hole. Set the plant over the cone; adjust the height of the cone so that the crown of the plant—the junction of roots and stems—sits at the recommended depth. (This may be level with or just below the surrounding ground.) Now hold the plant with one hand; with the other, gently separate the roots and spread them down over the cone in an evenly spaced arrangement. Refill the hole, working soil between the roots with your fingers to eliminate air pockets. Firm the soil with your hands, water well and insert the identifying marker that came with the plant. □

A BASIC PRESCRIPTION FOR KEEPING A GARDEN HEALTHY

Once a bed of perennials has been planted, it does not need a great deal of care—but it does need some. The first task is weeding, which is best begun in the spring to smarten a garden's appearance and get rid of rogue plants that will rob the perennials of water and nutrients. A preferred technique for weeding—one that enables you to excise weeds without disturbing nearby perennials—is shown at the top of the opposite page.

Then comes fertilizing. Even a well-prepared bed full of organic matter can use the boost provided by sprinkling fertilizer around the perimeter of the plant—a technique called side-dressing. A good mix for perennials will have the numbers 5-10-5 on the bag, meaning the fertilizer contains 5 percent nitrogen, which speeds plant growth; 10 percent phosphorus, for overall strength and health; and 5 percent potassium, to help plants resist diseases and cold. (The other 80 percent is filler, which is needed to dilute the strong chemicals and make them easier to spread.) Fertilizer should be applied in the spring and again in early summer, especially if heavy summer rains have leached the soil of its nutrients.

The next step is to spread a good warm-weather mulch, which performs a host of essential tasks—enriching the soil, protecting plants from excessive summer heat, conserving moisture and retarding the growth of weeds. Pine needles, pine bark, shredded leaves, salt marsh hay and peanut shells make excellent mulches—as do other materials that decompose.

A last task—but one that continues through the season—is watering. Perennials are chronically thirsty and need 1 inch of water each week. If nature does not provide enough rain, a garden should get a good soaking every four or five days. The best time is early morning, before the hot sun promotes evaporation, and the water should be directed onto the soil and the plant roots rather than the foliage, which is susceptible to mildew if it is dampened too much.

Opposite a bank of blue-flowering forget-me-nots and alongside a sun-dappled lawn, yellow and red primroses exhibit the bright blooms and lush foliage characteristic of plants living in a neatly weeded, fertilized, well-mulched and -watered garden.

1 With a weeding tool, slice into the soil and yank out the weeds and their roots. Get rid of weeds as early in the spring as possible, before they grow large, produce seeds and propagate more weeds. Dispose of them in the trash.

2 Dust dry fertilizer around the circumference of each plant and scratch it into the soil with a pronged cultivator *(right)*. After the fertilizer has been worked in, water the flower bed; plants can absorb nutrients only in liquid form. Three or four pounds of fertilizer for each 100 square feet of garden is sufficient.

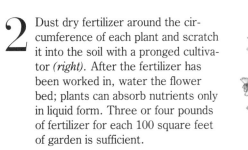

3 Spread your mulch—here pine bark nuggets—in a layer 2 or 3 inches thick, keeping it away from contact with the plants' tender stems. You can buy mulch at a garden center or shred your own *(box, right)*. ☐

A GRINDER FOR LEAVES

If you have deciduous trees, a leaf-shredding machine will prove to be a good investment, converting fallen leaves into large amounts of free mulch year after year. Some such machines are powered by electricity; others are powered by gasoline.

HELPING PERENNIALS HOLD THEIR HEADS UP

Some perennials need a helping hand to grow straight and tall. Plants such as peonies and dianthus have long, slender stems that cannot support the weight of the flower heads without drooping. If such plants are not to flop over as they mature, they need to be braced with inconspicuous stakes that surround the plant like a tiny fence.

A good support system gets the job done without calling attention to itself. Stakes should be thin but sturdy, firm but flexible. Garden supply centers sell preshaped peony hoops made of galvanized wire. These hold flower stalks upright while curbing the plant's tendency to sprawl untidily.

You can achieve the same results less expensively by building a small fence of wooden stakes and twine. Bamboo canes that have been dyed dark green make ideal stakes, since they are nearly invisible against the foliage of a fully grown plant.

There are two keys to successful staking. The first is timing. As shown in the illustrations at right, peonies (and other clumpy, weak-stemmed perennials) should be staked in the spring before buds appear. Early staking allows a plant to grow in a natural manner, so it makes full use of the supports and hides them at the same time.

The second key to successful staking is space. Leave enough room for the plant to mature inside the support area. You don't want a cramped, "corseted" look by midsummer, or flower stalks that droop because they have outgrown their support. Consult the Dictionary of Perennials *(pages 90-148)* for plant sizes and spacing requirements.

Peripheral staking with slender bamboo canes and twine keeps this luxuriant clump of yarrow upright, its outlines neat but natural.

1 To stake a peony, begin when the plant is about 1 foot high *(right)* and before buds have begun to form. Push three or four stakes firmly into the ground at equal intervals around the clump. The stakes should not be taller than the expected height of the mature plant. Cut a piece of twine long enough to go around the stakes, with a little extra for good measure. Tie one end of the twine to a stake, about 6 to 8 inches above the ground. Surround the clump with the twine, looping it around each stake in turn. Tie the loose end to the first stake and cut off any excess.

2 As the peony matures and begins to flower, you will need to add a second piece of twine. The first piece braces the growing stems; the second supports the weight of the opened flower heads. When the plant is 2 or 3 feet high and beginning to bloom *(left),* tie and loop the second piece of twine to the supporting stakes 15 to 18 inches above the ground. □

SINGLE STAKING
FOR TOP-HEAVY PERENNIALS

Even with their strong stems, tall spiky perennials like delphinium, aconitum and lupine may become top-heavy when in bloom. To prevent them from falling over, stake each plant separately to its own support with loops of twine.

Choose a stake that will be inconspicuous; green-painted bamboo cane is ideal. It should be about ½ inch in diameter and about 8 inches taller than the plant's expected height at maturity; the extra inches will allow the stake to be sunk firmly in the ground. Refer to the Dictionary of Perennials *(pages 90-148)* for plant heights.

A young delphinium tied to a stake twice its height may look ungainly for a few weeks. But keep in mind that a stem is weakest at the top. A mature delphinium that grows too far without support is in danger of losing its head in a strong wind or a heavy rain.

The time to stake spiky perennials is in the spring, as soon as the plant shows signs of budding—or even earlier if the stem starts to lean. The purpose of staking is to help a plant maintain an upright posture; you will find it difficult, if not impossible, to straighten a plant once it has begun to bend under its own weight.

While taking care to anchor the plant against the elements and its own weight, avoid looping the twine too tightly around the stem. Twine that is too tight may injure the plant by obstructing the flow of water and nutrients through the stem.

Before a wall of weathered planks, a picket of delphiniums stands guard, each flowery head held at attention by a spine of sturdy bamboo.

1 When young spiky perennials first begin to show buds, drive a stake firmly into the ground behind the main stem of each plant *(above)*. Loop a piece of twine loosely around the stem about three-quarters of the way up from the ground; then tie the twine securely to the stake *(inset)*. As the plant matures, check from time to time to make sure the loop does not choke the stem.

2 When a plant grows taller than its first tie, add a second and then a third tie. For a 3½-foot-tall delphinium *(near right)*, tie the second loop of twine at the base of the flower head when the flower head is all in bud and just starting to bloom. When the delphinium reaches 4 feet and three-quarters of its flower head is in bloom *(far right)*, add the third tie halfway between the second tie and the top of the stem. □

BEDDING DOWN PERENNIALS FOR THE WINTER

A perennial garden needs an annual cleanup in the fall to make it look neater through the winter and to promote healthy growth the next season. After the first killing frost, the stems of perennials that die back to the underground crown (chrysanthemums, peonies, coreopsis) should be cut back so that only 3 or 4 inches of stalk remain *(opposite)*. The dead stems and other detritus should then be raked up, cleared away and disposed of with trash to rid your garden of any lingering insects or diseases.

After cold weather has frozen the ground hard, mulches should be spread for winter protection. Mulches put down too soon make cozy homes for rodents, which will feast on the plants and their roots. Once the ground is hard, rodents will seek shelter elsewhere.

In most regions where winters are cold, mulching is needed not to keep plants warm but, paradoxically, to make sure that they stay solidly frozen in the ground. The perennials that are normally grown in the cooler zones can survive frigid weather. What they cannot tolerate is sharp variations: freezes followed by thaws followed by more freezes. Such changes cause the ground to heave, to move the plants and break their roots. Winter mulches prevent heaving by shading the soil from the sun so that it stays frozen, while also allowing air and moisture to penetrate. Snow does the same job perfectly, and in regions where a winter-long cover of 4 or 5 inches of snow is predictable, no mulching is required.

Some of the best mulches provide nutrients as well as protection: shredded leaves from deciduous trees, shredded tree bark, partially decomposed organic matter. In the spring, such mulches can be worked into the soil after being carefully removed from the crowns of the emerging plants.

An autumn mulch of pine needles blankets the ground around cut-back stems of goldenrod, insulating the plant's roots for the coming winter.

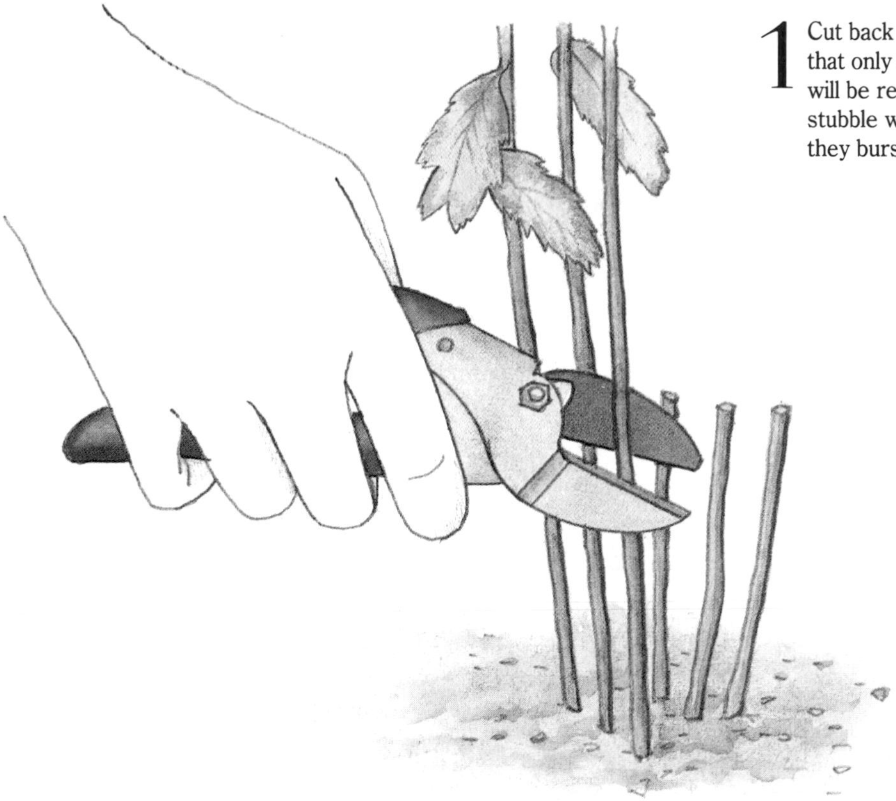

1 Cut back your perennials following the first hard frost so that only 3 or 4 inches of stalk remain; diseases and insects will be removed with the dead and dying foliage, and the stubble will serve to mark the locations of your plants till they burst forth with new growth in the spring.

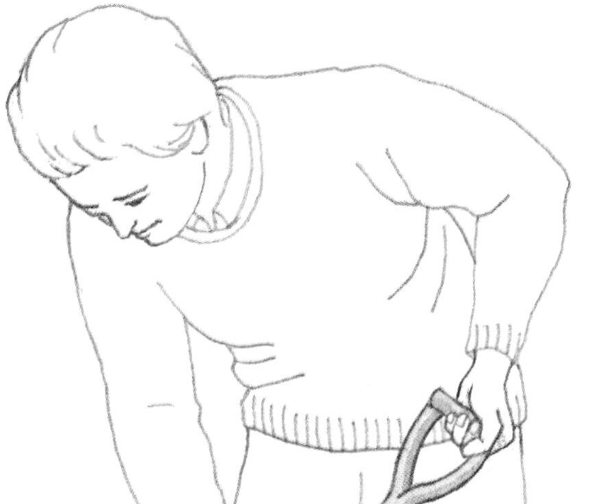

2 After waiting for the ground to freeze hard—it may be as long as two months after the initial killing frost—shovel a 2- to 3-inch layer of shredded tree leaves, as shown here, or other good mulch over your garden. Keep in mind that maple leaves are alkaline and oak leaves are acid. Delphiniums are a special case; they like an inch of coal ashes or sand to fend off their enemies, snails. □

3
PROPAGATING YOUR OWN PLANTS

Propagating your own perennials can be one of the most rewarding and intriguing parts of gardening. To watch plants grow that you have nurtured from seed is exciting in itself. Even more creative is the process of multiplying the perennials already growing in your garden by dividing their roots, or by cultivating what are called cuttings—small sections of stems or roots that, properly cared for, will grow into new plants. Either way, you will soon possess a wealth of fresh and healthy perennials with which to start a new garden if you wish, or that you can share and swap with friends.

There is nothing difficult or arcane about propagating plants, as the step-by-step explanations on the following pages make clear. And there are other rewards in addition to a sense of accomplishment. For one, the expense involved ranges from minimal to nonexistent. Buying seeds is far less costly than purchasing grown plants in pots from a nursery. Dividing your perennials, or planting cuttings from them, calls for no cash outlay whatever —except perhaps for an extra tool or two and the one-time cost of the materials for a cold frame in which to grow some of your infant plants. Further, seed catalogs offer a richer variety of species than you will ever find in a garden-supply center. Finally, propagating from root divisions or cuttings allows you to grow exact copies of the parent plants. You can therefore perpetuate the flowers and foliage of perennials that you have come to love and that are the proud focal points of your garden.

STARTING FROM SEED
FOR ECONOMY AND VARIETY

Foxglove seedlings flourish in nursery flats, awaiting transplanting to a garden. Adequate lighting has helped keep them compact and healthy; when deprived of light, seedlings become what horticulturists call leggy—tall and spindly.

Growing perennials from seed may be cheaper than buying established plants from a nursery and may also offer a greater range of species and colors than local garden centers have ready-grown. The planting and nurturing of the seeds, shown at right, is a simple process and affords the pleasure of watching small things grow day by day.

Some perennial seeds should be sown directly in the ground; they flourish that way and are averse to being transplanted later. Some of these are light-loving seeds and do best if simply spread on top of the soil and left uncovered; others need a thin covering of soil. The seed packets will give directions. In either case, the garden bed should be prepared in advance of planting—the soil turned over and enriched if necessary *(page 12)*—and then raked smooth.

Many perennials, however, can be started indoors, usually four to eight weeks before the coming of spring. When the weather turns warm, you can transplant the seedlings outdoors. For indoor containers you can use trays, wooden flats, pots made of peat, cell packs or a traditional terra-cotta planter like the one shown here.

Unless the container is new, it should be sterilized with a solution of one part bleach to nine parts water, to get rid of plant diseases. You should also use a disease-free planting medium. Soilless mixes available at garden centers are excellent because they are loose and make for easy root penetration, and they are presterilized. If you mix your own—equal parts of peat moss, soil and sand work well—you must rid it of disease by baking it in an oven for 40 minutes at 140° F.

A planting medium that contains no soil or other nutrients will require doses of diluted fertilizer to nourish the plants once they begin to sprout.

1 Fill the pot or other container to within ½ inch of the top with the planting mixture. Moisten with water all through, then sprinkle the seeds thinly and evenly over the surface. A few seeds each are enough for small pots and for cell packs. To determine how deep to plant the seeds and whether they need to be covered, follow the directions on the packet.

2 Spray the container with a gentle mist and cover it with a plastic bag to retain the moisture. Keep the container in a warm place—seeds germinate best at 75° to 80° F—but not in the sun; the top of a refrigerator can serve. When the plants begin to emerge —the stage pictured here—remove the plastic and move the planter to a location that is bright but not in direct sunlight. Fluorescent plant lights are excellent and can be kept on up to 18 hours a day.

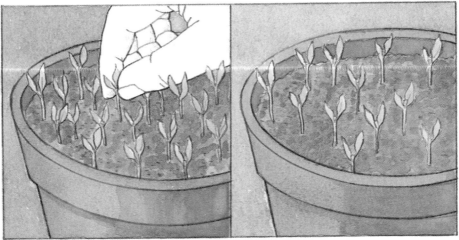

3 When the seedlings begin to crowd, start thinning them by pinching them off at the soil line or by pulling them out *(above, left);* retain the biggest and healthiest so that they are as far apart as they are high. In time, when growth further crowds the planter, transplant all the maturing seedlings into pots of their own and then outdoors *(page 56).* □

TRANSPLANTING SEEDLINGS AND CUTTINGS SAFELY

Whether they are started from seed or from stem or root cuttings, young perennials need plenty of room to grow. Plants started in flat containers should be transplanted into individual pots to prevent overcrowding and promote root development.

Timing is important. Transplanting too early can damage tender stem tissues; but if you wait too long, you risk injury to the competing root systems.

The right moment for transplanting usually comes about three weeks after sowing. With seedlings it occurs after the second pair of leaves begins to unfold. With cuttings you have to check for root development. Gently remove one plant from the rooting medium. If the roots are about 1 inch long, the cutting is ready for transplanting.

Seedlings may be transplanted into individual 2½-inch pots or into the compartments of plastic six-packs. For cuttings, which are generally larger than seedlings, you may need larger pots.

Whichever you use, fill the containers with a sterile planting medium that provides good drainage, such as 1 part loam, 1 part peat moss, and 1 part perlite or sand. The stem of each transplant should sit at the same level in the soil as it did in the rooting medium. Dig a hole deep and wide enough to seat each transplant at the proper height and to allow its roots to spread out.

Never handle a seedling by the stem. Immature stems are easily bruised, sometimes fatally. Instead, hold the plant by a leaf. To keep its roots from drying out, which can slow the plant's development, repot it immediately.

Young plants should be acclimated, over a period of several days, to the stronger light and more variable temperatures outdoors. Put the repotted plants in a cold frame *(page 72)* or in a spot where they are sheltered from the harshest extremes of wind, sun and rain.

Young chrysanthemum transplants stand in individual pots, where their roots can develop without competition. After about a week of "hardening off"—acclimating to the out of doors—they will be ready for permanent planting in the garden.

1 To lift seedlings from a rooting medium *(left),* hold one leaf carefully between your thumb and first finger, and gently dislodge the roots with the tip of a plant label. If the seedlings are massed together in a clump, separate them by lightly shaking the soil from the roots. Remove only a few plants at a time and transplant them immediately so they will not dry out from exposure to air.

2 Fill clean pots with a sterile planting mix. Tamp the mixture lightly to within ½ inch of the rim. Using a plant label *(right),* dig a hole in the center of each pot. Allow enough room for the roots to stretch out comfortably. Make sure the stem of each plant extends to the same height above the soil as it did in the rooting medium. Water the plant, then gently pat the soil down around it to eliminate air pockets. Place the pots in a cold frame or in any protected spot in your garden. □

ONE INTO MANY: PROPAGATION BY DIVISION

Spring-blooming primroses offer a wide spectrum of vivid flower color amid satiny-soft foliage. Their performance and appearance are best in the first three years after division.

Breaking up one large plant into several smaller plants suitable for replanting is called division. This is the most common method of propagating perennials. Not only does it increase your stock of plants, it also helps keep them healthy because it controls overcrowding and rejuvenates older plants that have begun to decline in vigor. Most perennials need periodic division—usually once every three years.

The easiest plants to divide are those that grow in clumps with loose, multiple crowns and shallow, fibrous roots. Some examples are aster, bellflower, gaillardia, phlox, shasta daisy and yarrow.

The best time for dividing perennials is in the early spring, when plants have just begun to grow, or in the fall, when growth has stopped and foliage has begun to die.

Make divisions on a cool, cloudy day, since uncovered roots will dry out quickly when exposed to the sun. Lift the plant from the ground and hose off the roots so you can see the base of the plant. The plant will have a clump of matted roots connected to the stems by crowns—the areas where root tissue joins stem tissue. Gently pull the plant apart at points where a crown or crowns have vigorous roots and healthy shoots of foliage. One plant may yield more than one offspring. Discard any diseased or insect-infested portions, along with any dry, woody material in the center of the clump.

Replant the healthy divisions as soon as possible in soil that has been improved with compost or peat moss, plus bone meal, superphosphate or some other fertilizer. If you are dividing plants in the late summer or fall, cut back their foliage to minimize water loss and to give the roots a chance to establish themselves before the next growing season.

1 Use a spading fork to dig all around the plant to be divided. When loosening the soil, work in a circle as broad as the plant's foliage so that the extended root system will not be damaged.

2 Carefully lift the plant out of the ground by hand *(left)*. In a protected location out of direct sunlight and strong wind, hold the plant at the crown area and gently shake off as much soil from the roots as possible.

59

3 Hose any clinging soil off the crown and roots so that you can see the base of the plant *(right)*. Competition for nutrients, water, light and air is most intense at the center of the clump, so roots and stems there may appear less healthy.

4 With your fingers, gently pull apart individual crowns and intertwining roots *(left)*. Make the divisions at points that seem to separate easily, where crowns connect with healthy stems. Each new division should include at least one crown. Discard any dry, woody portion at the center of the old crown.

5 Inspect each new division for insects, discolored roots or foul odors. The plants should have a pleasant fresh-earth scent. Discard plants that do not look and smell healthy. Use a sharp knife or pruning shears to trim off any old or dead roots *(right)*. Dust the roots with a fungicide.

6 If you are dividing in early fall, trim back all foliage to a few inches above the crowns with pruning shears *(right);* this will minimize water loss and the shock of replanting. If you are dividing in early spring, when the foliage is only a few inches high, this step is not necessary.

7 Before replanting, amend the soil in the newly dug holes—and in the original hole as well if you plan to reuse it. Replant the divisions as soon as possible to prevent the roots from drying out. Set each division at the same depth as in the original hole. Firm the soil and then water the plant well. Insert a label near each hole for future identification. □

PRYING APART
FLESHY-ROOTED PERENNIALS

Pastel yellow and peach-colored blossoms of daylilies stand in rich profusion against a stone wall. Daylilies and other plants with fleshy roots propagate themselves so vigorously that they may double and redouble annually, and need dividing every three or four years.

Plants that have fleshy rootstocks, as do daylilies and phlox, can be propagated by division if you use the proper tools. The basic method is similar to that used with fibrous-rooted perennials *(page 58).* But fleshy roots are tightly interwoven and matted at the crown—the area between the roots and the stem. Instead of separating the crown with your hands, you will need two spading forks to pry it in half. Each half can then be cut into smaller clumps with a sturdy knife.

Plan to divide fleshy-rooted plants in early fall. If possible, make divisions on a cool, cloudy day to protect the exposed roots from direct sunlight, which dries them out.

Before dividing any plant, prepare new holes so that you can replant the divisions without delay. The holes should be wide and shallow so the roots will have plenty of room to spread out horizontally. After digging the holes, improve the soil with a mix of amendments (compost, peat moss) and fertilizer (bone meal, dried manure, superphosphate).

When you divide an uprooted daylily *(opposite),* make sure that each piece has at least one fan of leaves and a segment of the crown with healthy roots attached. To prevent the roots from rotting, dust the cut surfaces with a fungicide before replanting.

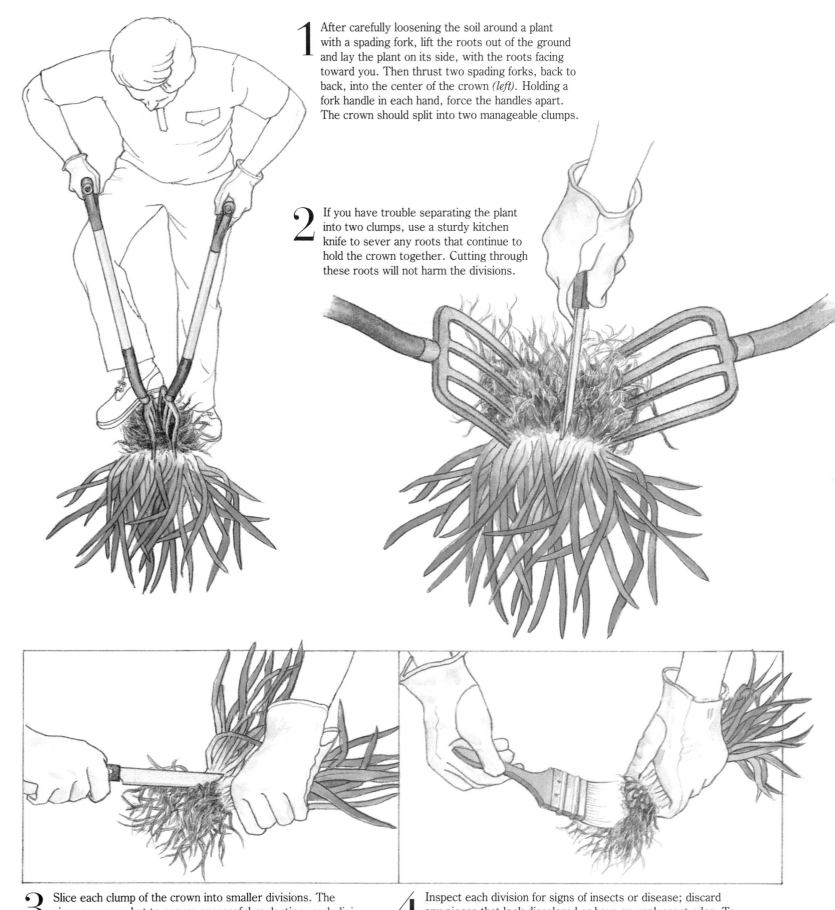

1 After carefully loosening the soil around a plant with a spading fork, lift the roots out of the ground and lay the plant on its side, with the roots facing toward you. Then thrust two spading forks, back to back, into the center of the crown *(left)*. Holding a fork handle in each hand, force the handles apart. The crown should split into two manageable clumps.

2 If you have trouble separating the plant into two clumps, use a sturdy kitchen knife to sever any roots that continue to hold the crown together. Cutting through these roots will not harm the divisions.

3 Slice each clump of the crown into smaller divisions. The sizes can vary, but to ensure successful replanting, each division must include at least one fan of healthy foliage, a portion of the crown and several healthy roots.

4 Inspect each division for signs of insects or disease; discard any pieces that look discolored or have an unpleasant odor. To guard against rot, dust the cut surfaces of the roots with a fungicide *(above)*. Replant in amended soil and water well. □

BRINGING RHIZOMES BACK TO LIFE

A rhizome is a stem that behaves like a root. It grows laterally along or just under the soil surface, and it consists of fleshy tissue that stores nutrients the plant lives on. It has many fine, hairlike feeder roots that extend downward and draw the nutrients from the soil.

Rhizomes need dividing because they are voracious feeders and vigorous spreaders that eventually exhaust and outgrow the soil they were planted in. Since they are located at or near the soil surface, they are easy to get at.

The most common perennials with rhizomes propagated by division are varieties of bearded iris *(opposite)*. Other perennials with rhizomes that can be divided include bergenia, red-hot poker and snakeroot. They need to be divided about once every four years. When they are ready for rejuvenation by division, they will give visible signals; the number and quality of blooms will decline, and the rhizomes themselves will begin to push out of the soil.

The time for division is after the flowers fade. Because the rhizomes are so close to the surface, the entire plant is easily lifted with a spading fork. After gently shaking the plant and rinsing off any clinging soil, you can distinguish the vigorous new rhizomes from the older, exhausted portions, which will be shriveled, hollow or darker in color. Cut out old or diseased growth with a sharp knife and discard, and then cut the remaining rhizome into as many sections as you want. Make sure each division has healthy leaves and a complement of roots attached to it.

Plant new divisions in soil improved with compost. The roots should be covered with 2 to 4 inches of soil; the rhizomes themselves sit half in, half out, of the ground. Sprinkle fertilizer around the new plants.

Hybrid bearded irises greet the spring with colorful, aromatic blossoms. Through periodic divisions, bearded iris and other plants with rhizomes can flourish in the same garden for 50 years or more.

1 Dig around a clump of rhizomes with a spading fork *(right)*. Carefully lift the clump from the ground. Each new plant should have healthy roots and foliage attached.

2 Some rhizomes will break into divisions when removed from the ground; separate others with your hands along natural divisions. Where two smaller rhizomes grow from a larger rhizome in the form of a Y *(inset, left)*, use a sharp knife to separate these divisions with double fans from the larger rhizome. Gently shake off dirt; then immerse the rhizome and root system in a pail of water *(left)*. Be careful not to break or tear the fine roots. Inspect for discoloration, which indicates disease or insect damage. Newer and more vigorous portions will come from the outer edge of the original clump.

3 Use a sharp knife to cut away old growth and any damaged, discolored or diseased sections *(right)*. Save as much of the new rhizome as possible, since its tissue contains nutrients essential for plant growth. Each division must have a healthy fan of leaves growing from it. Discard any pieces with dead or sickly-looking foliage.

4 Trim the foliage to one-third of its original height, maintaining a natural fan shape with the leaves in the middle slightly longer than those on the sides *(left)*. Dust the cut surfaces of the rhizome with a fungicide and let the rhizome dry in the sun for two to three hours; the sun helps heal the wounds, and the drying process makes the rhizome less susceptible to disease.

5 Dig shallow holes or a trench and build a low ridge of soil where the divisions are to be planted. Align the rhizomes horizontally on the ridge with the foliage fans running in the same direction and the roots dangling on either side. Cover the roots with 2 to 4 inches of soil, leaving the rhizome only half covered. Firm the soil by hand. Water the plants well.

6 Sprinkle bone meal or low-nitrogen fertilizer in a ring around each division, taking care not to get any fertilizer on the rhizome itself. Apply fertilizer again in early spring, before the plants bloom, and in late summer or fall, after they have flowered. □

PLANTING STEM CUTTINGS FOR TRUE-TO-FORM OFFSPRING

This perennial border displays hybrid chrysanthemums in white, gold and red. Such hybrids breed true when grown from stem cuttings.

When you want exact replicas of a plant, the best method of propagation is to take stem cuttings *(opposite)*. This leaves the parent plant intact to bloom as usual while producing several offspring. It is also less haphazard than starting from the plant's seeds because seeds carry the genes of all their ancestors, and there is no telling which traits will appear in a new generation. A stem cutting, which has the same cell tissue as the parent plant, is an exact replica.

Perennials that form vigorous, solid-stemmed leaf shoots are good candidates for stem cuttings. These include chrysanthemum, bee balm and sedum.

Take cuttings in early spring, when young shoots are plentiful, but before the plant produces blossoms. To ensure that the stems are not dried out, water your stock plant several hours before taking a cutting. You will need a sharp, clean knife; a dull edge can damage tender plant tissue.

Successful propagation depends on three factors. You will have to make the cut in the proper place on a healthy stem, provide a sterile growing medium to reduce the risk of disease, and keep the new cuttings warm, moist and out of direct sunlight. Once roots have formed—check in three weeks—the cuttings are ready for transplanting to individual flower pots *(pages 56-57)*.

1 Choose a firm, leafy stem; avoid shoots that are woody or wilted. With a sharp knife, cut 3 to 4 inches off the tip of the stem. Make the cut directly below a node where leaves sprout. Strip off the lowest pair of leaves. Place the cuttings in a plastic bag with a splash of water to keep them from drying out while you work.

2 Fill a flat container with a moistened, sterile growing medium, such as equal parts of perlite and peat moss. Make shallow holes 2 to 3 inches apart in the medium with the tip of a pencil. To promote root growth and prevent disease, dip the cut end of each stem in a rooting hormone that contains a fungicide. Insert the cut ends into the holes and gently firm the medium with your fingers.

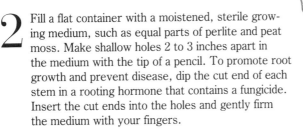

3 Place two hoops made from wire coat hangers in the container and cover with plastic. Keep the container moist, warm—about 70° F—and out of direct sunlight. When heavy drops accumulate inside the plastic, open it for a few hours to air out. After new leaves appear, check for root formation by tugging gently. If you feel resistance, the plant has rooted. Then leave the container uncovered for four to five days before transplanting. □

MULTIPLYING
WITH ROOT CUTTINGS

A profusion of bright orange Oriental poppies highlights a garden from early June through July. A single poppy may yield from three to six new plants through propagation by root cuttings.

Commercial gardeners often increase their stocks of certain perennials through root cuttings, small pieces taken from a plant's main root. This is the best way to propagate perennials such as butterfly weed, sea holly and Oriental poppy. These plants have neither the well-defined shoots that lend themselves to propagation by stem cuttings *(page 68)* nor the multiple crowns needed for propagation by division *(page 58)*. Instead they have one thick main root that descends from a single crown.

Take the cuttings from such a plant during its least active growth period, either in early spring or in early fall. After digging around the base of the plant, lift it out of the soil and hose it off so you can see the crown, the main root and its offshoots. Once you have cut the main root below the crown, the parent plant can be returned to its garden location. Before you replant it, trim back some of the foliage to lessen stress on the much-reduced root system.

The new cuttings should be planted with the same vertical orientation as the original root or they will not grow. To guard against mistakes, always make a straight cut on the end nearest the crown and a slanted cut on the bottom end; then plant with the slanted end down.

Keep the new cuttings in a protected location out of direct sunlight. When leaves develop—usually within a month—the cuttings are ready to transplant into larger pots *(page 56)*.

1 To take root cuttings from a freshly dug plant, rinse the soil from the root mass, then place the plant on a firm cutting surface. Trim the main root about 4 inches below the crown with a straight cut of a sharp knife *(above)*. If any of the offshoots from the main root are more than 2 inches long, they may also yield cuttings.

2 Position the usable root sections on a cutting surface and divide them into pieces 2 to 3 inches long *(right)*. Trim each piece so that you leave a straight cut at the crown end and a slanted cut at the lower end. This will help you orient each root section properly when planting. To reduce the risk of rot, dip both ends of each piece in a fungicide powder immediately.

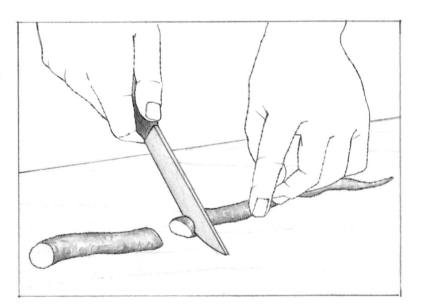

3 Fill a flower pot with a sterile potting mixture, such as equal parts of perlite and peat moss. Use the pointed end of a pencil to make holes in the mix 2 to 3 inches apart and deep enough to hold each cutting covered with ½ inch of soil. Moisten the soil; then insert the pieces of root, slanted end down, into the holes. Pat soil over each piece. Keep the pot in a warm, protected place until leaves begin to develop. □

A COLD FRAME
THAT KEEPS PLANTS WARM

A cold frame with a split top made of two window sashes shelters seedlings planted in the soil. Two sticks hold up the sashes, ventilating the seedlings and keeping them from overheating in the sun. Separate sashes make it possible to work in one section while the other side stays closed.

A cold frame is a greenhouse in miniature. It is a low, wooden, bottomless box with a glass lid that lets in sun when it is closed and can be held open to admit air on a warm day. Because the cold frame shelters plants from wind and cold, it enables you to germinate seeds outdoors weeks before nature would otherwise allow and to foster the growth of seedlings that would perish if left unprotected. You can use it to hold pots—or, because it has no bottom and stands in the garden, you can plant seeds directly in the soil inside it.

Cold frames can be bought ready-made in garden centers, but they are easy to make. The one shown here *(opposite)* consists of a 2-by-12 piece of lumber for the back piece, two trapezoidal side pieces cut out of another 2-by-12 and a front piece made out of a 2-by-6. The cover consists of a storm window hinged at the back. (You can use a window sash for a smaller cold frame, two or more sashes for a larger one.) The window overhangs the front piece of the cold frame so it can be raised with the fingers. It has adjustable supports so it can be opened high or low, depending on how warm or how cold the weather is and how much air you want to let in. But a lid can be propped open with any two sticks *(left)*.

In making the cold frame, it is best to use rot-resistant wood such as redwood, cedar or cypress. Pine that has been treated with a preservative is also acceptable—but be sure the preservative is copper or zinc naphthenate, not a compound containing creosote, which is harmful to plants.

To make the most of the sun's rays, the cold frame should face south and the lid should slope. The slope can run as little as 1 inch in 12 or as much as 1 inch in 5. If you live in an area where cold weather is particularly severe, you can retain heat by painting the interior white. Another precaution is to add weather stripping between the lid and the frame below.

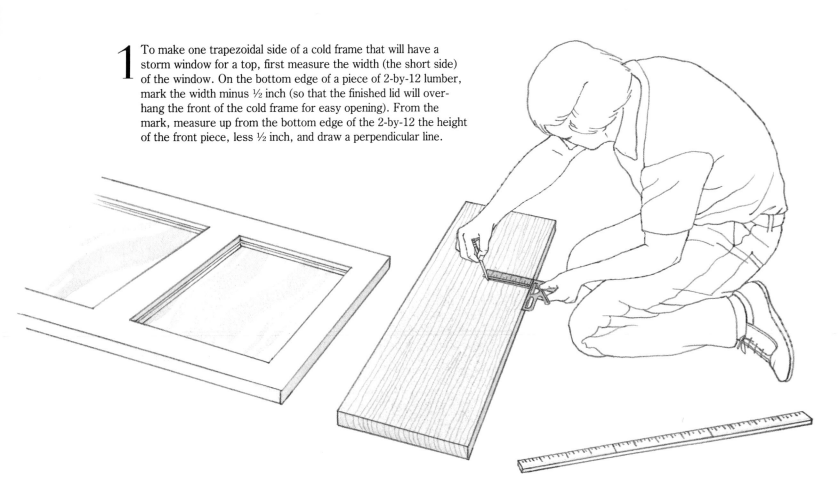

1 To make one trapezoidal side of a cold frame that will have a storm window for a top, first measure the width (the short side) of the window. On the bottom edge of a piece of 2-by-12 lumber, mark the width minus ½ inch (so that the finished lid will overhang the front of the cold frame for easy opening). From the mark, measure up from the bottom edge of the 2-by-12 the height of the front piece, less ½ inch, and draw a perpendicular line.

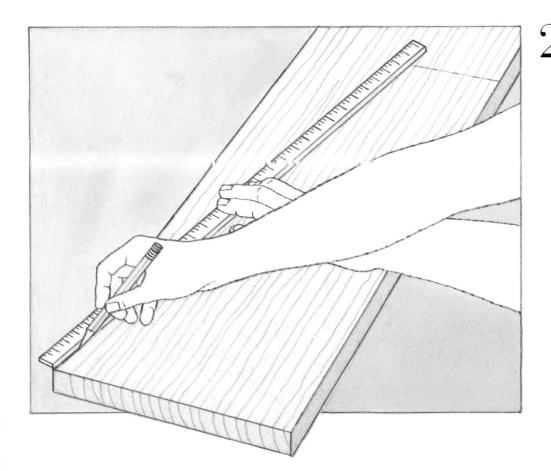

2 Draw a line from the upper corner of the 2-by-12 to the top of the perpendicular line drawn in Step 1, making the outline of a trapezoid. Saw along the lines and cut out the trapezoid to make one side piece. Use this side piece as a pattern to make the second side piece.

3 Measure the length (the long side) of the window. Cut a 2-by-12 for the back piece of the cold frame and a 2-by-6 for the front; make each piece the length of the window minus 3 inches (to account for the thickness of the side pieces). Using 4-inch-long No. 14 screws or sixteen-penny nails, attach the broad end of one trapezoidal side piece to one outside edge of the back piece. Attach the broad end of the other trapezoidal side piece to the other end of the back piece. Attach the short end of each trapezoidal side piece to an outside edge of the front piece. With a hand plane *(right)*, bevel the top edges of the front and back pieces to make them match the slope of the side pieces.

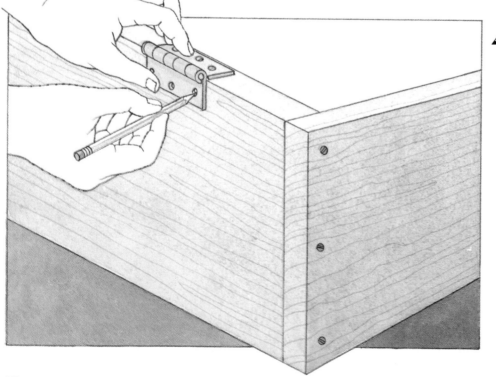

4 Place one leaf of a hinge on the outside of the back piece; position it so that it sits 6 to 8 inches in from the end and so the hinge pin lies parallel to the upper edge of the back piece. Mark the location of each hinge hole on the wood *(left)*. On the marks, drill pilot holes and then screw the leaf in place. In the same manner, attach a second hinge, making it equidistant from the other end of the back piece. Then place the window on the cold frame and mark on the window's edge the positions of the holes of the upper leaves of the hinges. Drill pilot holes and screw the leaves to the window edge.

5 To make lid supports, drill ⅝-inch holes every 2 inches in two 2-foot-long 1-by-2s. Lay the cold frame on its side. Place a 1-by-2 on the side so it is 4 inches from the front edge and so the lowest hole is on the side piece and the next lowest hole is centered on the window's edge. Mark the positions of both holes. Drill ½-inch holes on both marks—one in the frame, one in the window's edge. Repeat with the other 1-by-2 on the other side of the cold frame.

6 Cut four ½-inch dowels, making two of them 4 inches long and the other two 5 inches long. Set the 5-inch-long dowels in the two holes in the frame sides *(left)*. Set the 4-inch-long dowels in the two holes on the storm window edges. Slip a 1-by-2 over a pair of dowels. It should slip over the dowels without much resistance; if it sticks, enlarge the holes in the 1-by-2 or check to see if the angle of the holes needs straightening and redrill them if necessary. When the 1-by-2 can slip readily over the dowels, glue the dowels in position. On the other side, make any needed adjustments and glue the dowels in place.

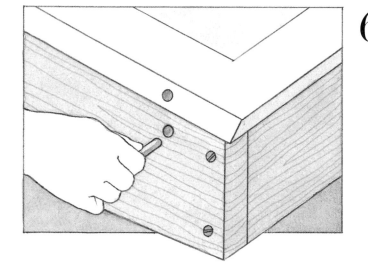

7 Dig a 2-inch-deep trench to match the perimeter of the cold frame and set the cold frame in the trench. If you do not intend to move the cold frame from this location, you can secure it by driving 18-inch 2-by-2 stakes into the ground inside each corner and nailing them to the cold frame. Place potted seedlings inside the frame *(right)*—or prepare the soil and plant seeds. □

4

MAKING THE MOST OF NATURE

Perennials are well known for their ruggedness and adaptability. Many varieties easily survive the long, hard winters of Maine and Minnesota, yet tolerate the torrid summers of, say, North Carolina and Missouri. But not many perennials thrive in every climate. A garden on the Gulf Coast, where the climate is warm and humid all year round, must be quite different from one in Michigan, where temperatures may remain below freezing as late as April or May. To find out about temperatures in your part of the country, turn to the map included here *(pages 78-79),* which divides North America into 10 climatic zones. To find out which zones plants flourish in, consult the Dictionary of Perennials *(pages 90-148).*

Wherever you live and whatever perennials you grow, your garden will go through seasonal changes—which bring with them regular seasonal tasks such as cutting back and mulching. To help you schedule the maintenance of your garden, this section includes a calendar that lays out the gardening year month by month and zone by zone. Also included here is a list of common bugs and diseases that can assail your plants, along with the effective remedies for the problems. In addition, there is a section that offers some professional tips on gardening techniques— handy tips for enhancing your garden.

THE ZONE MAP AND PLANTING

Gardeners love perennials for their faithful flowering year after year. But perennials, like all other growing plants, have individual predilections. Some like hot weather, some cold—and some cannot survive winter temperatures in certain areas of the country.

The map at right divides the United States into 10 climatic zones based on average minimum temperatures, as compiled by the United States Department of Agriculture. Zone 1 is the coldest; Zone 10, the warmest. The zone information given in the Dictionary of Perennials *(pages 90-148)* indicates the zones in which a given perennial will flourish and survive the winter. By checking the map to see which zone you live in, you can predict that perennials listed as winter-hardy in your zone are likely to return each year to your garden.

Zone information is only a loose guide to plant survival, however, because it is based on average temperatures over fairly large geographic areas. Your garden may be in a so-called microclimate—one that differs from the zone average. If it is in a low spot where cold air collects, you may have difficulty with plants already at the limit of their ability to tolerate low temperatures. If you have a sunny bed that lies on a southern slope or is tucked up near a masonry wall that reflects light, you may be able to grow plants usually considered too tender for your zone. To determine what plants will flourish in your garden, check local weather-bureau temperatures and compare them with those in your garden. You can also consult garden centers in your area; what they sell is what has proved to grow successfully.

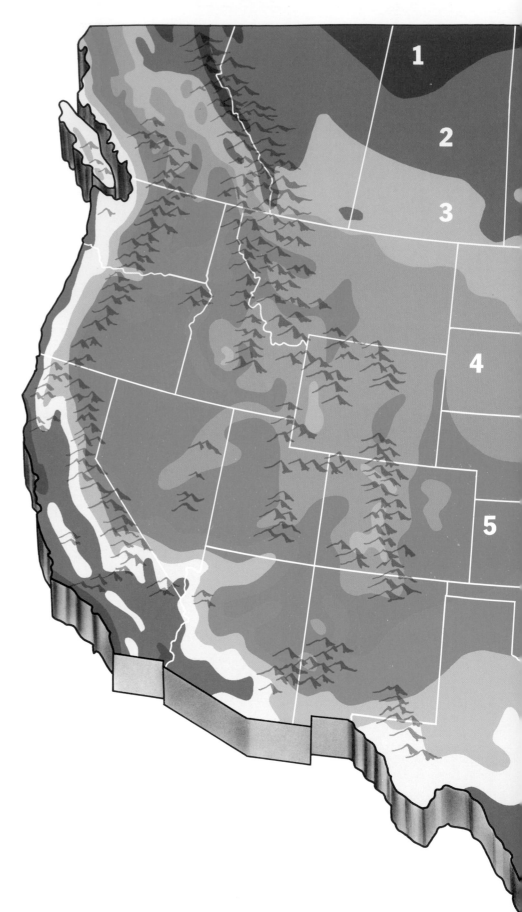

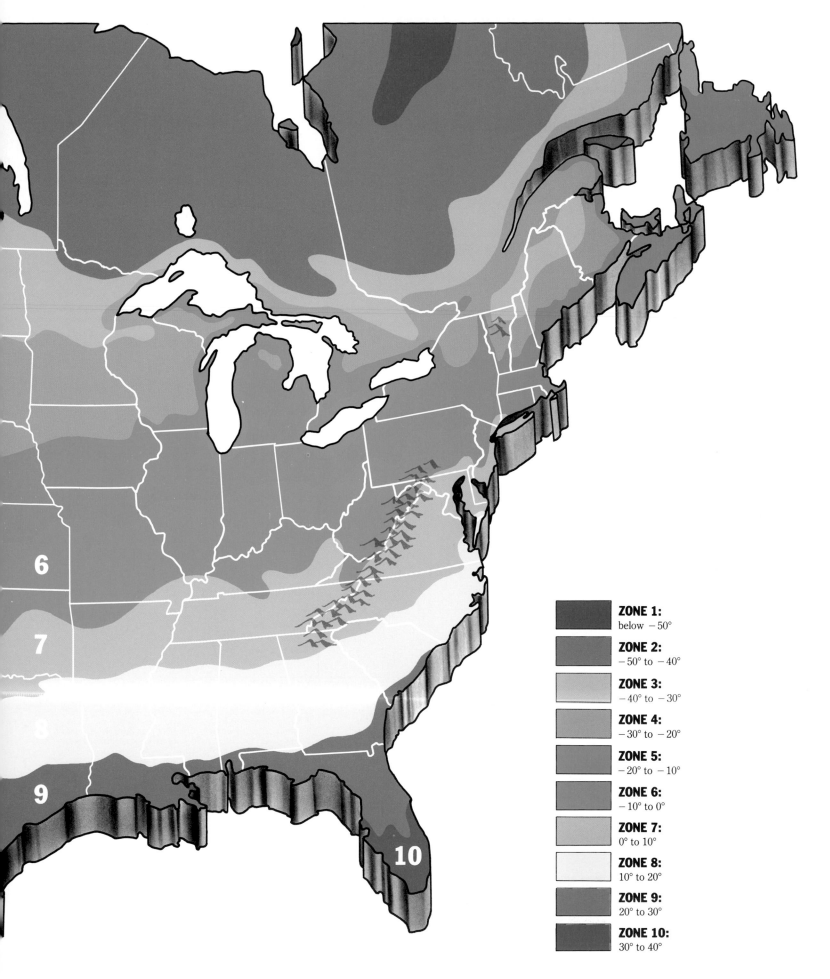

ZONE 1:
below −50°

ZONE 2:
−50° to −40°

ZONE 3:
−40° to −30°

ZONE 4:
−30° to −20°

ZONE 5:
−20° to −10°

ZONE 6:
−10° to 0°

ZONE 7:
0° to 10°

ZONE 8:
10° to 20°

ZONE 9:
20° to 30°

ZONE 10:
30° to 40°

A CHECKLIST FOR MAINTENANCE MONTH BY MONTH

	ZONE 1	ZONE 2	ZONE 3	ZONE 4	ZONE 5
JANUARY/FEBRUARY	• Study seed and plant catalogs for new ideas for spring • Sharpen and repair garden tools • Press heaved plants back into soil • Check winter mulch; add extra if necessary	• Study seed and plant catalogs for new ideas for spring • Sharpen and repair garden tools • Press heaved plants back into soil • Check winter mulch; add extra if necessary	• Study seed and plant catalogs for new ideas for spring • Sharpen and repair garden tools • Press heaved plants back into soil • Check winter mulch; add extra if necessary	• Study seed and plant catalogs for new ideas for spring • Sharpen and repair garden tools • Press heaved plants back into soil • Check winter mulch; add extra if necessary	• Study seed and plant catalogs for new ideas for spring • Sharpen and repair garden tools • Press heaved plants back into soil • Check winter mulch; add extra if necessary
MARCH/APRIL	• Sow perennial seeds indoors	• Sow perennial seeds indoors	• Sow perennial seeds indoors	• Sow perennial seeds indoors • Plant bare-root perennials	• Remove fallen leaves, twigs and branches from garden • Repair fences, edging • Remove winter mulch • Sow perennial seeds indoors • Plant bare-root perennials
MAY/JUNE	• Remove fallen leaves, twigs and branches from garden • Repair fences, edging • Remove winter mulch • Sow perennial seeds outdoors • Set indoor-started seedlings outdoors • Plant bare-root perennials • Plant container perennials • Divide and transplant perennials • Root chrysanthemums; then plant • Thin out overgrown plantings • Fertilize as growth starts • Stake plants as they start to grow • Apply summer mulch • Cut back ornamental grasses • Disbud peonies • Apply pre-emergent herbicide; weed • Water if ground is dry • Check for insects, disease	• Remove fallen leaves, twigs and branches from garden • Repair fences, edging • Remove winter mulch • Sow perennial seeds outdoors • Set indoor-started seedlings outdoors • Plant bare-root perennials • Plant container perennials • Divide and transplant perennials • Root chrysanthemums; then plant • Thin out overgrown plantings • Fertilize as growth starts • Stake plants as they start to grow • Apply summer mulch • Cut back ornamental grasses • Disbud peonies • Apply pre-emergent herbicide; weed • Water if ground is dry • Check for insects, disease	• Remove fallen leaves, twigs and branches from garden • Repair fences, edging • Remove winter mulch • Sow perennial seeds outdoors • Set indoor-started seedlings outdoors • Plant bare-root perennials • Plant container perennials • Divide and transplant perennials • Root chrysanthemums; then plant • Thin out overgrown plantings • Fertilize as growth starts • Stake plants as they start to grow • Apply summer mulch • Cut back ornamental grasses • Disbud peonies • Apply pre-emergent herbicide; weed • Water if ground is dry • Check for insects, disease	• Remove fallen leaves, twigs and branches from garden • Repair fences, edging • Remove winter mulch • Sow perennial seeds outdoors • Set indoor-started seedlings outdoors • Plant bare-root perennials • Plant container perennials • Divide and transplant perennials • Root chrysanthemums; then plant • Thin out overgrown plantings • Fertilize as growth starts • Stake plants as they start to grow • Apply summer mulch • Cut back ornamental grasses • Disbud peonies • Apply pre-emergent herbicide; weed • Water if ground is dry • Check for insects, disease	• Sow perennial seeds outdoors • Set indoor-started seedlings outdoors • Plant container perennials • Divide and transplant perennials • Root chrysanthemums; then plant • Thin out overgrown plantings • Fertilize as growth starts • Stake plants as they start to grow • Apply summer mulch • Cut back ornamental grasses • Disbud peonies • Apply pre-emergent herbicide; weed • Water if ground is dry • Check for insects, disease

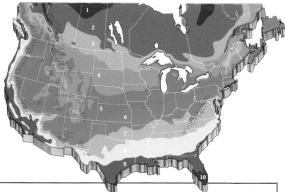

ZONE 6	ZONE 7	ZONE 8	ZONE 9	ZONE 10	
• Study seed and plant catalogs for new ideas for spring • Sharpen and repair garden tools • Press heaved plants back into soil • Check winter mulch; add extra if necessary	• Study seed and plant catalogs for new ideas for spring • Sharpen and repair garden tools • Press heaved plants back into soil • Check winter mulch; add extra if necessary	• Study seed and plant catalogs for new ideas for spring • Sharpen and repair garden tools • Press heaved plants back into soil • Apply mulch if frost threatens • Sow perennial seeds indoors • Plant bare-root perennials	• Study seed and plant catalogs for new ideas for spring • Repair fences, edging • Apply mulch if frost threatens • Sow perennial seeds indoors and outdoors • Plant bare-root perennials • Plant container perennials • Divide and transplant summer- and fall-flowering perennials • Root chrysanthemum cuttings • Thin out overgrown plantings • Fertilize as growth starts • Apply pre-emergent herbicide; weed • Water if ground is dry • Check for insects, disease	• Study seed and plant catalogs for new ideas for spring • Sharpen and repair tools • Remove fallen leaves, twigs and branches from garden • Sow perennial seeds indoors and outdoors • Plant bare-root perennials • Plant container perennials • Divide and transplant summer- and fall-flowering perennials • Root chrysanthemum cuttings • Thin out overgrown plantings • Fertilize as growth starts • Apply pre-emergent herbicide; weed • Water if ground is dry • Check for insects, disease	**JANUARY/FEBRUARY**
• Remove fallen leaves, twigs and branches from garden • Repair fences, edging • Remove winter mulch • Sow perennial seeds indoors • Plant bare-root perennials • Fertilize as growth starts • Cut back ornamental grasses	• Remove fallen leaves, twigs and branches from garden • Repair fences, edging • Remove winter mulch • Sow perennial seeds indoors • Plant bare-root perennials • Plant container perennials • Thin out overgrown plantings • Fertilize as growth starts • Cut back ornamental grasses • Stake plants as they start to grow	• Repair fences, edging • Remove winter mulch • Sow perennial seeds • Set seedlings outdoors • Plant bare-root perennials • Plant container perennials • Divide and transplant summer- and fall-flowering perennials • Root chrysanthemum cuttings • Thin overgrown plantings • Fertilize as growth starts • Cut ornamental grasses • Stake plants as they start to grow • Apply pre-emergent herbicide; weed • Water if ground is dry • Check for insects, disease • Apply summer mulch • Disbud peonies	• Sow perennial seeds outdoors • Set indoor-started seedlings outdoors • Plant container perennials • Divide and transplant summer- and fall-flowering perennials • Thin out overgrown plantings • Fertilize as growth starts • Cut back ornamental grasses • Stake plants as they start to grow • Apply pre-emergent herbicide; weed • Water if ground is dry • Check for insects, disease • Apply summer mulch • Plant chrysanthemums • Disbud peonies	• Sow perennial seeds outdoors • Set indoor-started seedlings outdoors • Plant container perennials • Divide and transplant summer- and fall-flowering perennials • Thin out overgrown plantings • Fertilize as growth starts • Cut back ornamental grasses • Stake plants as they start to grow • Apply pre-emergent herbicide; weed • Water if ground is dry • Check for insects, disease • Apply summer mulch • Plant chrysanthemums • Disbud peonies	**MARCH/APRIL**
• Sow perennial seeds outdoors • Set indoor-started seedlings outdoors • Plant container perennials • Divide and transplant perennials • Root chrysanthemums; then plant • Thin out overgrown plantings • Fertilize as growth starts • Stake plants as they start to grow • Apply summer mulch • Disbud peonies • Remove spent blooms • Shear candytuft and basket-of-gold • Apply pre-emergent herbicide; weed • Water if ground is dry • Check for insects, disease	• Sow perennial seeds outdoors • Set indoor-started seedlings outdoors • Plant container perennials • Divide and transplant perennials • Root chrysanthemums; then plant • Thin out overgrown plantings • Fertilize as growth starts • Stake plants as they start to grow • Apply summer mulch • Disbud peonies • Remove spent blooms • Pinch stem tips off chrysanthemums until mid-July • Shear candytuft and basket-of-gold • Apply pre-emergent herbicide; weed • Water if ground is dry • Check for insects, disease	• Plant container perennials • Divide and transplant perennials • Plant chrysanthemums • Thin out overgrown plantings • Apply summer mulch • Remove spent blooms • Pinch stem tips off chrysanthemums until mid-July • Shear candytuft and basket-of-gold • Apply pre-emergent herbicide; weed • Water if ground is dry • Check for insects, disease	• Plant container perennials • Divide and transplant perennials • Thin out overgrown plantings • Apply summer mulch • Remove spent blooms • Pinch stem tips off chrysanthemums until mid-July • Apply pre-emergent herbicide; weed • Water if ground is dry • Check for insects, disease	• Plant container perennials • Divide and transplant perennials • Thin out overgrown plantings • Apply summer mulch • Remove spent blooms • Pinch stem tips off chrysanthemums until mid-July • Apply pre-emergent herbicide; weed • Water if ground is dry • Check for insects, disease	**MAY/JUNE**

	ZONE 1	ZONE 2	ZONE 3	ZONE 4	ZONE 5
JULY/AUGUST	• Sow perennial and biennial seeds outdoors • Remove spent blooms • Shear ground covers and rock-garden plants • Cut off phlox blooms before seeds drop • Pinch stem tips off chrysanthemums until mid-July • Dig up iris; check for borers and root rot • Divide and replant iris • Cut flowers and ornamental grasses for drying • Weed; check summer mulch • Water if ground is dry • Check for insects, disease • Plant chrysanthemums in bud and bloom • Plant poppies and peonies	• Sow perennial and biennial seeds outdoors • Remove spent blooms • Shear ground covers and rock-garden plants • Cut off phlox blooms before seeds drop • Pinch stem tips off chrysanthemums until mid-July • Dig up iris; check for borers and root rot • Divide and replant iris • Cut flowers and ornamental grasses for drying • Weed; check summer mulch • Water if ground is dry • Check for insects, disease • Plant chrysanthemums in bud and bloom • Plant poppies and peonies	• Sow perennial and biennial seeds outdoors • Remove spent blooms • Shear ground covers and rock-garden plants • Cut off phlox blooms before seeds drop • Pinch stem tips off chrysanthemums until mid-July • Dig up iris; check for borers and root rot • Divide and replant iris • Cut flowers and ornamental grasses for drying • Weed; check summer mulch • Water if ground is dry • Check for insects, disease • Plant chrysanthemums in bud and bloom • Plant poppies and peonies	• Sow perennial and biennial seeds outdoors • Remove spent blooms • Shear ground covers and rock-garden plants • Cut off phlox blooms before seeds drop • Pinch stem tips off chrysanthemums until mid-July • Dig up iris; check for borers and root rot • Divide and replant iris • Cut flowers and ornamental grasses for drying • Weed; check summer mulch • Water if ground is dry • Check for insects, disease • Plant chrysanthemums in bud and bloom • Plant poppies and peonies	• Sow perennial and biennial seeds outdoors • Remove spent blooms • Shear ground covers and rock-garden plants • Cut off phlox blooms before seeds drop • Pinch stem tips off chrysanthemums until mid-July • Dig up iris; check for borers and root rot • Divide and replant iris • Cut flowers and ornamental grasses for drying • Weed; check summer mulch • Water if ground is dry • Check for insects, disease • Plant chrysanthemums in bud and bloom • Plant poppies and peonies
SEPTEMBER/OCTOBER	• Water if ground is dry • Cut back tops of withered plants • Move semihardy young plants to a cold frame • Clean up leaves and other litter • Turn off water; drain hose • Apply winter mulch after a hard freeze	• Water if ground is dry • Cut back tops of withered plants • Move semihardy young plants to a cold frame • Clean up leaves and other litter • Turn off water; drain hose • Apply winter mulch after a hard freeze	• Water if ground is dry • Cut back tops of withered plants • Move semihardy young plants to a cold frame • Clean up leaves and other litter • Turn off water; drain hose • Apply winter mulch after a hard freeze	• Water if ground is dry • Cut back tops of withered plants • Move semihardy young plants to a cold frame • Clean up leaves and other litter • Turn off water; drain hose • Apply winter mulch after a hard freeze	• Sow perennial and biennial seeds outdoors • Remove spent blooms • Prepare soil for fall planting • Divide and transplant spring-flowering perennials • Water if ground is dry • Move semihardy young plants to a cold frame
NOVEMBER/DECEMBER				• Rake leaves from perennial beds	• Rake leaves from perennial beds • Water if ground is dry • Turn off water; drain hose • Apply winter mulch after a hard freeze

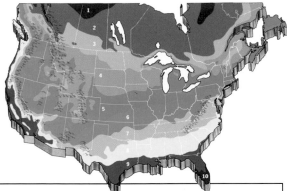

ZONE 6	ZONE 7	ZONE 8	ZONE 9	ZONE 10	
• Sow perennial and biennial seeds outdoors • Remove spent blooms • Shear ground covers and rock-garden plants • Cut off phlox blooms before seeds drop • Pinch stem tips off chrysanthemums until mid-July • Dig up iris; check for borers and root rot • Divide and replant iris • Cut flowers and ornamental grasses for drying • Weed; check summer mulch • Water if ground is dry • Check for insects, disease • Plant chrysanthemums in bud and bloom	• Sow perennial and biennial seeds outdoors • Remove spent blooms • Shear ground covers and rock-garden plants • Cut off phlox blooms before seeds drop • Pinch stem tips off chrysanthemums until mid-July • Dig up iris; check for borers and root rot • Divide and replant iris • Cut flowers and ornamental grasses for drying • Weed; check summer mulch • Water if ground is dry • Check for insects, disease	• Remove spent blooms • Shear ground covers and rock-garden plants • Pinch stem tips off chrysanthemums until mid-July • Dig up iris; check for borers and root rot • Divide and replant iris • Cut flowers and ornamental grasses for drying • Weed; check summer mulch • Water if ground is dry • Check for insects, disease	• Remove spent blooms • Shear ground covers and rock-garden plants • Pinch stem tips off chrysanthemums until mid-July • Dig up iris; check for borers and root rot • Divide and replant iris • Cut flowers and ornamental grasses for drying • Weed; check summer mulch • Water if ground is dry • Check for insects, disease	• Remove spent blooms • Shear ground covers and rock-garden plants • Pinch stem tips off chrysanthemums until mid-July • Dig up iris; check for borers and root rot • Divide and replant iris • Cut flowers and ornamental grasses for drying • Weed; check summer mulch • Water if ground is dry • Check for insects, disease	**JULY/AUGUST**
• Sow perennial and biennial seeds outdoors • Remove spent blooms • Prepare soil for fall planting • Plant poppies and peonies • Dig, divide and replant iris • Divide and transplant spring-flowering perennials • Water if ground is dry • Move semihardy young plants to a cold frame	• Sow perennial and biennial seeds outdoors • Remove spent blooms • Prepare soil for fall planting • Plant poppies and peonies • Dig, divide and replant iris • Divide and transplant spring-flowering perennials • Water if ground is dry • Move semihardy young plants to a cold frame	• Sow perennial and biennial seeds outdoors • Remove spent blooms • Prepare soil for fall planting • Plant poppies and peonies • Dig, divide and replant iris • Divide and transplant spring-flowering perennials • Water if ground is dry • Move semihardy young plants to a cold frame	• Sow perennial and biennial seeds outdoors • Remove spent blooms • Prepare soil for fall planting • Plant poppies and peonies • Dig, divide and replant iris • Divide and transplant spring-flowering perennials • Water if ground is dry • Move semihardy young plants to a cold frame	• Sow perennial and biennial seeds outdoors • Remove spent blooms • Prepare soil for fall planting • Plant poppies and peonies • Dig, divide and replant iris • Divide and transplant spring-flowering perennials • Water if ground is dry • Move semihardy young plants to a cold frame	**SEPTEMBER/OCTOBER**
• Cut back tops of withered plants • Clean up leaves and other litter • Water if ground is dry • Turn off water; drain hose • Apply winter mulch after a hard freeze	• Cut back tops of withered plants • Clean up leaves and other litter • Water if ground is dry • Turn off water; drain hose • Apply winter mulch after a hard freeze	• Plant chrysanthemums • Sow perennial and biennial seeds outdoors • Cut back tops of withered plants • Divide and transplant spring-flowering perennials until mid-November • Clean up leaves and other litter • Water if ground is dry • Turn off water; drain hose	• Plant chrysanthemums • Sow perennial and biennial seeds outdoors • Divide and transplant spring-flowering perennials until mid-November • Water if ground is dry • Turn off water; drain hose	• Plant chrysanthemums • Sow perennial and biennial seeds outdoors • Divide and transplant spring-flowering perennials until mid-November • Water if ground is dry	**NOVEMBER/DECEMBER**

WHAT TO DO
WHEN THINGS GO WRONG

PROBLEM	CAUSE	SOLUTION
Leaves curl, are distorted in shape and may have a black, sooty appearance; plant is stunted. Many perennials may be affected, including columbine, delphinium, iris, poppy, primrose and chrysanthemum.	Aphids (plant lice), ⅛-inch cream, green, red, black or brown semitransparent insects found on buds, leaves and stems.	Wash plants with a spray of water and a diluted soap solution or with an insecticide. Ladybug beetles, which eat aphids, may also be introduced into the garden.
Peony flowers fail to open or have browned petals. Other perennials, such as chrysanthemum, foxglove, daylily, hollyhock and delphinium, have darkened buds and leaves with a silvery appearance. The plants may be stunted.	Thrips, which are tiny, thin insects barely visible to the naked eye.	Destroy damaged buds and foliage. Spray plants with an insecticide.
Small, round holes are eaten into leaves and flowers.	Japanese, Asiatic, snout, blister or other beetles—dark red, brown or bronze-colored, hard-shelled insects ¼ to ½ inch long.	Small colonies can be handpicked. Japanese beetles can be caught in baited traps. The larval stage can be controlled with *Bacillus popillias,* a bacterium, called milky spore, that causes milky disease, which is lethal to beetles but harmless to plants.
Chrysanthemum buds are distorted and do not open; stems and leaves are severely twisted.	Midges, maggots that bore into leaves and stems; not visible to the naked eye.	Pick off and destroy affected buds and foliage.
Iris plants wilt, discolor and eventually die. Leaves become loose at the base and the rhizomes become soft and rotten.	Iris borer, a 1½-inch-long, fat, wormlike larva.	In fall, pick off and destroy damaged leaves. In spring, young borers are visible in the leaves and may be removed by hand. Heavily infested rhizomes should be dug out and discarded.
Leaves become speckled with white dots, which later turn yellowish brown. Leaves and stems curl or become distorted.	Leafhoppers, small, yellow-green, cricket-like insects.	Damaged foliage should be removed and destroyed. Spray plants with an insecticide.
White or light green tunnels are bored into leaves of columbine, chrysanthemum, delphinium or primrose. Older tunnels turn black. Leaves may lose color, dry up and eventually die.	Leaf miners, microscopic, pale green fly maggots.	Control is difficult. Pick off and destroy infested leaves as they appear. In the fall, cut the plant to the ground and discard it. Since organic waste attracts maggots, keep the garden well weeded.

PROBLEM	CAUSE	SOLUTION
Foliage of hibiscus, columbine, lupine, primrose or chrysanthemum turns yellow and plants are stunted. Shaking of the plants causes a white cloud to appear.	Whiteflies, insects ⅟₁₆ inch long that generally collect on the undersides of young leaves.	Keep the garden weeded. Spray affected plants with a diluted soap solution or an insecticide. Whiteflies are attracted to yellow, so flypaper can be hung in the garden to help control the population.
Leaves become speckled, then discolored and curled; flowers and buds discolor or dry up and webbing is seen. This is particularly evident in hot, dry weather. Susceptible plants are columbine, daylily, delphinium, iris, phlox, shasta daisy, foxglove, hollyhock, candytuft and chrysanthemum.	Mites, which are pinhead-sized, insect-like creatures.	Keep the plants well watered, and spray the undersides of the leaves with water or a diluted soap solution regularly. An insecticide may also be used.
Holes appear in leaves; buds, flowers and stems may also be eaten.	Any variety of caterpillar.	Small populations can be destroyed by hand. *Bacillus thuringiensis,* called Bt, causes milky disease, which kills many types of caterpillars but does not harm plants. If caterpillars return to your garden every spring, Bt can be sprayed in anticipation of the problem.
Light-colored spots appear on the upper surfaces of leaves. Foliage may wilt or discolor and fall from the plant. Flower buds may be deformed.	Plant bugs, also called true bugs, green or shiny black insects, ¼ inch long, with antennae and wings.	Spray with an insecticide.
A sudsy, white substance resembling foam appears in the area between leaf and stem.	Spittlebugs. Eggs hatch in spring and young insects produce the foamy substance for protection while they feed on sap from tender leaves and stems.	Wash plants off with water and a diluted soap solution or use an insecticide.
Chrysanthemum or phlox plants wilt, stop growing and may die. Sometimes brown or yellow blotches appear on leaves.	Nematodes, very tiny worms that live in the soil and feed on roots.	Since nematodes cannot be seen, only a soil test will confirm their presence. Be suspicious if roots appear swollen or stunted. There are no effective chemical controls; remove and dispose of infected plants and the soil that surrounds them.
Holes are eaten in leaves, starting with leaves at the bottom of plants. Entire young seedlings may disappear. Telltale silver streaks appear on leaves and garden paths.	Slugs or snails, which hide during the day and feed at night.	Slugs and snails can be trapped in saucers of beer. Slugs will also collect under grapefruit halves or melon rinds turned upside down. Both slugs and snails are killed by salt, but salt may damage plants. Bait is available at garden centers.

PROBLEM	CAUSE	SOLUTION
Leaves develop spots or lesions that can lead to yellowing and the death of the plant. Aster, chrysanthemum, delphinium, foxglove, iris and phlox are particularly susceptible.	Leaf spot disease, caused by a number of fungi or bacteria and spread by insects, contaminated tools or even splashing water. The organisms thrive in moisture.	Remove infected leaves as they appear and do not allow infected material to remain in the garden through winter. Water overhead only in the morning; damp foliage in cool night air fosters the spread of the disease. Do not overcrowd plants. A fungicide can protect healthy foliage but will not destroy fungus on infected leaves.
Young seedlings suddenly topple over, especially when started indoors.	Damping-off, a disease caused by a fungus that forms in the soil and attacks seeds and the roots of young seedlings at ground level.	Use a fresh, sterile planting medium. Do not overwater seed flats. Provide good air circulation. Drench the seed flat with a systemic fungicide before sowing.
Upper leaf surfaces have pale spots; undersides of leaves are covered with an orange or reddish brown powder. Plants may be stunted in severe cases. Bee balm, black-eyed Susan, chrysanthemum, columbine, hollyhock, liatris and lupine are susceptible.	Rust, a disease caused by fungus.	Water early in the day so plants can dry before nightfall; cool air and damp foliage foster the spread of the disease. In the fall, collect and discard all infected leaves and stems. Spray with sulfur or a garden fungicide. Some varieties of chrysanthemum are rust-resistant.
Leaves turn yellow or are stunted and wilted. Entire plant may wilt and die. Roots are discolored, dark brown or black. Many perennials, especially aster, chrysanthemum and delphinium, may be affected.	Root rot, caused by pythium, rhizoctonia or sclerotinia fungus in the soil.	Remove and discard affected plants and the surrounding soil. These fungi grow in moist soils; improved soil drainage is one means of control. Drench the soil with a garden fungicide.
White, powdery growth appears on upper leaves, causing leaf distortion. Signs may also be seen on stems and buds—especially in late summer and fall, when nights are cool. Susceptible plants include aster, bee balm, delphinium and phlox.	Powdery mildew, a disease caused by fungus.	Plant susceptible plants in full sun with good air circulation. Water overhead only in the early morning. Cut off infected plants to the ground in fall and discard. Fungicides may be used; also effective are lime-sulfur sprays and antidesiccants.
Foliage of gaillardia, English daisy, coreopsis and delphinium suddenly yellows; flowers are stunted and have a greenish color; new growth is distorted in shape.	Aster yellows, a disease caused by microscopic organisms similiar to bacteria.	Aster yellows is often spread by leafhoppers *(page 84)*. Remove and destroy infected plants; do not use the same type of plant in the same spot. Keep the garden weeded; aster yellows and leafhopper eggs thrive in untended, weedy areas.

PROBLEM	CAUSE	SOLUTION
Entire plant becomes yellow, wilts, fails to grow and eventually dies; a cut across a stem reveals dark streaks or other discoloration on the inside. Chrysanthemum, peony, bleeding heart, aster, coreopsis, poppy, phlox and delphinium may be affected.	Vascular wilt, caused by fungi or bacteria in the soil.	Remove and destroy infected plants; substitute wilt-resistant varieties. There are no effective chemical controls.
Tips and leaves of peonies blacken. Buds may not open; if they do, flowers are likely to be streaked with brown.	Botrytis blight, a disease caused by various fungi.	Cut stalks to the ground in fall and destroy. As growth starts in spring, spraying with a systemic fungicide can help prevent recurrence.
Leaves of peony, columbine, delphinium, iris, aster or gaillardia become mottled with light green or yellow discoloration. Plant growth is often stunted.	Mosaic virus.	Virus infections cannot be controlled, but since they are often spread by aphids, treat affected areas for aphids *(page 84)*. Keep the garden well weeded. Remove infected plants.
Iris plants fall over; rhizomes are soft to the touch.	Soft rot, a disease caused by bacteria.	Cut out the infected parts of the rhizomes with a sharp knife or scrape them out with a spoon. Mix a 10 percent solution of chlorine bleach in water and pour it over the rhizomes and the surrounding soil.
Leaves and stems of iris or columbine turn yellow, wilt and rot, then die. White fibers are visible at the base of the plant. Roots show signs of decay.	Crown rot, a disease caused by a fungus that enters stems at soil level.	Remove and discard all infected plants and the surrounding soil. Thin out overcrowded plants and improve soil drainage. Clean and disinfect all garden tools, which can spread the disease.
Foliage of hollyhock and peony develops irregular, purplish brown spots. Purplish lesions form along the stem; plant growth is often stunted.	Anthracnose, a disease caused by fungus.	The best control is preventive spraying with a fungicide in early spring. Remove and discard any infected plant parts.
Leaves of aster, geum, veronica, lupine and potentilla turn yellow. The undersides of the foliage develop gray or tan fuzzy growths that resemble tufts of cotton.	Downy mildew, a disease caused by fungus.	Do not water plants overhead after morning. Remove and destroy infected plant parts or the entire plant if the infection is severe. Spray with fungicide.

TIPS AND TECHNIQUES

FRAGRANCE IN THE GARDEN

Fill the air with the scent of perennial flowers, and you'll add an enriching dimension to the garden.

Among the most popular fragrant perennials are bee balm, peony and phlox *(left),* dianthus, gas plant, lavender, evening primrose, wormwood, viola, yarrow, yellow primrose and white primrose. Some varieties of daylily, hosta and iris also have pleasing aromas. Since different types of perennials mature and blossom at different times, you can have a series of garden fragrances from late spring through early autumn.

When designing a garden for fragrance, select a site where the sweet scents can be enjoyed. Locate aromatic plants alongside a porch or a patio where you sit, in a border beside a path you regularly walk along or in a bed outside a window you sometimes open so the perfume can be wafted indoors.

MAKING GARDENING EASY

If you want to keep gardening chores to a minimum, select plants that require little maintenance. Among the perennials rarely bothered by pests and diseases are butterfly weed, coreopsis, bleeding heart, coneflower, daylily, candytuft, veronica, globeflower, monkshood, sedum, Solomon's-seal, coralbells, statice, poppy and yarrow.

The time that you must devote to gardening chores will be reduced even further if you plant perennials that do not need staking, frequent deadheading, dividing or thinning. In this category are butterfly weed, coneflower, bleeding heart, fleabane, daylily, coralbells, gay-feather, lythrum, Virginia bluebells, false dragonhead, geum, hosta, bergenia and veronica.

ACCENTS AT NIGHT

One of the most delightful times of day in a garden is the evening, when the air is still and cool. To make the most of it, select perennials with white or pastel flowers, because pale colors show up better against the night sky than dark ones. Garden lighting will help to accent them and show off their beauty. Some flowers, especially the evening primrose, become more fragrant at night.

The gas plant is a perennial that can lend a little fun to the night garden. Its foliage and flowers exude a volatile gas that can be ignited. For a momentary flare that is bright (but not hot enough to be dangerous), hold a lighted match alongside the plant. Choose a still night; wind disperses the gas and you won't get any flare at all.

THE MONOCHROMATIC GARDEN

A perennial garden of a single color can be an extension of your personality; it can also suggest and influence mood. Since some perennials bloom in spring and others bloom in fall, you can change colors with the seasons.

For a tranquil scene, use flowers in shades of cool colors such as blue and lavender. Good candidates are bellflower, mist flower and monkshood (above), balloon flower, Italian bugloss, Stokes' aster, fleabane, forget-me-not, false indigo, pincushion flower, lavender, delphinium or veronica. A serene mood can also be achieved with a selection of white flowers such as phlox, gas plant, veronica, candytuft, shasta daisy, trillium, white iris, cimicifuga and feverfew.

A bright, bold colorscape can be created with the red hues of astilbe, bee balm, chrysanthemum, poppy, gaillardia, peony, daylily, cardinal flower, red-hot poker or penstemon. For a warm, lively color display, use the oranges of geum, daylily, lychnis, butterfly weed, iris, poppy or blackberry lily; or the golds and yellows of daylily, evening primrose, globeflower, goldenrod, coreopsis, chrysanthemum, leopard's-bane, sunflower, sneezeweed, black-eyed Susan, loosestrife, basket-of-gold and yarrow.

For a soft, delicate effect, plant pink varieties of geranium, dianthus, peony, phlox, turtlehead or bleeding heart.

ATTRACTING BUTTERFLIES

Attracting butterflies to the garden requires a combination of selecting the right plants and arranging them in a manner that looks natural. But-terflies need water, shelter from wind, sunlight for warmth and flower nectar for energy. And they have certain preferences; they seem to favor plants with small clusters of flowers rather than large blooms. Among the perennials they like are black-eyed Susan, globe thistle, goldenrod, aster, fleabane, catmint, red valerian, sedum, lavender, bee balm and phlox.

THE JOY OF CUT FLOWERS

Show off your creativity by cutting flowers from the garden and bringing them indoors to liven up the dining table, the living room, the bedroom and even the bath. The arrangements you make can be as simple as one or two poppies floating in a bowl or as complicated as a mix of spiky foxgloves, rounded peonies and leafy greens in an upright vase. When planning a cutting garden, use different perennials for different effects. Delphinium, iris, gay-feather, lupine and phlox have long stems. Lavender, red-hot poker and veronica provide tall spikes of color. Peonies and poppies are large, broad-faced flowers. Aster, gaillardia, marguerite, black-eyed Susan and shasta daisy have informal-looking blossoms. Baby's-breath and coralbells have airy clusters of tiny flowers that can fill out an arrangement.

It is not necessary to have a separate area for a cutting garden. These plants are attractive in their own right and can be incorporated into any perennial garden. Some of the plants will continue producing new blossoms after they have been cut.

MAXIMIZING ON MUMS

Chrysanthemums are favorite perennials for the fall garden, but from early spring until late August, they take up space and do not provide blossoms. To solve this problem without purchasing new mums every fall, and still have flower beds that are filled with color all summer long, take stem cuttings (page 68) from the chrysanthemums in spring, when new mum growth begins. As soon as the cuttings have taken root, remove the mother plants from the ground and discard them. In their place, fill the beds with annuals for color that lasts throughout the summer. In early fall, when the annuals begin to fade and the new chrysanthemums begin to bloom, remove the annuals from the beds. Plant the mums, leave them in the ground all winter and start the process over again the following spring.

5
DICTIONARY OF PERENNIALS

erennials come in varieties by the hundreds, and many are available in countless colors and sizes. Some are early-spring bloomers; others wait to flower in autumn. A majority prosper in soil that is slightly to moderately acid, but a few do well in soil that is alkaline or strongly acid. Then there is the question of which species provide long-lasting cut flowers. Some cut blooms remain brisk for weeks; less sturdy ones droop almost before you can get them in the house.

The dictionary that follows should help you devise plantings rich in color and foliage throughout the growing season. It lists 185 perennials, from acanthus to yucca, under their Latin names, with cross-references under their common names. Within each entry there is a description of what the plant looks like, what climatic zone it flourishes in, when it blooms, and what it requires in the way of soil conditions, sunlight, moisture and special care.

The entries also include specific help in planning your garden. Sections called "Landscape uses" suggest how and where each plant will show up most effectively—as bright color accents in a shady spot, as massed waves of foliage, as tall centerpieces in beds or borders, or as low-growing but decorative additions to a rock garden. Perennials, with their enormous diversity, offer limitless opportunities to create gardens and other plantings to suit any taste. The dictionary should help you put together a graceful, varied landscape that is particularly, delightfully your own.

ACANTHUS SPINOSUS

ACHILLEA MILLEFOLIUM 'FIRE KING'

ACONITUM × CARMICHAELII

Acanthus (a-KAN-thus)
Bear's-breech

Sun-loving plant resistant to drought with broad, deeply lobed leaves up to 2 feet long that rise from the base of the plant. Large spikes of white, rose or purple tubular flowers blossom on 3- to 4-foot stalks in summer. Zones 6-9.

Selected species and varieties. *A. mollis,* soft-leaved acanthus: broad clumps of dark green leaves and rose or white flowers. The variety 'Latifolius,' broad-leaved acanthus, has glossy arching leaves and purplish pink flowers. *A. spinosus:* dark green spiny, thistle-like leaves and profuse blossoms.

Growing conditions. Grow bear's-breeches in well-drained soil in full sun, except in the South, where a soil with more moisture and light shade is needed. Allow 3 feet of space between plants. Propagate in the spring by seeds or in the fall from root cuttings. Clumps can be divided in early spring or in fall after the plant has blossomed for at least three years. In rich soil, the rapidly spreading roots can become a problem and may need to be contained.

Landscape uses. Plant bear's-breeches where their large, bold decorative forms can show to best advantage: in the front of a perennial bed or a shrub border or bordering a walk. Acanthus leaves are a common motif in classical sculpture.

—

Achillea (ak-il-EE-a)
Yarrow

Sun-loving plant with ferny foliage and flat clusters of white or yellow flowers. Noted for its ability to grow in poor soil and dry conditions. Zones 3-8.

Selected species and varieties. *A. filipendulina,* fernleaf yarrow: grayish green foliage and showy clusters of small yellow flowers that blossom throughout the summer on plants 4 feet tall. Varieties include 'Coronation Gold,' with 3-inch deep-yellow flower clusters that bloom on stiff, upright 3-foot stems from late spring through midsummer; and 'Gold Plate,' the tallest of the achilleas, with 6-inch yellow flower heads on 4½-foot stems from late spring to midsummer. *A. × lewisii* 'King Edward': a hybrid 8 inches high with downy gray foliage and small pale yellow flowers from late spring to midsummer. *A. millefolium,* common yarrow: small flat clusters of grayish white flowers, and foliage that smells spicy when crushed. Height 2 feet. The variety 'Fire King' has clusters of bright pink flowers with white centers growing on 2-foot stems rising from a low mat of light green leaves. Blooms middle to late summer. The variety 'Rosea' has lighter pink flowers. *A. × 'Moonshine':* a 2-foot hybrid with silver-gray foliage and yellow blossoms ringed with green. Blooms late spring to late summer.

Growing conditions. Plant yarrow in full sun in a well-drained soil. Although it tolerates poor soil, yarrow will flourish in soil enriched with organic matter. Space 'King Edward' yarrows 1 foot apart and the other yarrows about 2 feet apart. Stake tall species. Divide clumps every three or four years or whenever they become crowded. If the dead flowers are cut off, the plant will bloom again later in the season.

Landscape uses. Low forms of yarrow make good rock garden plants. Grow the taller kinds in a perennial border or in a cutting garden. The large, flat flower heads are long-lasting as cut flowers and are easily dried for winter bouquets.

—

Aconitum (ak-o-NY-tum)
Monkshood

Tall spikes of rounded blue to purple flowers shaped like little helmets in summer or early fall. Glossy, finely cut leaves on plants from 2 to 5 feet tall. Zones 3-8.

Selected species and varieties. *A. × bicolor* 'Bicolor': 4 feet tall with blue-and-white flowers on loosely branching spikes in summer. *A. × bicolor* 'Bressingham Spire': 3 feet tall with bluish purple flowers. *A. × carmichaelii,* azure monkshood: 3 to 4 feet tall with blue flowers in late summer to early fall. *A. napellus,* English monkshood: indigo-blue flowers on 4-foot stems from middle to late summer. *A. napellus* 'Sparks Variety' has deep blue flowers.

Growing conditions. Plant monkshood in light shade in moist soil enriched with compost, cow manure or leaf mold. It can also be grown in full sun in Zones 3-6. Space plants 1½ feet apart. Water well in dry seasons. Monkshood grows slowly and once established should not be moved. Mulch the roots with straw or evergreen boughs during the first winter after planting. Propagate by seed. All parts of these plants are extremely poisonous.

Landscape uses. Grow monkshood in the middle or rear of a perennial border or in dappled sunlight in moist woods. Azure monkshood is an excellent plant for late-season bloom.

Actaea (ak-TEE-a)
Baneberry

Dense clusters of small white spring flowers held above 1- to 2-foot clumps of toothed foliage. Clusters of glistening berries ripen in late summer or fall. Zones 2-8.

Selected species and varieties. *A. pachypoda,* doll's-eyes: sharply toothed, deeply cut leaves and white flowers. The white berries that ripen in late summer have black tips, making them resemble dolls' eyes. Zones 2-8. *A. rubra,* red baneberry: similar to doll's-eyes but with leaves less deeply cut and less sharply toothed. Shiny red berries ripen in fall. Zones 3-8.

Growing conditions. Grow baneberries in partial shade in a moist soil rich in organic matter such as peat moss, compost or leaf mold. Space new plants 1½ feet apart. Propagate by dividing plants in the spring or by sowing seeds in the fall. The berries are poisonous.

Landscape uses. Use baneberries among shrubs or as accents in a woodland garden or plant them in a rock garden.

Adam's-needle see *Yucca*

Adenophora (ad-en-OFF-or-a)
Ladybells

Deep blue bell-shaped flowers that bloom in branching spires atop 3-foot stems from middle to late summer. Zones 5-8.

Selected species and varieties. *A. confusa,* Farrer's ladybells: ¾-inch flowers borne above low clumps of 3-inch toothed oval leaves.

Growing conditions. Plant ladybells in full sun in a light, well-drained soil supplemented with leaf mold, peat moss or compost. Plant ladybells in a permanent location, since they will not do well if they are moved or divided. Space plants 1½ feet apart. Propagate from seed planted in fall.

Landscape uses. Though bloom is sparse, the flowers provide a handsome blue in a perennial border.

Adonis (a-DON-is)

A member of the buttercup family with fernlike foliage and 2- to 3-inch saucer-shaped flowers in white and shades of red, yellow and orange from late winter to early spring. Grows 1 to 1½ feet tall. Zones 3-7.

Selected species and varieties. *A. amurensis,* Amur adonis: blooms so early that it sometimes comes up through the snow. The flowers are usually borne several to a stem. The deeply cut foliage curls around the flower buds later in the season but is barely visible when the plant first blossoms.

Growing conditions. Plant in full sun or light shade in well-drained sandy soil, setting plants 9 to 12 inches apart. Late in the spring the plant becomes dormant and disappears underground. Be sure to mark where adonis is planted. Propagate by dividing in the fall.

Landscape uses. Amur adonis looks best planted in groups. Site the plants where their early flowers can easily be seen and appreciated. Grow them close to plants with abundant foliage to fill the empty spaces left when they go dormant.

Aegopodium (ee-go-PO-dee-um)
Goutweed

Low, rapidly spreading plant grown mainly for its foliage, which consists of compound, oval, toothed leaflets. Inconspicuous clusters of small white flowers in spring. Zones 3-9.

Selected species and varieties. *A. podagraria:* deep-rooted 12-inch-tall plant with green foliage. The variety 'Variegatum,' silver-edged goutweed, grows only 6 inches tall and has leaves attractively edged and splotched with white. It is less invasive than the species.

Growing conditions. Plant goutweed in sun or partial shade in poor or fertile moist but well-drained soil. It spreads rapidly but it can be controlled by planting it in a bottomless plastic flower pot or other container sunk in the soil. Propagate by division. The flowers of the variegated form should be sheared off before they go to seed.

Landscape uses. Use goutweed as a fast-spreading ground cover where its invasive habit will not be a problem. Silver-edged goutweed is an attractive foliage plant for a perennial border if care is taken to control its spread.

ACTAEA RUBRA

ADENOPHORA CONFUSA

ADONIS AMURENSIS

AEGOPODIUM PODAGRARIA 'VARIEGATUM'

AGAPANTHUS ORIENTALIS

ALCEA ROSEA

ALCHEMILLA CONJUNCTA

ALOE STRIATA

Agapanthus (ag-a-PAN-thus)
African lily, lily of the Nile

Large round clusters of blue or white funnel-shaped flowers on tall stems for many weeks in summer. Clumps of handsome long, narrow leaves are evergreen in warm winters. Zones 8-10.

Selected species and varieties. *A. africanus:* stems 1½ to 2 feet tall with up to 30 or more blue flowers. Curving leaves ½ inch wide. *A. orientalis:* flower stems up to 5 feet tall with clusters of as many as 100 blue flowers. The cultivar 'Albidus' has white flowers. *A.* × 'Peter Pan' has 12- to 18-inch flower stems and foliage clumps up to 1 foot tall. Large clumps of leaves 2 inches wide.

Growing conditions. Plant agapanthus in moist, well-drained soil in full sun. It tolerates periods of drought but grows best when well watered during the growing season. Allow 2 feet between plants. Divide only when plants become overcrowded. North of Zone 8 agapanthus can be grown in a container that is brought indoors for the winter.

Landscape uses. Use agapanthus next to a terrace or at the end of a bed where both its flowers and its attractive foliage will be visible.

—

Ageratum see *Eupatorium*

—

Alcea (al-SEE-a)
Hollyhock

Tall, sturdy stalks up to 10 feet high lined with rough, hairy foliage and tipped with spires of 3- to 5-inch flowers that open in succession from the bottom up from early summer through early fall. Zones 3-8.

Selected species and varieties. *A. rosea:* white, pink, red, yellow or purple flowers with either single or double rows of petals on 5- to 10-foot stalks. The variety 'Charter's Doubles' has double-petaled flowers on 5- to 6-foot stalks, 'Powder Puff' has fluffy double flowers on 4- to 5-foot stalks and 'Singles' has single flowers on 7-foot plants.

Growing conditions. Grow hollyhocks in full sun in moist but well-drained soil that is rich in organic matter such as peat moss, compost or leaf mold. Protect plants from strong winds. Hollyhocks live only two years but they propagate themselves by the many seeds they drop in the fall. Transplant seedlings when they come up the following spring, spacing them 1½ feet apart. They will flower the following year. Hollyhocks are prone to rust, especially in the South.

Landscape uses. Hollyhocks make dramatic specimen plants when used in small groups. Plant them at the back of a wide border or in the shelter of a fence or a wall.

—

Alchemilla (al-kem-ILL-a)

Low-growing plant with flower clusters on slender stems up to 18 inches tall in late spring through early summer. Handsome lobed or fan-shaped leaves. Zones 3-8.

Selected species and varieties. *A. conjuncta:* pale yellow-green ⅛-inch flowers borne high on 4- to 6-inch clumps of lobed green foliage edged in silver. *A. mollis,* lady's-mantle: lacy chartreuse ⅛-inch flowers are held in elongated clusters above grayish green fan-shaped leaves.

Growing conditions. Plant alchemilla in full sun or light shade in any moist but well-drained soil enriched with organic matter. Propagate by digging up and replanting the seedlings that self-sow or by division. Space new plants 1½ feet apart.

Landscape uses. Use alchemilla to edge a perennial border or as an attractive ground cover. Flowers are excellent fillers in small arrangements and can be dried.

—

Aloe (AL-lo)

Clusters of tubular spring flowers grow on long stalks above evergreen rosettes of thick green, bluish green or gray leaves with bristly edges. Zones 9 and 10.

Selected species and varieties. *A. striata,* coral aloe: pink to orange flower clusters on 3-foot stalks. Pointed lance-shaped leaves edged with pink are up to 20 inches long.

Growing conditions. Grow aloe in full sun in a well-drained to dry soil. Space plants 2 feet apart. Propagate from seed or by removing young shoots from the base of the plant.

Landscape uses. Its stiff sculpturesque form and varied textures make aloe a valuable specimen plant in a dry, hot climate. It can also be planted in groups at the front of a border or used to outline a walk or a terrace.

Alstroemeria
(al-stree-MEER-ee-a)
Peruvian lily

Clusters of up to 20 funnel-shaped flowers with curled lips bloom in midsummer atop sturdy stems lined with narrow, ribbon-like leaves. Zones 8-10.

Selected species and varieties. *A. ligtu:* red to rosy lilac 2-inch flowers with upper petals streaked with purple, orange or yellow on 4-foot stems rising at intervals from creeping horizontal roots. There are many hybrids ranging from 2 to 4 feet tall with pastel pink or yellow flowers.

Growing conditions. Plant Peruvian lilies in full sun in a moist, well-drained soil enriched with peat moss or other organic matter, spacing plants 1 foot apart. Provide light shade where summers are hot and dry. Let soil dry out after plants flower, and mulch in fall to protect from frost. Propagate by division in spring.

Landscape uses. Use Peruvian lilies at the middle or the back of a wide border or as the centerpiece in an island bed. They make excellent cut flowers.

—

Alumroot see *Heuchera*

—

Amsonia (am-SO-nee-a)
Bluestar

Shrubby plants with narrow willow-like leaves. Bluish star-shaped spring or early-summer flowers in clusters are followed by narrow seedpods. Zones 3-8.

Selected species and varieties. *A. ciliata:* blue flowers on stiff 3-foot stems and extremely narrow feathery leaves. Zones 6-8. *A. tabernaemontana,* willow amsonia: dense clusters of steel blue flowers almost an inch in diameter blossom on the ends of 3½-foot-long stems. The leaves change from green to yellow in the fall. Zones 3-8.

Growing conditions. Grow bluestars in almost any soil in full sun or light shade. Space plants 1½ feet apart. If the soil is very fertile, plants may need to be cut back to make them bushier. Propagate by division or by sowing seeds in spring.

Landscape uses. Plant bluestars singly or in small groups in the middle of a border. Willow amsonia does well in damp soil and is a good choice for planting by the side of a stream or a pool. Both species are dependable and easy to grow.

Anaphalis (an-AFF-al-is)
Pearly everlasting

Silver-gray to green lance-shaped leaves on erect stems holding small flat clusters of fluffy ¼-inch white flowers in summer. Zones 3-9.

Selected species and varieties. *A. margaritacea,* common pearly everlasting: grows to 2 feet with slender pointed leaves that are green on top, gray and downy underneath. Zones 4-9. *A. triplinervis:* silvery gray leaves in the spring turn a soft gray-green toward the end of summer. Clusters of flowers bloom on foot-tall stems from midsummer through frost. The cultivar 'Summer Snow' is more compact. Zones 3-9.

Growing conditions. Plant pearly everlasting in full sun in any ordinary, well-drained soil. Common pearly everlasting tolerates dry conditions; *A. triplinervis* does best when the soil is constantly moist but not wet. Plants live for years with little attention. Start new plants by division in spring. Space them 1 foot apart. Seed sown in spring will produce flowering plants the second year.

Landscape uses. The foliage of pearly everlasting remains attractive throughout the growing season. Locate plants toward the front of a perennial border, group them in an all-white border or grow them in a rock garden. The flowers can be gathered and dried for winter bouquets.

—

Anchusa (an-KOO-sa)
Bugloss

Branching clusters of showy blue flowers resembling forget-me-nots above rough tongue-shaped leaves. Blossoms appear in late spring and last for a month or more. Zones 3-8.

Selected species and varieties. *A. azurea,* Italian bugloss: blue flowers ½ inch across bloom abundantly on 3- to 5-foot stems. *A. azurea* 'Little John' is a compact 1-foot variety with deep blue flowers. 'Loddon Royalist' has large clear blue flowers on 3-foot stems.

Growing conditions. Plant in full sun or light shade in any good well-drained soil. The roots will rot if water collects around them in winter. Tall buglosses need staking. After plants blossom, their stems and leaves become limp and unattractive. Cut them back to the ground for another show of blossoms later in the season. Propagate by division every two to three years. Space the new divisions 1½ to 2 feet apart.

ALSTROEMERIA LIGTU

AMSONIA TABERNAEMONTANA

ANAPHALIS TRIPLINERVIS

ANCHUSA AZUREA 'LODDON ROYALIST'

ANEMONE × HYBRIDA

ANIGOZANTHUS FLAVIDUS

ANTENNARIA DIOICA ROSEA

Seedlings seldom resemble the parent varieties.

Landscape uses. Plant bugloss in a perennial border where the foliage of other plants can mask the space left when it is cut back.

Anemone (a-NEM-o-ne)
Windflower

Graceful single or double flowers in white, cream, and shades of red, purple and blue. Sizes range from 3-inch alpines to 2-foot hybrids. Branched stems with leaves composed of several divided or ferny leaflets. Zones 2-8.

Selected species and varieties. *A. canadensis,* meadow anemone: white flowers 1 to 2 inches wide on 2-foot stems above light green three-lobed leaves in spring. Zones 3-7. *A. × hybrida,* Japanese anemone: single pink or white flowers 2 to 3 inches wide from late summer into fall on 3-foot stems. Zones 5-8. Among the many hybrid varieties are 'Alba,' with 2- to 3-inch white flowers; 'September Charm,' with pink flowers having a silvery sheen; and 'September Sprite,' a 15-inch plant with single pink flowers that bloom through fall. *A. magellanica:* cream-colored flowers on 1½-foot stalks from late spring through summer. Zones 2-8. *A. pulsatilla,* pasque flower: blue or purple bell-shaped flowers on foot-tall plants in the spring. Zones 5-8. *A. sylvestris* 'Snowdrops,' snowdrop windflower: sweet-scented white flowers, sometimes drooping, on stems 1½ feet tall. Blossoms in late spring. Zones 3-8. *A. vitifolia* 'Robustissima,' grape-leaved anemone: branching clusters of pink flowers on 2- to 3-foot stalks. Blooms from late summer into fall. Zones 4-8.

Growing conditions. Grow anemones in partial shade in moist, but not soggy, woodland soil or in garden soil supplemented with organic matter such as compost or well-rotted leaves. Pasque flower requires full sun and well-drained soil in cool locations. Grape-leaved anemone also thrives in ordinary garden soil and tolerates both full sun and drought. Japanese anemones should have some protection from the wind. Space the smaller anemones 1 foot apart and the taller ones 2 feet apart. New plants can be started from seed or by dividing established plants carefully in the spring. Meadow, Japanese and grape-leaved anemones will all grow quickly under good conditions and may require division every

three years or so. The other anemones grow more slowly and division is rarely needed except for propagation purposes.

Landscape uses. It is possible to have anemones flowering in three seasons. Plant the spring-blooming pasque flower in a rock garden or in a partially shaded border. The snowdrop windflower is best naturalized in a lightly shaded woodland garden or in a shrub border where it can be allowed to spread unhampered. Plant *A. magellanica* for summer bloom in a lightly shaded perennial border and Japanese anemones for late-summer and autumn bloom. Use grape-leaved anemone for late-season flowers in sun or light shade.

Anigozanthus (an-i-go-ZAN-thus)
Kangaroo-paw

Tubular downy red, yellow or green flowers on hairy stems with sword-shaped leaves. Zones 9 and 10.

Selected species and varieties. *A. flavidus:* clusters of 1½-inch flowers with divided lips on 5-foot stalks. Blossoms spring through fall.

Growing conditions. Plant kangaroo-paw in full sun in a well-drained sandy soil, spacing plants 1 foot apart. Water well from spring through fall and sparingly in winter. Propagate by division in spring.

Landscape uses. Kangaroo-paw may be grown as a specimen plant or used as a decorative accent in a container on a terrace.

Antennaria (an-ten-AY-ree-a)
Pussy-toes

Small plant with woolly leaves and stems and tight clusters of small flowers in spring. Zones 3-8.

Selected species and varieties. *A. dioica,* common pussy-toes: leaves that are green on top and white and furry beneath form a low ground cover. Little oval tufts of gray, pinkish or white flowers bloom atop 1-foot stems. *A. dioica rosea* has rose-colored flowers.

Growing conditions. Grow pussy-toes in well-drained sandy or gravelly soil in full sun. Space plants 1½ feet apart. Propagate by division or by sowing seeds in spring or fall.

Landscape uses. Pussy-toes spread rapidly in a rock garden, where their foliage remains attractive after the plants have flowered.

Anthemis (AN-them-is)

Daisy-like blossoms from midsummer through early fall on stems up to 3 feet tall with ferny, aromatic foliage. Zones 3-8.

Selected species and varieties. *A. sancti-johannis,* St. John's camomile: deep orange flowers 2 inches across on branching gray-green stems. Zones 5-8. *A. tinctoria,* golden marguerite: 2-inch golden yellow flowers held well above a low clump of foliage. Zones 3-8. Varieties include 'Kelwayi,' with deeper yellow flowers; 'Moonlight,' with pale yellow flowers; and 'E. C. Buxton,' with flowers usually pale yellow but occasionally white.

Growing conditions. Grow St. John's camomile and golden marguerite in full sun in a well-drained to dry infertile soil. In moist, fertile soils the plants become leggy and have fewer blossoms. Remove spent flowers to ensure continuous bloom for more than two months and stake the floppy stems for support. Divide plants annually in spring or fall, and set new plants 1½ feet apart. Sow seeds in spring.

Landscape uses. Use St. John's camomile and golden marguerite as edging plants at the front of an informal border. They are excellent for cutting.

Aquilegia (ak-wil-EE-jee-a)
Columbine

Graceful plants with attractive ferny foliage and yellow, blue, lavender, red, white or bicolored flowers. Long narrow spurs extend backward from the flower. Zones 3-8.

Selected species and varieties. *A. caerulea,* Colorado columbine: 1½ to 3 feet tall, with blue-and-white flowers 2 inches across that have slender curved spurs. Blooms spring through early summer. *A. canadensis,* American columbine: branched stems 1 to 2 feet tall bear nodding red-and-yellow flowers 1½ inches wide. The smooth leaves are lobed and divided into three sections. Blossoms spring through early summer. *A. chrysantha,* golden columbine: large yellow flowers up to 3 inches across with exceptionally long spurs bloom from late spring to midsummer. The variety 'Silver Queen' is 2½ to 3 feet tall with showy white spring flowers. *A. flabellata,* fan columbine: a low-growing species with blue to purple flowers 2 inches wide on 1- to 1½-foot stems. The variety

'Nana Alba' is barely 1 foot tall with white spring flowers. *A. longissima* 'Maxistar': a robust columbine with clear yellow flowers and long yellow spurs. Grows 2 to 3 feet tall. Hybrid forms of columbine are the ones most often used in flower borders. These include *A.* × 'Crimson Star,' with long red spurs and white centers tinted with red; *A.* × 'Nora Barlow,' an unusual columbine with numerous petals, no spurs, and a soft red, pink and green color combination; and *A.* × 'Rose Queen,' with many pink-and-white flowers.

Growing conditions. Plant in full sun or light shade in well-drained soil. After several years the plants will begin to deteriorate. Discard and replace them. To start plants from seed, sow outdoors early in the spring in fine soil and transplant into the garden the following autumn or spring. Set plants 1½ feet apart.

Landscape uses. American columbine and fan columbine are appealing plants for a rock garden or the front of a flower border. Use the taller forms in the middle of a border, where they will bloom for several weeks. The flowers are excellent for cutting. Columbines have abundant nectar and attract hummingbirds.

Arabis (AR-a-bis)
Rock cress

Low-growing plant 1 foot tall or less with pink or white spring blossoms. Zones 3-8.

Selected species and varieties. *A. caucasica,* wall rock cress: fragrant white flowers ½ inch across and downy whitish leaves 1 to 3 inches long. The variety 'Flore-Pleno' has gray furry leaves and double-petaled white flowers; 'Snow Cap' grows to 8 inches and bears fragrant white flowers with a single row of petals. *A. procurrens:* numerous spikes of white flowers on 1-foot stems above a thick mat of small oval evergreen leaves. *A.* × 'Rosabella': a compact 5-inch plant with pinkish rose flowers.

Growing conditions. Grow rock cresses in full sun; *A. procurrens* may also be planted in light shade. All rock cresses require a light, well-drained soil. Humid weather and standing water will cause wall rock cress to rot. After the flowers have faded, shear plants lightly to make sure that they remain compact. Propagate by division in late summer or by sowing seeds in spring. Space new plants 1 foot apart.

ANTHEMIS TINCTORIA 'KELWAYI'

AQUILEGIA CHRYSANTHA

ARABIS CAUCASICA

ARCTOTHECA CALENDULA

ARENARIA MONTANA

ARISAEMA TRIPHYLLUM

ARMERIA PLANTAGINEA

Landscape uses. Plant arabis in a rock garden or among spring bulbs in a border.

—

Arctotheca (arc-to-THEE-ca)

Yellow daisy-like spring flowers above deeply divided gray-green leaves. Zones 9 and 10.

Selected species and varieties. *A. calendula,* Cape weed: yellow flowers 2 inches across on spreading foot-high plants.

Growing conditions. Plant Cape weed in full sun in a well-drained fertile soil. It is drought-tolerant and in good conditions spreads quickly. Space plants 1 to 1½ feet apart. Cape weed grows well on the West Coast but does not prosper in the high heat and humidity of Zones 9 and 10 in the Gulf Coast area and Florida.

Landscape uses. Cape weed may be used in a wildflower garden. It is an excellent ground cover for large, dry sunny areas.

—

Arenaria (a-ren-AIR-ee-a)
Sandwort

Mat-forming evergreen plant with small white flowers, singly or in clusters, in spring or early summer. Zones 5-9.

Selected species and varieties. *A. montana:* flowers in late spring or early summer on stems lined with slender, glossy leaves. *A. verna caespitosa,* moss sandwort, Irish moss: mosslike leaves up to ¾ inch long. Flowers appear in spring.

Growing conditions. Plant sandwort in full sun in constantly moist but well-drained soil, spacing plants 6 to 12 inches apart. Propagate by division in late summer or early fall.

Landscape uses. Sandwort may be planted in a rock garden or between the paving stones of a sunny terrace or walk.

—

Arisaema (a-ris-EE-ma)

A pair of large three-lobed leaves on a stout stem shelter an intricate green and purple or green flower structure resembling a small figure in a hooded pulpit. Arisaema blooms in spring. Zones 4-8.

Selected species and varieties. *A. triphyllum,* Jack-in-the-pulpit: tiny flowers surround the base of a cylindrical spike, or Jack, beneath a green and purple or green hood 4 to 7 inches long, called the pulpit. Plants grow 1 to 3 feet tall. Flowers are fol-

lowed by clusters of red berries after the hood shrivels and falls away.

Growing conditions. Plant Jack-in-the-pulpit in light to deep shade in a constantly moist but not wet soil that is high in organic matter such as leaf mold. Space plants 1 foot apart. Foliage dies down in summer. Propagate from seed in fall.

Landscape uses. Use Jack-in-the-pulpit in a woodland garden among plants that will fill in the empty space left when its foliage dies down.

—

Arkwright campion see *Lychnis*

—

Armeria (ar-MEER-ee-a)
Thrift, sea pink

White, pink or rose globe-shaped clusters of flowers borne on leafless stems above low tufts of grassy evergreen leaves in spring or summer. Zones 3-8.

Selected species and varieties. *A. maritima,* common thrift: white to deep pink ½-inch flower heads bloom throughout spring on 1-foot stems above 6-inch clumps of blue-green leaves. There are several dwarf forms, including 'Alba,' with white flowers on 5-inch stems, and 'Laucheana,' with rose to pink flowers on 6-inch stems. *A. plantaginea,* plantain thrift: 1- to 1¾-inch clusters of rosy pink or white flowers on 2-foot stems above 4- to 6-inch clumps of grassy leaves from late spring through midsummer.

Growing conditions. Plant thrift in full sun in a well-drained sandy soil. Plants will flower less if soil is too rich. Clumps eventually die out in the center. To rejuvenate old plants and propagate new ones, divide thrift every three to four years in spring or fall, and space new plants 9 to 12 inches apart.

Landscape uses. Use common thrift in a rock garden or between paving stones. Plantain thrift is a good plant for the front of a border.

—

Artemisia (ar-tem-IS-ee-a)

Plant prized for its ornamental, aromatic gray or silver foliage. Inconspicuous white or yellow flowers. Zones 3-9.

Selected species and varieties. *A. absinthium,* common wormwood: woody plant 2 to 4 feet tall. Silvery leaves divided into narrow segments. Zones 4-9. *A. canescens:* forms a lacy

1- to 1½-foot-tall mound of silver-gray foliage. Zones 5-9. *A. ludoviciana,* Western sage: 2 to 3 feet high, has narrow gray leaves up to 4 inches long with downy white undersides. Spreads rapidly. Zones 5-9. The variety 'Silver King' has smaller, more silvery leaves. 'Silver Queen' resembles 'Silver King' but has downier leaves. *A. schmidtiana* 'Nana': grows only 4 inches tall. Finely cut foliage is covered with white hairs. Zones 4-9. *A. schmidtiana* 'Silver Mound' forms a feathery mound 4 to 6 inches high and 1 foot or more across. Zones 4-9. *A. stellerana,* dusty-miller: grows to 2 feet with grayish white finely divided leaves. Spreads rapidly. Zones 3-9.

Growing conditions. These artemisias are hardy and easy to grow. Plant them in sun in well-drained soil of average or poor quality. The plants will become scraggly and floppy if the soil is fertile. They grow best if the temperature is cool and, like most gray-leaved plants, they tend to rot in hot and humid climates. Dusty-miller tolerates heat and humidity better than most. Plant the smaller artemisias 1 foot apart and the taller ones 2 feet apart. Propagate artemesias by division. 'Silver King' spreads rapidly and needs to be divided every year in spring or fall. 'Silver Mound' rarely needs dividing and is best left undisturbed.

Landscape uses. Artemisias are grown for their attractive foliage rather than for their modest flowers. Plant the lowest ones in a rock garden or use as edging plants. Plant taller artemisias in drifts in a border where their silver-gray foliage provides an interesting contrast to green leaves and is a good foil for bright flowers. Dusty-miller is the best choice for seaside gardens, where it will prosper even among sand dunes. Many artemisias, notably 'Silver King,' are attractive in both fresh and dried arrangements.

Arum (AY-rum)

Tuberous-rooted plant with large ornamental leaves and spikes of white flowers in spring followed by colorful berries. Zones 7-9.

Selected species and varieties. *A. italicum* 'Pictum,' painted arum: long arrow-shaped dark green leaves with white marbling in the center. White flowers resembling small calla lilies on thick, erect 1½-foot stalks. Orange-red berry clusters.

Growing conditions. Plant arum

tubers in spring or fall in partial shade in a rich soil that remains moist throughout the growing season. In the summer the plants go dormant and require less moisture. Space plants a foot apart. Plant arum deep, since roots emerge close to each tuber's top. In the fall, when new leaves begin to appear, apply a leaf mulch around the plants. Propagate by removing offshoots from the tubers and planting them.

Landscape uses. Plant painted arum in small groups in a woodland garden among other plants that will fill in the empty space left when it becomes dormant. Arums are prized as foliage plants and their leaves are attractive in flower arrangements.

Aruncus (a-RUNK-us)
Goatsbeard

Robust shrubby plant with ferny foliage and large plumes of small white flowers for about two weeks in late spring or early summer. Zones 4-9.

Selected species and varieties. *A. dioicus,* goatsbeard: foliage clump grows up to 4 feet tall and 3 feet across. Flower stalks are 4 to 6 feet tall. The broad, handsome leaves remain in good condition for many months. *A. dioicus* 'Kneiffii' is smaller and slower-growing and has more finely cut leaves. Its flower stalks are 2 to 3 feet tall.

Growing conditions. Grow goatsbeard in partial shade in rich, moist soil. Plant it in a permanent site, since the tough root system makes transplanting and dividing difficult. Space plants 4 feet apart.

Landscape uses. Plant singly as a specimen, at the back of a large perennial border or in a lightly shaded woodland garden. Goatsbeard makes an impressive display when several plants are grouped together.

Asarum (as-AR-um)
Wild ginger

Low-growing mat-forming plant with inconspicuous spring flowers almost hidden by glossy foliage. Zones 4-9.

Selected species and varieties. *A. canadense,* Canada wild ginger: heart-shaped leaves up to 6 inches wide hide reddish brown cup-shaped flowers with three pointed lobes growing close to the ground. Plants grow 4 to 12 inches high. Zones 4-9. *A. europaeum,* European wild ginger: evergreen heart-shaped leaves

ARTEMISIA SCHMIDTIANA

ARUM ITALICUM 'PICTUM'

ARUNCUS DIOICUS

ASARUM CANADENSE

ASCLEPIAS TUBEROSA

ASTER × FRIKARTII

between 2 and 3 inches wide. Reddish brown or greenish purple flowers ½ inch across. Zones 4-8. *A. virginicum,* Virginia wild ginger: evergreen leaves 2 inches wide on plants up to 1 foot tall. Brownish flowers 1 inch wide. Zones 5-8.

Growing conditions. Plant wild ginger in partial to deep shade in well-drained soil that is rich in leaf mold, compost or some other organic matter. Wild ginger is easily propagated by division in spring or autumn. Plant the new sections no deeper than 1 inch and space them 8 to 12 inches apart.

Landscape uses. Wild ginger makes an attractive ground cover that spreads by creeping roots. Plant it in a woodland garden beneath shrubs or in a shaded wildflower garden, or use it as an edging plant.

—

Asclepias (as-KLEE-pee-as)

Showy flat flower clusters on stems with milky sap in summer and early fall. Ornamental seedpods packed with many seeds attached to silky hairs, which are carried by the wind. Zones 3-9.

Selected species and varieties. *A. incarnata,* swamp milkweed: pairs of lance-shaped leaves on 2- to 4-foot stems. Clusters of fragrant rose-colored ¼-inch flowers bloom from summer to early fall. Zones 3-8. *A. tuberosa,* butterfly weed: showy 2-inch clusters of bright orange ⅓-inch flowers from early to late summer. Broad 4½-inch-long leaves on stems 2 to 3 feet high. Favored by the monarch butterfly. Leaves and stems poisonous to animals. Zones 3-9.

Growing conditions. Plant swamp milkweed and butterfly weed in full sun. Swamp milkweed grows best in moist to wet soil and butterfly weed in dry soil. It is resistant to drought and needs to be watered only during an extended dry spell. Both species can also be grown in ordinary garden soil. Space plants 1½ to 2 feet apart. Propagate both by seed or from root cuttings.

Landscape uses. Use swamp milkweed in a wildflower garden or an informal border or allow it to naturalize in a boggy meadow. Plant butterfly weed in a border or a wildflower garden, where its brilliant color is most effective in groups of three or more plants. Its flowers are excellent for drying. The seedpods of both species are attractive when used in dried arrangements.

Aster (AS-ter)

A large group of dependable plants whose daisy-like yellow-centered flowers come in white and a variety of blues, purples and pinks. Blooming time ranges from early summer to late fall. Zones 3-9.

Selected species and varieties. *A. × frikartii:* fragrant lavender-blue flowers 2 to 2½ inches wide on stems 2 to 3 feet high. Exceptionally long blooming period from early summer through fall. Zones 6-9. *A. laevis,* smooth aster: white, light blue or purple flowers in clusters on the upper part of stems with heart-shaped lower leaves. Blooms late summer through fall. Zones 4-8. *A. novae-angliae,* New England aster: purple flowers 1½ inches wide and lance-shaped leaves on branching stems 5 feet tall or more. Blooms summer through fall. Zones 4-8. Varieties of *A. novae-angliae* include 'Alma Potschke,' with soft pink flowers on 3-foot plants from late summer through fall; 'Harrington Pink,' with pink flowers on 4-foot stems in fall; and 'Treasure,' with deep purple flowers on 3½- to 4-foot stems from late summer through fall. *A. novi-belgii,* Michaelmas daisy: bluish violet flowers 1 inch across on 3- to 5-foot stems from late summer until frost. Zones 5-8. Among the many varieties are 'Audrey,' a compact dwarf aster only 15 inches high with lavender-blue flowers from midsummer through fall; 'Boningdale White,' with double white flowers on sturdy 3½-foot stems from early fall through frost; and 'Coombe Violet,' with violet to purple flowers on 4-foot plants. *A. tartaricus,* Tartarian daisy: violet-purple flowers on 6- to 8-foot stems with lower leaves up to 2 feet long. Zones 3-8.

Growing conditions. Asters are sturdy plants that are easy to grow. Plant them in full sun in well-drained fertile soil. If soil is chronically wet in winter, they are prone to rot. Space low-growing asters 1 to 1½ feet apart and the taller ones 2 to 3 feet apart. Fading flowers should be removed before they set seed, since the seedlings will not be identical to the original plant. Divide asters every three or four years, or when they become crowded. To propagate, remove sections from the outside of the clump and replant in spring or fall.

Landscape uses. Asters are important perennials for summer and autumn bloom. Plant species asters in a wildflower garden. Grow the cultivated varieties in a flower border, and use the dwarf forms as edging plants.

Whether they are wild or cultivated, asters are lovely in arrangements, by themselves and combined with other cut flowers.

Astilbe (as-TIL-be)

Graceful, glossy ferny foliage in loose mounds below fluffy summer flower spikes in white and shades of pink, red and lavender on erect stems. Zones 4-8.

Selected species and varieties. *A. × arendsii*, garden spirea: a varied group of 1½- to 3½-foot-tall hybrids. 'Fanal' is a 2-foot variety with early-summer to midsummer deep red flowers above finely divided foliage tinged with red; 'Ostrich Plume' has salmon pink flowers on 3½-foot stems; 'Peach Blossom' has light salmon pink flowers on 18- to 26-inch plants; 'Snowdrift' is 2 feet tall and bears white flowers in midsummer. *A. chinensis* 'Pumila': a dwarf astilbe 8 to 12 inches tall with numerous spikes of pink flowers that bloom from midsummer to late summer. Zones 5-8. *A. tacquettii* 'Superba': rosy purple spikes in midsummer to late summer on reddish green stems 3 to 4 feet tall.

Growing conditions. Plant astilbes in light shade in moist soil that is rich in organic matter. Although they do best in shade, astilbes can be grown successfully in full sun if they are given plenty of water and mulch in summer. *A. chinensis* 'Pumila' and *A. tacquettii* 'Superba' tolerate drought better than the others. The plants multiply rapidly and should be divided in spring or fall every two or three years. Space new plants 1½ to 2 feet apart.

Landscape uses. Plant astilbes in groups in a perennial border or mass them as ground cover in a shady location. Plant the tall forms singly, as specimen plants. If the weather is not too hot, the shiny foliage will remain attractive all summer. The flower spikes are excellent in arrangements, whether fresh or dried. If left standing they will provide interest in a winter garden.

Aubrieta (o-bree-AY-ta)

Low mat of evergreen foliage with pink to purple flowers that are large in relation to the size of the plant. Tiny oval leaves crowd downy stems. Zones 5-8.

Selected species and varieties. *A. deltoidea*, purple rock cress: lilac or purple flowers ¾ inch across bloom at the ends of 3- to 6-inch stems from early to late spring. Leaves form a thick mat. *A. × hybrida* 'Cascade Strain': pink or purple ¾-inch flowers.

Growing conditions. Plant aubrietas in full sun or light shade in sandy, well-drained soil, spacing them 9 inches apart. If the plants are sheared back after the flowers have faded, they may bloom again in fall. Propagate in spring by division or by seed. Aubrietas grow best in cool, moist climates and may not live long where summers are hot and humid.

Landscape uses. Use aubrietas as edging for a perennial border or plant in a rock garden; they combine well with white- or pink-flowered arabis.

Aurinia (o-RIN-ee-a)
Basket-of-gold

Low-growing plant topped with frothy clusters of yellow or apricot flowers above rosettes of silver-gray foliage in early spring. Zones 4-10.

Selected species and varieties. *A. saxatilis*, basket-of-gold: forms mat 6 to 12 inches high with open clusters of dainty four-petaled yellow flowers. Varieties include 'Citrinia,' with pale yellow flowers; 'Compacta,' with vivid yellow flowers on dwarf plants; and 'Dudley Neville,' with pale apricot flowers.

Growing conditions. Plant basket-of-gold in full sun in a well-drained sandy or gravelly soil that is not too fertile, spacing plants 9 to 12 inches apart. It does not grow well where summers are hot and humid. Cut plants back by a third after they flower. Basket-of-gold is difficult to divide but is easily propagated from seed sown in spring or fall.

Landscape uses. Mass basket-of-gold in a rock garden, use as an edging plant for a border, or allow it to cascade over a low retaining wall or the edge of a raised bed.

Avena grass see *Helictotrichon*

Avens see *Geum*

Azure sage see *Perovskia*

Baby's-breath see *Euphorbia;* see *Gypsophila*

Balloon flower see *Platycodon*

Baneberry see *Actaea*

ASTILBE × ARENDSII 'FANAL'

AUBRIETA DELTOIDEA

AURINIA SAXATILIS

BAPTISIA AUSTRALIS

BEGONIA GRANDIS 'ALBA'

BELAMCANDA CHINENSIS

BERGENIA CRASSIFOLIA

Baptisia (bap-TIZ-ee-a)
Wild indigo

Blue or white spring flowers shaped like small butterflies in loose spikes on mounded 3- to 4-foot plants with bluish green to gray-green foliage. Zones 3-9.

Selected species and varieties. *B. australis,* blue wild indigo, blue false indigo: large clumps of stems with clover-like leaves and spires of 1-inch blue flowers. Zones 3-9. *B. pendula,* white wild indigo: inch-wide white flowers on 3-foot plants. Zones 5-9.

Growing conditions. Grow wild indigos in full sun in well-drained to dry sandy soil. In partial shade they will grow but not flower profusely. They may need to be staked. Propagate by seed, cuttings or division in spring. Set new clumps 2 to 3 feet apart.

Landscape uses. Wild indigos are valuable for both their beautiful form and their flowers in drier sections of a wildflower garden or a perennial border. Both flowers and foliage are excellent in arrangements.

—

Barrenwort see *Epimedium*
Basket-of-gold see *Aurinia*
Beard-tongue see *Penstemon*
Bear's-breech see *Acanthus*
Bee balm see *Monarda*

—

Begonia (be-GO-nee-a)

Loose, branched clusters of 1½-inch pink or white flowers appear on reddish stems amid colorful hairy leaves in late summer or autumn. Zones 7-10.

Selected species and varieties. *B. grandis,* hardy begonia: green heart-shaped leaves with reddish veins beneath sprays of pink flowers on 1- to 2-foot stems. The variety 'Alba' has white flowers.

Growing conditions. Plant hardy begonias in deep, fertile soil in full sun at the northern end of the range or in partial shade where summers are hot and dry. In colder areas, plant in a protected location and apply a winter mulch. Little bulbs that grow at the junctions of leaves and stems drop to the ground and root. Propagate by digging up and transplanting these bulblets in spring, when new growth appears. Space 1½ feet apart.

Landscape uses. Plant hardy begonias in groups in a perennial border, as an edging for a shrub border or as a ground cover in a woodland setting.

—

Belamcanda (bel-am-CAN-da)
Blackberry lily

Sprays of lily-like summer flowers on branched stems above 1½-foot grasslike leaves. Seedpods open to reveal columns of shiny seeds that resemble blackberries. Zones 5-10.

Selected species and varieties. *B. chinensis:* red-spotted orange flowers up to 2 inches wide on 3-foot stems.

Growing conditions. Plant blackberry lilies in full sun or light shade in a moist but well-drained soil enriched with organic matter. Provide mulch where winters are severe. Propagate from seed, by division of the tubers in spring, or by digging up and replanting the seedlings that crop up. Space them 1 foot apart.

Landscape uses. Use blackberry lilies in a perennial border or an island bed, where they will bloom for at least two weeks. The plant's unusual seedpods are attractive in the garden and in arrangements, either fresh or dried.

—

Bellflower see *Campanula*
Bergamot see *Monarda*

—

Bergenia (ber-JEN-ee-a)

Large clusters of pink, red or magenta spring flowers on 1- to 1½-foot stalks. Attractive large fleshy leaves are evergreen in milder climates. Zones 4-9.

Selected species and varieties. *B. cordifolia,* heartleaf bergenia: clusters of ¼- to ½-inch pink flowers on short stalks amid leaves 1 foot across. *B. crassifolia,* leather bergenia: clusters of pink or reddish pink flowers held above 8-inch leaves on 1- to 1½-foot stalks. *B.* hybrids: plants to 18 inches tall with varying colors in flowers and leaves. 'Evening Glow' has clusters of single or semidouble magenta flowers on 1½-foot plants and maroon and plum-colored leaves in winter; 'Sunningdale' has crimson flowers on foot-high flower stalks tinged with red and reddish leaves in winter.

Growing conditions. Bergenia grows best in light shade in a moist, well-drained soil, but it tolerates full sun in Zones 4-7. Propagate from seed sown in spring or by division in spring or fall. Space new plants 1½ to 2 feet apart. Protect bergenia with a light winter mulch at the northern end of its range, where it may not be fully evergreen.

Landscape uses. Use clumps of bergenia as underplantings in a shrub border, let it spread as a ground cover by a stream or a garden pool, or plant it at the front of a shady border, where its leaves will provide year-round interest in milder zones. The leaves are used in arrangements.

Bethlehem sage see *Pulmonaria*

Betony see *Stachys*

Bishop's-hat see *Epimedium*

Blackberry lily see *Belamcanda*

Black-eyed Susan
see *Rudbeckia*

Blanket flower see *Gaillardia*

Blazing star see *Liatris*

Bleeding heart see *Dicentra*

Blue-eyed grass
see *Sisyrinchium*

Blue marguerite see *Felicia*

Blue oat grass see *Helictotrichon*

Bluestar see *Amsonia*

Boltonia (bowl-TO-nee-a)

White daisy-like flowers with bright yellow centers from late summer into fall. Zones 4-8.

Selected species and varieties. *B. asteriodes* 'Snowbank,' white boltonia: numerous ¾-inch white flowers grow on sturdy 3- to 5-foot branched stems lined with narrow bluish green leaves.

Growing conditions. Plant white boltonia in full sun in either dry or moist garden soil. Plants do not require staking. Propagate by division in spring or fall. Space new plants 3 feet apart.

Landscape uses. Use white boltonia in a naturalistic meadow garden or at the back of a border. Pick for fall bouquets.

Bouncing bet see *Saponaria*

Bowman's-root see *Porteranthus*

Bridal-wreath see *Francoa*

Brunnera (BRUN-er-a)

Clusters of dainty blue spring flowers on 1- to 2-foot slender stems above handsome heart-shaped leaves. Zones 4-9.

Selected species and varieties. *B. macrophylla,* Siberian bugloss, heartleaf brunnera: ¼-inch bright blue flowers resembling forget-me-nots in branched open clusters. Boldly textured leaves up to 8 inches across. The cultivars 'Hadspen Cream' and 'Variegata' have leaves edged with pale cream or yellow; 'Langtrees' has spotted leaves.

Growing conditions. Plant brunnera in full sun or light shade in a deep, moist, well-drained soil enriched with organic matter. Propagate by digging up and replanting seedlings or by division in spring. Space new plants 1 foot apart. The seedlings are deep-rooted and can be invasive.

Landscape uses. Plant Siberian bugloss in an informal perennial garden where its seedlings will not be objectionable, among shrubs or in a woodland garden, where it can spread to form a ground cover. It is an attractive companion for spring bulbs.

Bugbane see *Cimicifuga*

Bugloss see *Anchusa;*
see *Brunnera*

Burnet see *Sanguisorba*

Bush pea see *Thermopsis*

Buttercup see *Ranunculus*

Butterfly lily see *Hedychium*

Butterfly weed see *Asclepias*

Calamagrostis
(kal-a-ma-GROS-tis)
Reed grass

Dense clump of narrow, arching leaves and bristly flower spikes on tall stems in summer. Leaves turn golden tan in late fall and can be left standing to provide winter interest. Zones 6-9.

Selected species and varieties. *C. acutiflora stricta,* feather reed grass: 5 to 7 feet tall; clump width is 2 feet or more, increasing slowly by underground stems. Slender buff flower spikes on erect stems rise about 2 feet above the foliage.

Growing conditions. Plant feather reed grass in well-drained soil in full sun or light shade, spacing plants 3 feet apart. Cut the clump to within 6

BOLTONIA ASTERIODES 'SNOWBANK'

BRUNNERA MACROPHYLLA

CALAMAGROSTIS ACUTIFLORA STRICTA

CALCEOLARIA × 'JOHN INNES'

CALLIRHOE INVOLUCRATA

CALTHA PALUSTRIS 'FLORE PLENO'

inches of the ground before new spring growth appears. Propagate by division in early spring

Landscape uses. The narrow, erect form of feather reed grass makes it a good accent plant for an island bed or a perennial border, where its slender leaves and stems are a nice foil for large-leaved plants such as plume poppy. Its winter color is handsomely displayed against an evergreen background.

—

Calceolaria
(kal-see-o-LAIR-ee-a)
Slipperwort, pocketbook plant

Brightly colored summer flowers with large inflated lower lips that resemble little slippers or pouches. Zones 7-9.

Selected species and varieties. C. × 'John Innes': golden yellow flowers with small red spots are borne on erect stems above tufts of pointed oval leaves. This dwarf plant grows only 6 inches tall.

Growing conditions. Plant slipperwort in light shade in a moist, well-drained soil enriched with organic matter. Propagate from seed or by division. Space the new plants a foot apart.

Landscape uses. Use slipperwort as an edging for a shady perennial bed, in a rock garden or among ferns.

—

California tree poppy
see *Romneya*

—

Callirhoe (kal-LI-ro-ee)
Poppy mallow

Showy deep pink to purple flowers on trailing 1- to 3-foot stems bloom throughout summer. Zones 3-8.

Selected species and varieties. C. involucrata, low poppy mallow, wine-cups: 2½-inch cup-shaped flowers with creamy conical centers. The leaves are lobed and deeply cut.

Growing conditions. Grow low poppy mallow in full sun in well-drained to dry soil. Its long taproot makes watering unnecessary except in drought. Propagate by seed, by stem cuttings or by division in spring or fall. Space new plants 1½ feet apart.

Landscape uses. Use low poppy mallow in a sunny, dry wildflower garden or let it spill over the edge of a retaining wall or a raised bed.

Caltha (KAL-tha)
Marsh marigold

Low-growing plant with small branched clusters of bright yellow spring flowers held above shiny heart-shaped leaves. Zones 4-9.

Selected species and varieties. C. palustris, marsh marigold, cowslip: yellow 2-inch flowers with single rows of petal-like sepals resembling buttercups grow on 1- to 2-foot stalks. The variety 'Flore Pleno' has ruffly double-petaled flowers.

Growing conditions. Plant marsh marigolds in full sun in a moist, even boggy soil that is rich in organic matter. Propagate from seed or by division before or after flowering. Space new plants 1 to 2 feet apart.

Landscape uses. Plant clumps of marsh marigolds along the edges of ponds and streams.

—

Campanula (kam-PAN-ew-la)
Bellflower

Spikes or clusters of showy blue, violet, purple or white bell- or star-shaped flowers in spring, summer or fall, depending on the species. Broad oval, toothed leaves in tufts at the bases of stems, becoming thinner and smaller toward the tips. Zones 3-9.

Selected species and varieties. C. carpatica, Carpathian bellflower: many delicate blue 2-inch bell-shaped flowers on compact plants less than 1 foot tall from late spring to early summer, followed by a few flowers throughout the summer. The variety 'Alba' has white flowers. Zones 3-9. C. glomerata, clustered bellflower, Danesblood bellflower: clusters of up to 12 deep purple inch-wide flowers blossom on 2-foot stems from spring through early summer, followed by another show of blossoms late in the season. Zones 3-8. The cultivar 'Crown of Snow' has clusters of large white flowers and blooms continuously from late spring through early summer on stems up to 20 inches; 'Superba' has purple flowers on 12- to 18-inch stems. C. latifolia, great bellflower: single purple flowers up to 1½ inches wide bloom from early summer to midsummer on 3-foot plants with long rough leaves. Zones 4-8. C. persicifolia, peach-leaved bellflower: modest numbers of blue or white 1½-inch summer flowers on 3- to 5-foot stems above sturdy rosettes of bright green evergreen or semi-evergreen foliage. Zones 4-8. Varieties that flower more abundantly than the species include 'Grandiflora Alba,' with large snowy white flowers on 2-foot-long stems from late spring through early summer, and 'Telham Beauty,' with large violet flowers on stems 3 feet long. *C. portenschlagiana*, Dalmatian bellflower: blue ¾- to 1-inch-wide flowers in late spring and early summer on dwarf 6- to 8-inch plants above attractive heart-shaped foliage. Zones 5-7. The cultivar 'Resholt' has violet blossoms on 6-inch plants from late spring into midsummer. *C. poscharskyana*, Serbian bellflower: light blue star-shaped flowers on 1- to 2-foot-long trailing stems from late spring until frost. Zones 3-8. *C. rotundifolia*, Scottish bluebells: delicate bright blue-violet inch-wide flowers grow in profusion at the tips of wiry 1- to 2-foot-long stems from late spring through late summer. Zones 3-9.

Growing conditions. Most bellflowers thrive in sun or light shade in a moist but well-drained soil enriched with organic matter such as peat moss or compost. The Dalmatian and Serbian bellflowers grow best in sandy or gritty soil; Scottish bluebells grow in almost any kind of soil from gravelly ledges to marshy meadows. Dig up and divide bellflowers every three or four years to maintain plant vigor. Space small species and cultivars 9 to 12 inches apart and larger ones up to 2 feet apart. Clip faded flowers to encourage further bloom. In winter protect bellflowers with a light mulch.

Landscape uses. Plant dwarf and trailing bellflowers in a rock garden or in the crevices of a wall, next to steps or in a wildflower garden. Use taller species of bellflower in a perennial border. The flower sprays are excellent for cutting.

—

Campion see *Lychnis;* see *Silene*
Candytuft see *Iberis*
Cape weed see *Arctotheca*
Cardinal flower see *Lobelia*

—

Catananche (kat-a-NAN-ke)
Cupid's-dart

Lavender-blue or white daisy-like summer flowers on slender stems above clumps of grasslike grayish green leaves. Zones 5-9.

Selected species and varieties. *C. caerulea:* lavender-blue 2-inch flowers with notched petals and darker centers on 1½-foot plants with woolly foliage. The variety 'Alba' has white flowers.

Growing conditions. Plant Cupid's-dart in full sun in well-drained soil. It tolerates dry conditions and must not be planted where water collects in winter. Cupid's-dart is often short-lived. Propagate from seed planted in spring or by division in fall. Space new plants 12 inches apart.

Landscape uses. Use Cupid's-dart in groups of at least three at the front of a border. It goes well with artemisias and other gray-leaved plants. The flowers are excellent for cutting and long-lasting when dried.

—

Catchfly see *Lychnis;* see *Silene*
Catmint see *Nepeta*
Celandine poppy see *Stylophorum*

—

Centaurea (cen-TOR-ee-a)

Spring or summer flowers with fringes of purple, blue, pink or white petal-like bracts. Gray-green leaves with woolly undersides. Zones 4-8.

Selected species and varieties. *C. dealbata*, Persian centaurea: showy pink 2-inch thistle-like flowers grow singly on 2- to 3-foot stems above large finely divided leaves up to 1½ feet long from late spring through midsummer. *C. hypoleuca* 'John Coutts': rosy pink 2-inch flowers with white centers from early summer to midsummer on sturdy stems 2 to 3 feet long. Attractive silver seed heads follow the flowers. *C. macrocephala*, globe centaurea: yellow 4-inch thistle-like early-summer flowers on 4-foot plants with coarse leaves up to 1 foot long and thick hairy stems. *C. montana*, mountain bluet: deep blue 3-inch flowers with red-tinged centers on 2-foot-long stems from the middle of spring to early summer.

Growing conditions. Plant centaureas in full sun in moist but well-drained soil. Propagate by division every two to three years. Space new plants 1 to 2 feet apart. Centaureas self-sow readily and can be invasive.

Landscape uses. Centaureas are attractive additions to a sunny border. Allow mountain bluet to spread in a naturalistic meadow garden. Grow the large, bold globe centaurea as a specimen and use its bright yellow flowers for dried arrangements.

CAMPANULA GLOMERATA

CATANANCHE CAERULEA

CENTAUREA MACROCEPHALA

CENTRANTHUS RUBER

CERATOSTIGMA PLUMBAGINOIDES

CHELONE LYONII

Centranthus (sen-TRAN-thus)
Red valerian

Dense clusters of small spurred summer or fall flowers grow at the tips of 1- to 3-foot stems above pairs of toothed oval leaves. Zones 4-9.

Selected species and varieties. *C. ruber*: fragrant ½-inch red flowers with slim red or white spurs. The variety 'Alba' has white flowers.

Growing conditions. Plant red valerian in full sun or partial shade in any well-drained soil. The species self-sows readily and may be invasive, but 'Alba' produces few seeds. Propagate in spring by division or by digging up and replanting self-sown seedlings. Space new plants 1½ feet apart.

Landscape uses. Plant red valerian in a perennial border. It is especially valuable for poor, dry locations that will not support other plants. The blossoms are excellent for cutting and add a delightful scent to a bouquet. Blooming may continue until frost.

Ceratostigma (ser-at-OS-tig-ma)
Plumbago

Spreading 1-foot plants with clusters of brilliant blue flowers from late summer through midfall. Zones 5-9.

Selected species and varieties. *C. plumbaginoides*, blue plumbago, leadwort: cobalt blue flowers ¾ inch across. Handsome bright green leaves lining wiry, slightly zigzag stems turn reddish in fall.

Growing conditions. Plant blue plumbago in full sun or light shade in a moist, well-drained light soil. Its creeping roots spread rapidly and may be invasive. Propagate by division in spring. Space new plants 1½ feet apart. Protect with a winter mulch in Zone 5.

Landscape uses. Use blue plumbago to edge a sunny flower border, or plant clumps in a lightly shaded shrub border, or grow it as a ground cover where its spreading habit can be used to advantage.

Chelone (kell-O-ne)
Turtlehead

Short spikes of white or pink-lipped flowers resembling a turtle's head with open mouth above glossy dark green toothed leaves on 3-foot stems. Blooms from late summer into fall. Zones 4-9.

Selected species and varieties. *C. glabra*, white turtlehead: white to pink 1-inch flowers with white beards on the lower lips. *C. lyonii*, pink turtlehead: deep rose pink 1-inch flowers with yellow beards on the lower lips.

Growing conditions. Plant turtleheads in full sun or light shade in constantly moist or wet soil that is rich in organic matter such as peat moss or leaf mold. Propagate from seed or cuttings taken in summer or by division in the fall or early spring. Space new plants 18 inches apart.

Landscape uses. Plant turtleheads in groups by a stream or a garden pool or in a bog garden. They are excellent additions to a perennial border.

Chinese indigo see *Indigofera*
Chinese lantern see *Physalis*
Christmas rose see *Helleborus*

Chrysanthemum
(kri-SANTH-em-um)

Showy flowers in a wide range of sizes and shapes from small buttons to large globes in all colors except blue. Chrysanthemum is valued for its profusion of blooms above ferny foliage at varying times from late spring through fall. Zones 3-10.

Selected species and varieties. *C. frutescens*, marguerite chrysanthemum: white or yellow flowers up to 2½ inches across on bushy plants up to 3 feet tall throughout summer. Zones 9 and 10. *C. leucanthemum*, oxeye daisy: white 2-inch flowers with yellow centers bloom on 2-foot plants in late spring and early summer. Zones 3-9. *C. × morifolium*, florist's chrysanthemum: a huge group encompassing hundreds of varieties with late-summer through fall blooms in myriad forms. Florist's chrysanthemums are divided into six categories. Cushion chrysanthemums are low, compact plants with numerous blossoms; varieties include 'Allure,' with yellow flowers on 14-inch plants, and 'Glamour,' with 3½-inch lavender flowers on 15-inch plants. Daisy chrysanthemums have large yellow centers and daisy-like petals; 'Pink Daisy' is a variety with 2-inch pink flowers on plants to 2 feet tall. Decorative chrysanthemums grow in a taller and looser form than cushion mums and have larger flowers; 'Nutmegger' is a variety with soft orange-tan flowers on 2-foot-tall plants. Pompom chrysanthemums have dainty round flower balls on loosely formed plants up to 1½ feet tall; 'Sassy' has yellow 1½-inch flowers on plants a foot tall and twice as wide. Spider chrysanthemums have rolled petals of irregular lengths; varieties include 'Carousel,' with large silvery purple flowers 3 to 4 inches wide with yellow centers, and 'Sun Quill,' with bright yellow 3-inch flowers on low, compact plants. Spoon chrysanthemums have rolled petals with expanded and flattened tips that resemble spoons; varieties include 'Crystal Star,' with cream-colored flowers on 16-inch plants, and 'Starlet,' with 2½-inch orange-buff flowers on 20-inch plants. Florist's chrysanthemums grow in Zones 5-10. *C. nipponicum*, Nippon daisy: shrubby plants 1½ to 2 feet tall covered by a mass of yellow-centered 1½- to 3½-inch white flowers in fall. Zones 6-9. *C. parthenium*, feverfew: ¼-inch button-like flowers with short white petals and light yellow centers on 1- to 3-foot plants with strongly scented leaves, from early summer through fall. Varieties include 'Golden Ball,' a dwarf plant with yellow flowers, and 'White Star,' another dwarf plant with white flowers. Zones 5-8. *C. × superbum*, shasta daisy: parent of many single- and double-petaled varieties with white flowers up to 5 inches across. Among them are 'Alaska,' with profuse large daisy-like flowers on 2-foot stems, Zones 4-9; 'Little Miss Muffet,' with semidouble flowers with yellow centers on compact 12- to 15-inch plants, Zones 5-9; and 'Polaris,' with large daisy-like flowers, Zones 5-9.

Growing conditions. Plant chrysanthemums in full sun in a moist, well-drained soil enriched with organic matter. Water during dry periods. To develop sturdy plants with many flowers, pinch back chrysanthemums when they are 6 to 8 inches tall; repeat a second time before plants set flower buds. Where winters are cold, protect plants with a light mulch. Divide chrysanthemums every one to two years in the spring, discarding the woody center and replanting the outer sections 1 to 2 feet apart. The shrubby Nippon daisy cannot be divided, but it sometimes sends out branches near the base roots; these new branches can be removed and replanted. Feverfew and oxeye daisy self-sow. All chrysanthemums can be propagated from cuttings taken in spring or summer.

Landscape uses. The range of heights and colors makes chrysanthemums extremely versatile plants for use in borders. They also do well in containers. Florist's chrysanthemums are among the best perennials for fall flowers and make a handsome show in a bed or a border of their own as well as in combination with other fall bloomers such as the eupatoriums and sedums. Chrysanthemums are excellent cut flowers.

—

Chrysogonum (kris-OG-o-num)
Golden star

Spreading plant with five-petaled yellow spring flowers above tufts of grayish green toothed oval leaves. Zones 6-9.

Selected species and varieties. *C. virginianum:* yellow star-shaped flowers 1½ inches wide on plants 6 to 12 inches tall. In cooler areas blooming continues into summer.

Growing conditions. Golden star grows best in full sun or partial shade in a moist, well-drained soil, but it can also tolerate dry conditions. Propagate from seed sown in spring or by division in the spring or fall. Space new plants 12 inches apart.

Landscape uses. Use golden star in groups or as a ground cover in a woodland garden, or plant it in a rock garden.

—

Chrysopsis (kri-SOP-sis)
Golden aster

Clusters of bright yellow daisy-like flowers in late summer and fall. Zones 5-9.

Selected species and varieties. *C. mariana*, Maryland golden aster: 1½-inch yellow flowers with bristly yellow centers on 2- to 3-foot plants with twisted, pointed, hairy leaves. *C. villosa* 'Golden Sunshine,' hairy golden aster: bright yellow flowers up to 1⅓ inches wide on 3- to 4-foot stems rising from a low-growing rosette of evergreen or semi-evergreen lance-shaped leaves.

Growing conditions. Plant golden asters in full sun or light shade in a moist, well-drained soil. They will also tolerate hot, dry locations well. Where winters are cold do not cut old stems back until spring to protect the crowns over winter. Propagate golden asters from seed or by division in spring. Space new plants 1½ to 2 feet apart.

Landscape uses. Use golden asters in a sunny meadow garden or a border for bright color well into fall. They make excellent cut flowers.

CHRYSANTHEMUM × MORIFOLIUM

CHRYSOGONUM VIRGINIANUM

CHRYSOPSIS VILLOSA

CIMICIFUGA SIMPLEX

CLEMATIS RECTA 'PURPUREA'

COREOPSIS LANCEOLATA 'SUNRAY'

Cimicifuga (si-mi-SIFF-yew-ga)
Bugbane

Long, narrow spikes of tiny white flowers rise above a mound of handsome ferny foliage in summer or fall. Zones 3-9.

Selected species and varieties. *C. racemosa*, cohosh bugbane, black snakeroot: branching 4- to 8-foot-tall stalks with summer flowers resembling bottle brushes. The large dark green compound leaves are divided into leaflets up to 8 inches long. *C. simplex*, Kamchatka bugbane: arching spikes of white flowers on 3- to 4-foot stalks in fall. The foliage is similar to that of *C. racemosa*.

Growing conditions. Plant bugbane in full sun or shade in constantly moist, well-drained soil enriched with organic matter such as leaf mold. In deep shade it has luxuriant foliage but few flowers. The tall spikes of cohosh bugbane may need staking. Propagate from seed or by division. Space new plants 2 feet apart. Bugbane grows slowly and can remain in place indefinitely; it seldom needs dividing except for propagation.

Landscape uses. Use bugbane singly or in small groups in a woodland garden or as a vertical accent at the back of a perennial border.

—

Cinquefoil see *Potentilla*

—

Clematis (KLEM-a-tis)

Fragrant, showy blue or white flowers shaped like bells or stars in summer. Zones 3-9.

Selected species and varieties. *C. heracleifolia davidiana*, tube clematis: shrubby 2- to 4-foot plant with elongated bell-shaped blue flowers in 1-inch-long clusters amid 5-inch-long dark green leaves. Feathery seed heads follow mid- to late-summer flowers. Zones 5-9. *C. integrifolia*, solitary clematis: light blue bell-shaped flowers up to 1½ inches long borne singly on vining stems from 1½ to 5 feet long. Zones 3-9. *C. recta*, ground clematis: starry white flowers up to 1 inch wide in fluffy clusters near the top of rangy 3- to 5-foot plants from early summer to midsummer. The variety 'Purpurea' has white flowers and purple-tinted leaves. Zones 4-9.

Growing conditions. Plant clematis in full sun in moist, well-drained soil enriched with organic matter. Apply 2 to 3 inches of mulch to keep the soil around the roots evenly moist and cool. Space plants 3 to 4 feet apart. Prune back tube clematis in the spring. To grow ground clematis and solitary clematis as erect plants, provide stakes to support them.

Landscape uses. Use clematis in a border; allow ground clematis and solitary clematis to tumble over the edges of raised beds or retaining walls. Use both the flowers and seed heads in arrangements.

—

Columbine see *Aquilegia*
Coneflower see *Echinacea;* see *Rudbeckia*
Coralbells see *Heuchera*

—

Coreopsis (ko-ree-OP-sis)
Tickseed

Single- or double-petaled daisy-like summer flowers in shades of yellow. Zones 4-10.

Selected species and varieties. *C. auricularia*, eared coreopsis: inch-wide bright yellow flowers on 18-inch plants with dark green oval leaves that have two lobes, or ears, where they join the stem. *C. lanceolata*, lance coreopsis: orange-yellow flowers up to 2½ inches wide on 2-foot stems above clumps of lance-shaped leaves. Among the many varieties are 'Brown Eyes,' golden yellow flowers with brown-rimmed centers on 1½- to 2-foot plants; 'Goldfink,' fringed yellow flowers on spreading clumps of 10- to 12-inch stems; and 'Sunray,' double 1½- to 2-inch flowers on 1½- to 2-foot stems. *C. verticillata*, threadleaf coreopsis: yellow 2-inch flowers on 3-foot plants with delicate, finely cut foliage. The variety 'Zagreb' has masses of small bright yellow flowers on 18-inch plants; 'Moonbeam' is 2 feet tall and has star-shaped pale yellow 2-inch flowers.

Growing conditions. Plant coreopsis in full sun in moist, well-drained soil. Stems of the taller species flop if grown in too fertile a soil. Threadleaf coreopsis withstands drought well. Remove dead flowers to encourage further bloom. Propagate from seed or by division every two to four years in the spring. Space plants 1 to 1½ feet apart.

Landscape uses. Use the low-growing 'Goldfink' coreopsis as an edging plant, as a ground cover or in a rock garden. Plant taller varieties in groups of three or more in the middle of a perennial bed or border. Gather the flowers for summer bouquets.

Corydalis (ko-RY-dal-is)

Small snapdragon-like flowers in loose clusters above delicate ferny foliage in late spring and summer. Zones 5-9.

Selected species and varieties. *C. lutea,* yellow corydalis: clusters of ¾-inch tubular yellow flowers with darker yellow tips on 12- to 15-inch stems. Leaves are blue-green above and grayish on the undersides.

Growing conditions. Plant yellow corydalis in shade in moist, well-drained soil. Propagate by division or by transplanting the seedlings that result from self-sowing. Space the new plants 8 to 10 inches apart.

Landscape uses. Use yellow corydalis in a shady rock garden or as an edging plant in a shady perennial border. The foliage is attractive through most of the growing season, and the flowers are pretty in small arrangements.

—

Cowslip see *Caltha*
Cranesbill see *Geranium*

—

Crocosmia (cro-COS-mee-a)

Drooping clusters of brilliant red-orange flowers on 3-foot stems in middle to late summer. Zones 6-9.

Selected species and varieties. *C. masoniorum,* montbretia: trumpet-shaped flowers 1½ inches across. Narrow sword-shaped leaves form clumps 2 feet tall.

Growing conditions. Plant crocosmia in full sun in moist, well-drained sandy soil. Space plants 1 to 1½ feet apart. Crocosmia spreads quickly into dense weedproof clumps. Propagate by division in spring or fall.

Landscape uses. Crocosmia's bright flowers and vertical leaves make it a strong focal point in a perennial border. Pale yellow flowers make a good foil for its intense red-orange, which also harmonizes with blues. Plant it in drifts in large sunny areas where it has room to spread.

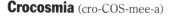

Culver's root see *Veronicastrum*
Cupid's-dart see *Catananche*

—

Cynoglossum (sy-no-GLOSS-um)
Hound's tongue

Brilliant blue flowers blossom in loose, branching clusters above the foliage during summer. Zones 5-7.

Selected species and varieties. *C. nervosum,* great hound's tongue: ½-inch flowers similar to forget-me-nots. Plants to 2 feet tall with narrow, pointed, hairy leaves 10 inches long at the bases of the stems, becoming smaller near the top.

Growing conditions. Grow great hound's tongue in full sun or light shade in a well-drained soil. It can tolerate hot, dry locations. Space plants 2 feet apart. They may need staking in rich soils. Propagate in spring from seed or by division.

Landscape uses. Use great hound's tongue in a rock garden. Its bright flowers are an attractive addition to an all-blue border and also make a pleasing contrast to golden yellow flowers.

—

Daisy see *Aster;* see *Chrysanthemum;* see *Gerbera*
Daylily see *Hemerocallis*
Dead nettle see *Lamium*
Deer grass see *Rhexia*

—

Delphinium (del-FIN-ee-um)
Larkspur

Tall, heavy spikes of spurred early- to late-summer blossoms, usually in shades from blue to purple but also in white and pink, often with a contrasting center called a bee. Handsome deeply cut foliage. Zones 3-10.

Selected species and varieties. *D. elatum,* candle larkspur, bee larkspur: bluish purple blossoms up to 2 inches across in dense spikes on stalks to 6 feet tall. The parent of many hybrids including the Belladonna delphiniums, with branched 3- to 5-foot stalks bearing multiple spikes of 2-inch white or blue flowers. Zones 3-10. *D. × belladonna* 'Bellamosa' has dark blue blossoms; *D. × belladonna* 'Casa Blanca' has white flowers. The *D. ×* 'Connecticut Yankee' hybrids have white or blue to purple blossoms on bushy plants 2½ feet tall. Zones 3-10. *D. grandiflorum chinense,* Siberian larkspur: blue or white 1-inch blossoms on slender 12- to 18-inch stalks. Zones 4-8. *D.* Pacific hybrids: plants up to 6 feet tall with pink, purple, blue, lavender or white blossoms with double rows of petals and, in some cultivars, centers of a contrasting color. Zones 3-10. The cultivar

CORYDALIS LUTEA

CROCOSMIA MASONIORUM

CYNOGLOSSUM NERVOSUM

DELPHINIUM

109

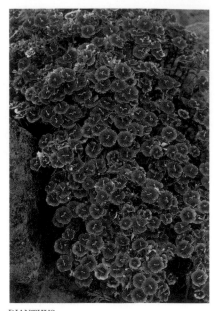
DIANTHUS

DICENTRA SPECTABILIS

DICTAMNUS ALBUS 'PURPUREUS'

'Black Knight' has deep violet blossoms, 'King Arthur' has purple blossoms, and 'Summer Skies' has soft blue blossoms with white centers.

Growing conditions. Grow delphiniums in full sun in moist but well-drained slightly acid to alkaline soil enriched with organic matter. Protect from wind and stake tall stems. Cut stems back after summer blooming for a second crop of flowers in fall. Propagate from seed or by division. Set new plants 2 feet apart for good air circulation. Delphiniums prefer cool summers and do well in Zones 8-10 only on the West Coast.

Landscape uses. Plant 'Connecticut Yankee' and other relatively short delphiniums in the middle of a perennial border and the taller ones at the back. Tall hybrids are also grown in beds of their own.

———

Dianthus (dy-AN-thus)
Pink

Fragrant red, pink or white spring and early-summer flowers above handsome clumps of blue or gray-tinted grassy leaves that are evergreen in mild climates. Zones 3-10.

Selected species and varieties. *D.* × *allwoodii,* Allwood pink: red, pink or white, usually semidouble 2-inch blossoms, sometimes with one color splotched on another. Plants grow up to 1½ feet tall. The cultivar 'Alpinus' grows only 6 inches tall, 'Doris' has salmon-colored blossoms with a darker eye on 15-inch plants and 'Robin' has bright scarlet blossoms. Zones 4-8. *D. barbatus,* sweet William: white, red, pink or multicolored blossoms in dense heads on 2-foot plants with broad leaves. Sweet William often grows as a biennial. Reliably perennial varieties include 'Scarlet Beauty,' 'White Beauty' and 'Newport,' with coral-colored blossoms. Zones 6-10. *D. deltoides,* maiden pink: red or pink flowers with crimson centers on 12-inch stems above dense mounds of narrow leaves. The cultivar 'Albus' has white blossoms; 'Samos' has deep red flowers and purple-tinged leaves. Zones 4-8. *D. gratianopolitanus,* Cheddar pink: single pink blossoms on 6-inch stems above a thick mat of blue-green foliage. Zones 4-8. *D. plumarius,* border pink, cottage pink, grass pink, Scotch pink: pink blossoms up to 1½ inches across with single or double rows of petals on 12- to 15-inch stems. Zones 4-8.

Growing conditions. Pinks do best in full sun in a well-drained, slightly alkaline sandy soil but will tolerate slightly acid soil. Space plants 12 to 18 inches apart. Shear mat-forming types in fall. In cold areas, protect with evergreen boughs in winter. Do not use a dense mulch, such as leaves, that fosters rot by reducing air circulation and trapping moisture. Propagate from seed or by division every three years in spring. Sweet William grows well in Zones 9 and 10 on the West Coast only.

Landscape uses. Grow pinks in the front of a perennial border or in a rock garden, plant as a ground cover in a small sunny area, or use to edge a walk or a terrace.

———

Dicentra (dy-SEN-tra)
Bleeding heart

Heart-shaped red, pink or white blossoms and attractive clumps of ferny foliage. Zones 3-9.

Selected species and varieties. *D. eximia,* fringed bleeding heart: clusters of pink flowers on erect foot-tall stems above mounds of feathery gray-green foliage from spring until frost. Zones 3-9. The variety 'Alba' has white blossoms. *D. formosa,* Pacific bleeding heart: similar to *D. eximia* but with deep pink flowers. The cultivar 'Sweetheart' has white blossoms. Zones 5-9. *D.* × *luxuriant:* bright reddish pink blooms on erect stems to 18 inches tall above finely cut gray-green foliage from spring to fall. Zones 5-9. *D. spectabilis,* common bleeding heart: pink to purple flowers along arching 3-foot stems in spring. Zones 3-9. The cultivar 'Alba' bears pure white blooms.

Growing conditions. Plant bleeding hearts in light shade in a well-drained soil enriched with organic matter. Space plants 1½ to 2 feet apart. Common bleeding heart dies down in summer. Propagate by division in early spring or from seed.

Landscape uses. Use bleeding heart in a shady border or allow it to naturalize in a woodland garden.

———

Dictamnus (dik-TAM-nus)
Gas plant, dittany

Loose spires of airy white or pinkish purple blossoms on shrubby 2- to 3-foot plants in late spring to early summer. Zones 3-8.

Selected species and varieties. *D. albus,* gas plant: white blossoms up to 2 inches across. A lighted match held under the blossoms will sometimes ignite the gas they give off and produce a slight flash of light, thus the common name. Glossy, aromatic dark green compound leaves are attractive all season long. Gas plant is a long-lived perennial. The variety 'Purpureus' has pinkish purple blossoms; 'Rubrus' has red flowers.

Growing conditions. Grow gas plant in full sun in a well-drained soil enriched with organic matter. Space plants 3 feet apart, setting them in their permanent locations. Gas plant should not be disturbed, since it is difficult to transplant or divide it successfully. It grows slowly and takes several years to become established. Propagate from seed, which will produce blooming plants in three or four years.

Landscape uses. Set gas plant in the middle of a perennial border, where its shrubby form and dark leaves form a good backdrop for shorter plants. White gas plants are attractive in a monochromatic border.

—

Digitalis (dij-i-TAL-lis)
Foxglove

White, yellow, pink to rose or purple bell-shaped flowers on erect spikes rising from low clumps of hairy, wrinkled leaves in late spring to early summer. Individual flowers open from the bottom to the top of each spike. Perennial or biennial, depending on the species. Zones 4-10.

Selected species and varieties. *D. grandiflora,* yellow foxglove: perennial with 2- to 3-inch creamy yellow flowers spotted with brown on 3-foot spikes. Zones 4-10. *D. lutea,* straw foxglove: perennial with white to pale yellow flowers on spikes 1 to 2 feet tall. Hairless foliage. Zones 5-10. *D. × mertonensis:* hybrid perennial with pink to rose or red flowers on spikes up to 6 feet tall. Zones 4-8. *D. purpurea,* common foxglove: biennial 2 to 4 feet tall with 2-inch flowers in white or shades of pink or purple. The variety 'Alba' has white flowers. Zones 5-8.

Growing conditions. Plant foxglove in a moist but well-drained soil enriched with organic matter. It grows best in full sun except in Zone 8, where it needs shade from the hot afternoon sun. Set new plants 1 to 1½ feet apart or sow seed in August for blooms the following year. Divide perennial species in spring. Biennial foxglove freely self-sows and will reappear each year if flowers are allowed to form seed before being removed. Foxglove does well

in Zones 9 and 10 only on the West Coast.

Landscape uses. Grow foxglove as a vertical accent at the middle or the back of a border, depending on the height of the species, or plant it in an informal naturalistic garden where it can self-sow and spread.

—

Disporum (dy-SPOR-um)
Fairy-bells

Nodding white or yellow bell-shaped flowers at the tips of branching stems in spring. The glossy, leathery leaves are deeply furrowed by numerous veins running lengthwise from base to tip. Spreads slowly by creeping underground stems. Zones 4-8.

Selected species and varieties. *D. flavum,* fairy-bells: inch-long yellow flowers on stems 2 to 3 feet tall with bright green oval leaves. *D. sessile* 'Variegatum,' variegated fairy-bells: white flowers 1 inch long on stems 1 to 2 feet tall. Lance-shaped leaves edged with white.

Growing conditions. Plant fairy-bells in well-drained soil enriched with organic matter in partial to full shade. Fairy-bells can compete with tree roots. Spreading clumps can be left undisturbed indefinitely or they can be divided to propagate new plants. Space plants 2 feet apart.

Landscape uses. A clump of fairy-bells foliage makes a unique textural accent for a shady border. Fairy-bells are ideal for planting in drifts beneath trees in naturalistic gardens.

—

Dittany see *Dictamnus*

—

Dodecatheon
(do-de-KATH-ee-on)
Shooting-star

Small flowers with swept-back petals on a single stout stem 1 to 2 feet tall. Early to late spring. Zones 4-10.

Selected species and varieties. *D. meadia,* common shooting-star: inch-long flowers with protruding cone-shaped reddish yellow anthers and white, rose or lavender petals. Fleshy toothed leaves 6 to 12 inches long form a tight rosette.

Growing conditions. Grow common shooting-star in partial shade in a moist, well-drained soil enriched with leaf mold or other organic matter. Leaves die back by midsummer.

DIGITALIS PURPUREA

DISPORUM SESSILE 'VARIEGATUM'

DODECATHEON MEADIA

DORONICUM CORDATUM

DRABA SIBIRICA

DRACOCEPHALUM

ECHINACEA PURPUREA

Plants do best when they receive ample moisture during their growing season but should be kept on the dry side while dormant. Propagate by dividing mature clumps every three or four years. Shooting-star grows well in Zones 9 and 10 only on the West Coast.

Landscape uses. Use shooting-star in groups in a shady shrub border or let it naturalize beneath deciduous trees. Plant it at the front of a border where perennials developing more slowly will fill in the gaps it leaves when it goes dormant.

Doll's-eyes see *Actaea*

Doronicum (do-RON-ik-um)
Leopard's-bane

Daisy-like bright yellow flowers blooming in spring on stems up to 1½ feet tall. Heart-shaped matte green leaves with toothed edges. Zones 4-8.

Selected species and varieties. *D. cordatum,* Caucasian leopard's-bane: single 2- to 3-inch flowers on stems 1 to 1½ feet tall. *D.* × 'Miss Mason' has slightly larger flowers and foliage that lasts longer than that of the species. *D.* × 'Spring Beauty' has double flowers.

Growing conditions. Plant leopard's-bane in full sun or partial shade in a constantly moist, well-drained soil. Leaves die back and disappear by midsummer. The shallow, fibrous roots spread into dense mats that develop dead centers unless the clump is divided in fall or early spring every two to three years. Space plants 1 to 2 feet apart.

Landscape uses. Use leopard's-bane as a brightly colored companion for spring bulbs and wildflowers, or use it in a border where it will be succeeded by other plants as its foliage dies back. Leopard's-bane is one of the earliest perennials for cutting.

Draba (DRAY-ba)

Clusters of dainty yellow flowers on slender 6-inch stalks above neat rosettes of foliage no more than 2 or 3 inches high. Zones 4-8.

Selected species and varieties. *D. densiflora,* rock-cress draba: dense cushion of hairy oval leaves and loose clusters of ⅛-inch yellow flowers from early spring to midspring. *D. sibirica,* Siberian draba:

small rosettes of hairy leaves strung along trailing 12-inch stems. Clusters of up to 20 tiny yellow flowers in both spring and fall.

Growing conditions. Grow draba in full sun in a well-drained sandy soil. Siberian draba tolerates some shade and is particularly easy to grow. Set new plants 6 inches apart. Propagate by sowing seed in spring.

Landscape uses. Plant draba in a rock garden or tuck it into small crevices in a wall or between stones of a terrace. Allow the stems of Siberian draba to trail over the edge of a retaining wall or a raised bed.

Dracocephalum
(dra-ko-SEF-a-lum)
False dragonhead, obedient plant

Spires of tubular pink or white blossoms resembling snapdragons in late summer and early fall. Flowers can be turned at any angle and will stay in position, hence the common name obedient plant. Zones 4-9.

Selected species and varieties. *D. virginianum* (also known as *Physostegia virginiana):* 8-inch clusters of bright pink flowers on plants up to 5 feet tall with attractive dark green lance-shaped leaves 5 inches long. *D. virginianum* 'Summer Snow' grows 3 feet tall with white flowers; *D. virginianum* 'Vivid' is 2 feet tall with dark rose pink flowers.

Growing conditions. False dragonhead grows well in a sunny, moist spot. It will also grow in a drier location if given light shade. Space plants 1½ to 2 feet apart. If conditions suit it well, false dragonhead may become invasive unless divided every other year. Propagate by division in spring or by seed.

Landscape uses. Use false dragonhead in a border or allow it to spread in large clumps in a naturalistic meadow garden.

Dropwort see *Filipendula*
Dusty-miller see *Artemisia*

Echinacea (ek-in-AY-see-a)
Purple coneflower

Summer-blooming large daisy-like flowers with gracefully drooping pink to purple or white petals and prominent conical centers. Zones 3-10.

Selected species and varieties. *E. pallida:* light to deep rosy purple flowers up to 3½ inches across on stems up to 3 feet tall. Zones 3-8. *E. purpurea:* flowers up to 6 inches across in white and shades of pink and purple on stems up to 4 feet tall. Zones 3-10. 'Bright Star' is a variety with rose-colored petals surrounding a deep purple center. 'The King' has deep reddish purple petals and a brown center. 'White Lustre' has creamy white petals surrounding a bronze center.

Growing conditions. Grow purple coneflowers in full sun or light shade. Set new plants 2 feet apart in well-drained sandy soil. Purple coneflower is easy to grow and flourishes even in dry, windy sites. It may need staking if soil is fertile. Propagate from root cuttings or by division in spring or fall. Plants also seed themselves freely.

Landscape uses. Use purple coneflowers at the back of a border or along the sunny edges of woodland areas for many weeks of color. They make excellent cut flowers, and stripped of petals, their prickly centers add textural variety to dried arrangements.

—

Echinops (EK-in-ops)
Globe thistle

Bristly blue globes bloom in summer on plants with spiny, deeply scalloped leaves that are glossy above and covered with downy white hairs on their undersides. Zones 3-9.

Selected species and varieties. *E. ritro:* spherical bright blue flower heads 1½ to 2 inches in diameter on stems to 2 feet tall. The variety 'Taplow Blue' has deep metallic blue flower heads 3 inches across on stems 3 to 4 feet tall with blue-green foliage.

Growing conditions. Plant globe thistle in full sun in well-drained soil. Because of its deep roots, it will tolerate drought; soggy soil will kill it. In very fertile soil it may require staking. Clumps can be left undisturbed indefinitely or new plants can be propagated by division every three or four years in spring. Set new plants 18 to 24 inches apart.

Landscape uses. Stiff and sculptural in appearance, globe thistle makes a bold statement in the middle of a border or at the back of one. Use it as the focal point of an island bed. If the flowers are cut before they are fully open, they can be hung upside down to dry for winter bouquets.

—

Edelweiss see *Leontopodium*

Epimedium (ep-i-MEE-dee-um)
Barrenwort, bishop's-hat

Clusters of nodding flowers whose buds resemble a bishop's-hat bloom in spring on stems up to 1 foot tall amid dense clumps of thin, leathery leaves. Each leaf is a trio of heart-shaped leaflets on a wiry stem. Foliage has a reddish cast in spring, turns green in summer and deep bronze in fall. Sometimes evergreen, depending on the climate. Zones 5-8.

Selected species and varieties. *E. grandiflorum* 'Rose Queen': mid- to late-spring pink flowers up to 2 inches across with whitish spurs. Zones 5-8. *E. × rubrum:* small bright pink to red flowers up to 1 inch across with white spurs. *E. × versicolor* 'Sulphureum': light yellow flowers 1 inch across. Zones 6-8. *E. × youngianum* 'Niveum': pure white ½-inch flowers. Zones 6-8.

Growing conditions. Plant epimediums in light to deep shade in a moist, well-drained soil enriched with organic matter. They tolerate full sun and dry soils. Leaves remain erect through winter unless crushed by snow. Where plants are deciduous, cut down old foliage in early spring before new growth begins. Epimediums spread slowly in widening clumps. Propagate by dividing the horizontal rootstocks, and space new plants 8 to 12 inches apart.

Landscape uses. Use epimedium at the front of a shady border or as a ground cover under shrubs or trees, where it competes well with roots.

—

Erigeron (e-RIJ-er-on)
Fleabane

Clusters of daisy-like flowers with bright yellow centers and a single or double row of white, pink, purple, lavender or blue petal-like fringe bloom from late spring to midsummer. Soft green pointed leaves on bushy plants. Zones 4-10.

Selected species and varieties. *E. pulchellus,* poor robin's plantain: blue, pink or white single flowers 1½ inches across on plants 1 to 2 feet tall. Zones 4-10. *E. speciosus,* Oregon fleabane: light purple 1½-inch single flowers in large clusters on plants 1½ to 2½ feet tall. Zones 4-8. It is the parent of many hybrids. The cultivar 'Azure Fairy' grows to 2½ feet with semidouble lavender flowers. 'Double Beauty' is an 18-inch hybrid with double blue-violet flowers. 'Foerster's Liebling' has deep pink semidouble flowers on

ECHINOPS RITRO

EPIMEDIUM × YOUNGIANUM 'NIVEUM'

ERIGERON SPECIOSUS

113

ERYNGIUM GIGANTEUM

EUPATORIUM FISTULOSUM

EUPHORBIA EPITHYMOIDES

plants 1½ to 2 feet tall. 'Sincerity' has single lavender flowers.

Growing conditions. Grow fleabanes in full sun in a light, sandy soil that is not too rich in organic matter. They do well in seaside conditions. Set plants about 1½ feet apart. Pick spent blossoms to prolong blooming. Fleabanes seed themselves freely. Plants can also be propagated by dividing clumps in early spring.

Landscape uses. Plant fleabanes in a perennial border or allow them to naturalize in a sunny meadow garden. They make excellent cut flowers.

—

Eryngium (e-RINJ-ee-um)
Sea holly

Collars of spiny leaflike bracts surrounding conical centers of many tightly packed tiny blue or green flowers in summer. Silvery gray-green leaves and stiff stems up to 3 feet tall give the plants a bristly, architectural quality. Zones 5-9.

Selected species and varieties. *E. alpinum:* finely divided blue bracts around blue 1¼-inch centers on plants 2 to 2½ feet tall. Spiny, deeply lobed leaves. Zones 5-9. *E. bourgatii:* stiff, toothed gray-green leaves veined with white on 2-foot plants. Greenish blue flowers in a ¾-inch cone encircled by silvery blue spiny bracts. Zones 5-7. *E. giganteum:* large blue or pale green centers 2 to 4 inches long surrounded by spiny gray-green bracts on stems to 2 feet or more. Zones 5-8. *E. × zabelii,* Zabel eryngium: inch-wide centers on stems 1½ to 2½ feet tall. Zones 5-8.

Growing conditions. Sea hollies do best in full sun in a well-drained sandy soil that is not too rich in organic matter. *E. alpinum* and *E. × zabelii* tolerate some shade. Space plants 1 to 1½ feet apart. *E. giganteum* dies out after flowering but self-sows freely to replace itself. Sea hollies are difficult to divide because of their long taproots. Propagate from seed sown in spring or fall or from root cuttings.

Landscape uses. The stiff, sculptural leaves and flowers of sea hollies make them superb specimen plants. Use them as accents in a border or in a sunny rock garden. They look good in a border composed of silver-, white- or gray-leaved plants. They make striking cut flowers.

—

Eulalia grass see *Miscanthus*

Eupatorium
(yew-pa-TOR-ee-um)

Clusters of small flowers in various shades of blue and purple that bloom from late summer into fall above whorls of coarse, pointed oval leaves. Zones 3-10.

Selected species and varieties. *E. coelestinum,* mist flower, hardy ageratum: numerous small flat clusters of bright blue or violet flowers on 2-foot plants. Zones 5-10. *E. fistulosum,* hollow Joe-Pye weed: large, rounded mauve flower clusters on plants 6 feet tall or more. Zones 3-9. *E. maculatum,* Joe-Pye weed, spotted Joe-Pye weed: stems up to 10 feet tall tipped with loose, flat clusters of tubular purple flowers. Coarse leaves 10 to 12 inches long. Zones 3-8.

Growing conditions. Plant mist flower and Joe-Pye weeds in full sun in moist soil. In light, fertile soils they spread rapidly, even invasively. In heavier clay soils they grow more slowly. They tolerate some shade but will flower less. Space mist flowers 1½ to 2 feet apart and the taller species 3 feet apart. Propagate from seed or cuttings taken in summer or by dividing clumps in spring. Set new plants 2 feet apart.

Landscape uses. Use mist flower in a border or in a wildflower garden for late-season color. Plant Joe-Pye weeds at the back of a border or along the marshy margins of a naturalistic meadow garden. Both mist flower and Joe-Pye weeds make good cut flowers.

—

Euphorbia (yew-FOR-bee-a)
Spurge

Clusters of tiny flowers surrounded by colorful petal-like bracts in white, yellow, chartreuse or red-orange in spring or summer. Zones 4-10.

Selected species and varieties. *E. characias:* narrow 4-inch blue-gray evergreen leaves spiraling closely around stiff 3- to 4-foot stems. Dense clusters of reddish brown flowers with collars of yellow-green bracts in spring. Zones 7-10. *E. corollata,* baby's-breath, flowering spurge: loose clusters of ¼-inch flowers and rounded white bracts on wiry stems bloom in summer at the ends of 3-foot stems with narrow blue-gray leaves that take on a burgundy hue in autumn. Zones 4-9. *E. epithymoides,* cushion spurge: 1- to 1½-foot hemispherical mound of neat foliage. Dense clusters of flowers are surrounded by bright chartreuse bracts in spring. Foliage reddens in autumn. Zones 4-10. *E. griffithii:* late-spring to early-summer clusters of tiny yellow flowers surrounded by deep red-orange bracts on 3-foot plants. Spirals of narrow pointed leaves with deep pink veins and reddish edges. Zones 5-9. The variety 'Fire Glow' has especially intense color.

Growing conditions. Grow spurges in full sun in well-drained to dry soil. Where summers are hot, provide some light shade. Cushion spurge does not do well in hot, humid conditions. Allow 3 feet of space for *E. characias,* 1½ feet for cushion spurge and 2 feet for baby's-breath and *E. griffithii.* Spurges are seldom propagated by division because they are difficult to transplant. They sow themselves freely, however, and small seedlings can be moved with a large soil ball. The milky sap of euphorbia stains and sometimes irritates skin. Wear gloves when picking spurges for arrangements and seal the cut end of each stem by searing it with a flame.

Landscape uses. Feature cushion spurge at the front of a border for its symmetrical mounded form, bright spring bracts and reddish fall foliage. Place the taller euphorbias in the middle or back of a border, where they are valuable for both their colorful bracts and their handsome foliage. 'Fire Glow' euphorbia's bronze-tinted leaves go well with red, orange or yellow flowers.

Evening primrose see *Oenothera*

Everlasting see *Helichrysum*

Fairy-bells see *Disporum*

False dragonhead
see *Dracocephalum*

False hellebore see *Veratrum*

False lupine see *Thermopsis*

False Solomon's-seal
see *Smilacina*

False sunflower see *Heliopsis*

Feather reed grass
see *Calamagrostis*

Felicia (fee-LISS-ee-a)

Daisy-like sky blue flowers on stalks up to 2 feet tall above a low mound of 1-inch oval leaves from early summer to late fall. Zones 8-10.

Selected species and varieties. *F. amelloides,* blue felicia, blue marguerite: ¼-inch flowers with bright

yellow centers surrounded by narrow sky blue petals on a mound of foliage that is 6 to 8 inches tall. The cultivar 'Astrid Thomas' is more compact; 'San Gabriel' produces especially large flowers; 'Variegata' has leaves marked with white.

Growing conditions. Grow blue felicia in full sun in a moist, well-drained soil. Space plants 6 to 12 inches apart. Remove spent blossoms to extend the flowering season and cut plants to half their size after they bloom. Propagate by seed in spring. Blue felicia is often grown as an annual north of its hardiness range.

Landscape uses. Use blue felicia in small groups near the front of a border or in drifts in a large informal bed. Cut blooms for bouquets.

Feverfew see *Chrysanthemum*

Filipendula (fil-i-PEN-dew-la)
Meadowsweet

Clusters of pink or white flowers in early or middle summer on plants with attractive compound leaves. Zones 2-9.

Selected species and varieties. *F. rubra,* queen-of-the-prairie, prairie meadowsweet: 4- to 7-foot plant with fluffy clusters of rosy pink flowers above deeply lobed dark green foliage. 'Venusta' is a variety with deeper pink color. Zones 2-9. *F. vulgaris,* dropwort: loose clusters of ¾-inch white flowers on 1- to 3-foot stems above mounds of dark green ferny foliage. The variety 'Flore Pleno' has blossoms with double rows of petals on shorter stems; 'Grandiflora' has mildly fragrant white flowers tinted with yellow. Zones 3-9.

Growing conditions. Plant queen-of-the-prairie in light shade in a moist soil. It can also be grown in full sun in northern areas. It does not do well where summers are hot and dry. Space plants 4 feet apart. Grow dropwort in full sun or light shade in a well-drained soil. Space plants 1½ to 2 feet apart. Propagate by division in spring or by seed sown in spring. Dropwort self-sows prolifically.

Landscape uses. Grow queen-of-the-prairie along the shaded edge of a naturalistic meadow garden or at the back of a perennial border. Use dropwort as part of a formal border or allow it to spread in a lightly shaded woodland garden. Pick flowers before they are fully open for long-lasting bouquets.

FELICIA AMELLOIDES

FILIPENDULA RUBRA

FRANCOA RAMOSA

GAILLARDIA × GRANDIFLORA 'GOBLIN'

GAURA LINDHEIMERI

Five-finger see *Potentilla*

Flax see *Linum*

Fleabane see *Erigeron*

Fleece flower see *Polygonum*

Forget-me-not see *Myosotis*

Fountain grass see *Pennisetum*

Foxglove see *Digitalis*

—

Francoa (fran-KO-a)

Long stems lined with delicate white or pink summer blossoms above a broad clump of evergreen foliage. Zones 8-10.

Selected species and varieties. *F. ramosa,* bridal-wreath: several 3-foot stems closely packed with four-petaled flowers rising from a clump of glossy, crinkled oval leaves 1 foot long.

Growing conditions. Grow bridal-wreath in light shade in a moist but not wet soil. Set plants 1½ feet apart. Its flowers wilt easily on hot days. Clumps grow slowly and seldom need division except for propagation. Bridal-wreath can also be propagated from seed and by rooting leaf cuttings in water.

Landscape uses. Use bridal-wreath in a shady border where its handsome evergreen foliage will add interesting textural variety after its flowers fade.

—

Gaillardia (gay-LAR-dee-a)
Blanket flower

Brightly colored daisy-like flowers up to 4 inches across bloom profusely from early summer through fall above mounds of narrow downy leaves. Zones 3-8.

Selected species and varieties. *G.* × *grandiflora:* narrow petals of red, yellow or a combination of the two colors surround prominent centers of red, yellow, purple or brown on stems up to 3 feet tall. The variety 'Burgundy' has solid wine-colored flowers on 2-foot stems. 'Goblin' grows in 12-inch mounds with yellow-tipped red petals; the 2-foot 'Yellow Queen' has solid golden yellow flowers.

Growing conditions. Blanket flowers do best in full sun in a well-drained to dry, average to poor soil. They tolerate drought and seaside conditions and tend to be short-lived in fertile, moist soils. Plants may need staking. For greater vigor, cut

them back after they flower. Propagate from seed or by division in spring. Set plants 1½ feet apart.

Landscape uses. Plant blanket flowers in groups of three or more at the front or middle of a sunny border or let them spread on sunny banks. They produce flowers for cutting throughout the summer and into fall.

—

Garden heliotrope see *Valeriana*

Garden sage see *Salvia*

Gas plant see *Dictamnus*

—

Gaura (GAW-ra)

From late spring into fall, white flowers opening successively from the bottom to the top of wiry stems that increase in height throughout the season. Zones 6-9.

Selected species and varieties. *G. lindheimeri,* white gaura: bushy perennial with flower stems 4 to 8 feet tall. The dainty 1½-inch-wide flowers have long, slender stamens and four curving petals that become pinkish as they age. Downy lance-shaped leaves 2 to 3 inches long in clumps up to 4 feet tall.

Growing conditions. White gaura thrives in full sun in a well-drained sandy soil. It tends to spread in moist soils with abundant organic matter. Set plants 3 feet apart. They seldom need division and are difficult to transplant because they have long taproots. Propagate from seed or by moving self-sown seedlings with a large soil ball.

Landscape uses. Use white gaura as a specimen plant, in a wildflower garden or at the rear of a perennial border where its continuously growing stems will not hide smaller plants.

—

Gay-feather see *Liatris*

Gentian see *Gentiana*

—

Gentiana (jen-she-AY-na)

Late-summer to early-fall 1½-inch blue flowers in small clusters from the junctions of pairs of tiny pointed leaves on 2-foot stems. Zones 4-8.

Selected species and varieties. *G. andrewsii,* closed gentian, bottle gentian: deep blue tubular flowers that do not open and somewhat resemble tiny bottles. Zones 4-8. *G. asclepiadea,* willow gentian: narrow pointed leaves on arching stems with bright blue flowers shaped like slender bells. Zones 6-8.

Growing conditions. Grow closed gentian and willow gentian in partial shade in a constantly moist, slightly acid soil enriched with peat moss or leaf mold. Closed gentian will also tolerate full sun. Space plants 1 to 1½ feet apart. Once established, closed gentian can be propagated by division in spring. Willow gentian should be propagated from seed only; leave established clumps undisturbed. They often self-sow.

Landscape uses. Use gentians in a cool woodland garden with other shade-loving plants such as hosta, hairy alumroot and barrenwort. Closed gentian is also a good plant for a marshy area or a bog garden.

—

Geranium (jer-AY-nee-um)
Cranesbill

Flat blossoms from 1 to 2 inches across in shades of pink, magenta, violet and blue on thin stems above clumps of attractively toothed and lobed leaves. The frost-sensitive bedding plants commonly called geraniums are members of the genus *Pelargonium*. Zones 3-10.

Selected species and varieties. *G. dalmaticum:* thick cushion of small, lobed, glossy leaves 6 inches high. Clusters of two to four rosy pink 1-inch flowers bloom in spring or early summer. Zones 4-8. *G. endressii,* Pyrenean cranesbill: spreading mound of deeply lobed leaves 12 to 18 inches high topped by dainty pink flowers no more than ½ inch across in early spring or summer. Zones 5-9. The variety 'A. T. Johnson' has silvery pink petals; 'Clarence Druce' has pink flowers with prominent purple veins; 'Wargrave Pink' has clear, bright pink blossoms. *G. × 'Johnson's Blue':* prolific crop of bright blue 1½- to 2-inch flowers veined in a deeper blue above a 1-foot mound of foliage in spring or early summer. Zones 4-8. *G. macrorrhizum,* bigroot cranesbill: 1-inch pink or magenta flowers with prominent stamens in spring or early summer. Deeply lobed leaves in a low, wide mound turn reddish in fall. Zones 3-10. 'Ingwersen's Variety' is a cultivar with pale pink blossoms. *G. maculatum,* wild geranium: pale rose to violet 1-inch spring flowers in loose clusters on plants 1 to 2 feet tall. Zones 3-8. *G. pratense,* meadow cranesbill: pairs of cupped ½-inch- to inch-wide violet to purple flowers in summer on

stems up to 3 feet tall. Zones 5-10. *G. psilostemon,* Armenian cranesbill: deep magenta flowers 1½ inches across with dark centers on stems up to 2 feet in summer. Dense clump of lobed, heart-shaped leaves. Zones 4-8. *G. sanguineum,* bloody cranesbill: deep magenta 1-inch spring or early-summer flowers above a 12-inch mound of finely cut lobed leaves that redden in fall. Zones 4-10. The variety 'Alba' has white flowers; 'Shepherd's Warning' has bright pink flowers.

Growing conditions. Plant hardy geraniums in full sun or light shade in a moist but well-drained soil. Where summers are hot and dry, grow them in light shade. Bloody cranesbill tolerates more heat and drought than other species. Allow 1 foot of space for *G. dalmaticum* and 1½ to 2 feet for the other geraniums. Propagate by dividing plants every three or four years in spring. Hardy geraniums do not grow well in Zones 9 and 10 in the Southern states.

Landscape uses. Use low-growing geraniums such as *G. dalmaticum,* Pyrenean cranesbill and bloody cranesbill in rock gardens. Plant other geraniums in a lightly shaded woodland garden or at the front of a border, where their foliage makes them an asset after flowering ceases. Meadow cranesbill is an attractive specimen plant. Bigroot cranesbill will spread by its creeping roots into a ground cover that is semi-evergreen in milder zones.

—

Gerbera (GER-ber-a)

Brilliantly colored flowers 4 or 5 inches across from spring through summer on sturdy 18-inch stems above deeply lobed rough, hairy leaves. Zones 8-10.

Selected species and varieties. *G. jamesonii,* Transvaal daisy: yellow, orange, red or white centers ringed with single or double rows of fringelike petals in a range of colors, including white, cream, pink, salmon, orange, red, violet and yellow.

Growing conditions. Transvaal daisies need full sun and a moist, well-drained soil rich in organic matter. Use a light mulch to protect plants from frost. Propagate by dividing plants every three or four years in early spring, setting new plants 1 to 1½ feet apart.

Landscape uses. Use Transvaal daisies as a colorful edging for a wide border or plant clumps as accents

GENTIANA ANDREWSII

GERANIUM × 'JOHNSON'S BLUE'

GERBERA JAMESONII

117

GEUM × 'BORISII'

GYPSOPHILA REPENS 'ROSEA'

HEDYCHIUM GARDNERANUM

along a fence or near a doorway. They make excellent cut flowers.

—

Geum (JEE-um)
Avens

One- to 1½-inch-wide flowers in red, yellow or white with softly ruffled petals surrounding conspicuous centers from spring into summer. Clumps of attractively toothed and lobed downy foliage. Zones 5-10.

Selected species and varieties. *G. quellyon,* Chilean avens: inch-wide scarlet flowers on stems up to 1½ feet tall. Zones 6-10. Cultivars include 'Mrs. Bradshaw,' with red-orange semidouble flowers on 2-foot stems; 'Red Wings,' with semidouble red flowers on 2-foot stems; and 'Starker's Magnificent,' with deep orange flowers on 1- to 1½-foot stems. *G. reptans:* a dwarf plant only 6 to 8 inches high with 1½-inch yellow blossoms. Spreads by reddish runners. Zones 5-9. *G. triflorum:* creamy yellow to purple flowers on 1½-foot stems. Zones 5-10. Hybrid geums include *G.* × 'Borisii,' with yellow-orange to deep orange flowers on 12-inch stems above neat low clumps of foliage. Zones 5-9; *G.* × 'Georgenberg,' with drooping yellow to pale orange flowers on 10- to 12-inch stems. Zones 6-9; and *G.* × 'Heldreichii,' with red-orange flowers on 12- to 18-inch stems. Zones 5-8.

Growing conditions. Plant geums in full sun or light shade in a moist but well-drained soil enriched with organic matter. Propagate by division every two or three years in fall. Set new plants 1 to 1½ feet apart. Geums grow well in Zone 10 only on the West Coast.

Landscape uses. Use the low-growing geums such as *G. reptans* and *G.* × 'Borisii' in a rock garden. Grow other geums near the front of a border. Taller species and hybrids make excellent cut flowers. In a mild winter, the foliage is evergreen.

—

Gillenia see *Porteranthus*

Ginger lily see *Hedychium*

Globeflower see *Trollius*

Globe thistle see *Echinops*

Gloxinia see *Incarvillea*

Goatsbeard see *Aruncus*

Golden dead nettle
see *Lamiastrum*

Golden marguerite
see *Anthemis*

Goldenray see *Ligularia*

Goldenrod see *Solidago*

Golden star see *Chrysogonum*

Goutweed see *Aegopodium*

—

Gypsophila (jip-SOFF-ill-a)
Baby's-breath

Thousands of minute, dainty summer flowers scattered on a lacy mass of wiry branched stems with tiny pointed leaves. Zones 4-9.

Selected species and varieties. *G. paniculata:* a mound of tangled stems 3 to 4 feet tall and wide with ¼-inch white flowers that become pinkish with age. Zones 4-9. The variety 'Bristol Fairy' has flowers with double rows of petals; 'Perfecta' grows to 2½ feet with double-petaled flowers. 'Pink Fairy' grows to 1½ feet with double-petaled light pink flowers. *G. repens,* creeping baby's-breath: trailing branched stems 6 to 8 inches tall with white, pale purple or pink flowers. The variety 'Alba' has white flowers; 'Rosea' has pink blossoms. Zones 6-8.

Growing conditions. Plant baby's-breath in full sun in a moist, well-drained alkaline soil, allowing 3 to 4 feet of space for *G. paniculata* and 18 inches for *G. repens.* The deep root system makes baby's-breath difficult to transplant or divide. Propagate from seed sown in spring. If plants are sheared before the flowers go to seed, they will flower again where growing seasons are long. Stake taller plants to avoid a straggly appearance. Baby's-breath does well in Zone 9 only on the West Coast.

Landscape uses. Baby's-breath makes an excellent filler plant in a border, a rock garden or bouquets.

—

Hardy ageratum see *Eupatorium*

Hardy gloxinia see *Incarvillea*

—

Hedychium (hed-IK-ee-um)
Ginger lily

Extremely fragrant flower resembling butterflies; blooms in long, bold spikes on tall stems having broad strap-shaped leaves from summer to fall. Zones 9 and 10.

Selected species and varieties. *H. coronarium,* butterfly lily, ginger lily: white flowers, sometimes marked with yellow, on spikes up to 1 foot long in summer. Stems up to 7 feet tall with leaves 5 inches wide and up to 2 feet long. *H. gardneranum,* Kahili ginger lily, Indian ginger lily: flower spikes more than 1 foot long lined with yellow flowers having prominent red stamens, from late summer to fall. Leaves up to 1 foot long on stems up to 8 feet tall.

Growing conditions. Plant ginger lilies in full sun or light shade in a moist to damp fertile soil, setting plants 3 feet apart. Keep the plants well watered during the growing season. Propagate by dividing the thick, fleshy roots in spring. In Zone 9 and the colder parts of Zone 10, protect the roots with a mulch in winter.

Landscape uses. Grow ginger lilies in bold groups in damp spots or as tall accents among foliage plants. Use them as cut flowers.

—

Helenium (hel-EE-nee-um)
Sneezeweed

Prominent pompoms of dark yellow, orange or red-brown encircled by drooping, narrow fan-shaped petals in lighter shades. Profuse flower clusters in summer and early fall at the tips of branched stems. Narrow leaves in clumps at the plant base, becoming sparser near the top of the stem. Zones 3-9.

Selected species and varieties. *H. autumnale,* common sneezeweed: flowers up to 2 inches across on rangy 5- to 6-foot stems in late summer and early fall. The variety 'Brilliant' grows only 3 feet tall with yellow, orange and mahogany flowers; 'Butterpat' has yellow flowers on 3-foot plants; and 'Crimson Beauty' is a bushy 2-foot plant with brick red to brownish red flowers. Zones 3-9. *H. flexuosum:* broad clusters of bright yellow flowers with reddish brown centers in midsummer on 2- to 2½-foot plants. Zones 5-9.

Growing conditions. Sneezeweed flourishes in full sun in a moist but not wet soil enriched with organic matter. Pinch taller sneezeweeds in spring to restrict their height and increase the number of flowers, and stake them for support. Propagate and renew plants by division every three to four years in spring. Space new plants 1½ to 2 feet apart.

Landscape uses. Use common sneezeweed at the back of an informal border, where it blends nicely with creamy white- or yellow-flowered perennials such as goldenrod. Plant lower-growing sneezeweeds at mid-border or in drifts in a sunny naturalistic garden. Sneezeweeds make good cut flowers.

—

Helianthus (hee-li-AN-thus)
Sunflower

Large bright yellow flowers, either single or double, at the tips of upright stems in summer or fall. Zones 5-9.

Selected species and varieties. *H. angustifolius,* swamp sunflower: daisy-like 2- to 3-inch flowers with conspicuous purple centers and yellow petals on 3- to 6-foot stems in middle to late fall. Zones 6-9. *H. × multiflorus,* hybrid sunflower: yellow summer flowers up to 5 inches across on a bushy plant 3 to 5 feet tall. Zones 5-9. The variety 'Flore Pleno' is 4 feet tall with clear yellow double-petaled blooms resembling chrysanthemums. 'Loddon Gold' is slightly taller with 4-inch double-petaled yellow flowers on short stems. 'Morning Sun' is a 5- to 6-foot plant with double-petaled golden yellow flowers.

Growing conditions. Plant sunflowers in full sun in a moist, well-drained soil. Swamp sunflower grows best where soil is constantly moist and should be kept well watered in hot, dry weather. Set plants 2 to 3 feet apart. Propagate by division every three to four years in spring.

Landscape uses. Use sunflowers at the rear of a border, in the center of an island bed or in drifts in a large meadow garden. They make excellent cut flowers.

—

Helichrysum (hee-li-KRY-sum)
Everlasting

Small clusters of tiny daisy-like summer flowers atop 18-inch stems with silvery gray foliage. Zones 5-8.

Selected species and varieties. *H. hybridum* 'Sulfur Light': clusters of ¼-inch brilliant yellow flowers with papery petal-like bracts. The narrow woolly leaves are aromatic.

Growing conditions. Plant everlasting in full sun in well-drained sandy soil, spacing plants 18 inches apart. Propagate from seeds in spring.

Landscape uses. Use everlasting near the front of a sunny border or as a filler in a rock garden, where its foliage is attractive all season. The flowers can be dried and used in winter bouquets.

HELENIUM AUTUMNALE

HELIANTHUS ANGUSTIFOLIUS

HELICHRYSUM HYBRIDUM 'SULFUR LIGHT'

119

HELICTOTRICHON

HELIOPSIS HELIANTHOIDES SCABRA

HELLEBORUS ORIENTALIS

Helictotrichon
(he-lik-to-TRY-kon)

Ornamental grass with stiff blue-gray leaves and graceful clusters of buff-colored flowers in summer. Zones 4-8.

Selected species and varieties. *H. sempervirens,* avena grass, blue oat grass: neat, erect clump of narrow 2-foot evergreen leaves. Flower clusters 4 to 6 inches long held above the leaves on slender stems.

Growing conditions. Blue oat grass requires full sun and well-drained soil. Space plants 1 foot apart. Remove dead or damaged leaves in early spring.

Landscape uses. Plant a single clump or small groups of blue oat grass near the front of a border for its attractive form and unusual color; its blue foliage makes it an excellent choice for a planting featuring white flowers and silver or gray foliage.

Heliopsis (he-li-OP-sis)
False sunflower, oxeye

Bright yellow flower up to 4 inches across from summer through fall. Blossoms are single, semidouble-petaled with visible centers or dome-shaped with many overlapping petals that cover the center. Zones 5-9.

Selected species and varieties. *H. helianthoides scabra,* rough heliopsis: orange-yellow semidouble or double flowers on stems up to 5 feet tall with rough-textured leaves. Among the available varieties are 'Golden Plume,' with dome-shaped double-petaled flowers on 2- to 3-foot plants; 'Incomparabilis,' with golden double-petaled flowers on bushy plants; and 'Summer Sun,' with orange-yellow flowers and darker centers on 4-foot plants.

Growing conditions. Plant rough heliopsis in full sun in any moist, well-drained soil. It will also tolerate a poor dry soil. Set plants 2 feet apart. Propagate rough heliopsis by dividing plants in spring or fall, or by seed in spring or summer.

Landscape uses. Rough heliopsis is a colorful late-season addition to a flower border and is an excellent cut flower.

Heliotrope see *Valeriana*
Hellebore see *Helleborus;* see *Veratrum*

Helleborus (hell-e-BOR-us)
Hellebore

Winter to early-spring flowers on thick stems rising from rosettes of usually evergreen leaves composed of leaflets arranged like the fingers on a hand. Cup- or bell-shaped flowers 1 to 3 inches across in white, pale green, pink or purple. Zones 3-10.

Selected species and varieties. *H. foetidus,* stinking hellebore: nodding pale yellow-green bell-shaped flowers up to 1¼ inches across on 18-inch stems. Evergreen leaves with dark green narrow, pointed leaflets. Zones 6-10. *H. lividus corsicus,* Corsican hellebore: large clusters of drooping pale green cup-shaped flowers up to 2 inches across with prominent yellow stamens. Blossoms appear on 1½- to 3-foot stems above toothed evergreen leaves veined with pale green or gray. Zones 7-9. *H. niger,* Christmas rose: white cup-shaped flowers, sometimes tinged pink, up to 3 inches across with conspicuous yellow stamens. Flowers appear on foot-high stems above dark green oval, pointed evergreen leaflets. Occasionally blooms in late fall. Zones 3-8. *H. orientalis,* Lenten rose: nodding cup-shaped flowers of cream, green, pink, rose or purple up to 2 inches across on 18-inch stems. Saw-toothed glossy leaves. Zones 4-9.

Growing conditions. Hellebores need partial shade and a constantly moist but well-drained soil enriched with organic matter. Water well and provide mulch where summers are dry. Corsican hellebore tolerates sun and dry conditions better than most hellebores. At the northern end of the range, hellebores may need protection from the weight of winter snows. They do not do well in Zones 9 and 10 in the Southern states. Set plants out in spring, leaving 12 inches between Corsican hellebores, 18 inches between stinking hellebores and Christmas roses, and 2 feet between Lenten roses. Propagate from seed or by division after flowering, although brittle roots make division of mature clumps difficult and older plants may not bloom for a year after being disturbed. Lenten rose self-sows readily. All parts of the plant are poisonous and the juices from bruised stems may cause skin irritation.

Landscape uses. Grow hellebores in a shaded perennial or shrub border or plant them in the shade of a wall. Allow Lenten rose to spread in a naturalistic woodland garden. Flowers are long-lasting, and the foliage is attractive most or all of the year.

Hemerocallis (hem-er-o-KAL-is)
Daylily

Bold trumpet-shaped flower from 1 to 10 inches across, sometimes with double row of petals or ruffled edges, in spring, summer or fall. The hundreds of hybrids offer a broad choice of hues, from off-white or cream through yellow, melon, pink and red to mauve and orchid, often with two or three colors in the same blossom. Clusters of up to 30 flowers grow on stiff 1- to 7-foot stalks rising from a thick clump of narrow, arching leaves. The long flower buds in each cluster open successively, and each flower lasts only a day, hence the name. Zones 3-10.

Selected species and varieties. *H.* hybrids: 'Admiral Nelson' bears red flowers on 3-foot stalks in midsummer. 'Autumn Red' has red flowers with yellow to green throats that bloom from late summer to fall. 'Bonanza' is a dwarf daylily with pale orange flowers having maroon centers on 15-inch stalks that appear in abundance from summer to fall. 'Golden Chimes' has 30-inch stalks with golden yellow flowers that are 3 inches across and flecked with red and striped with burgundy on the underside of each petal. Blooms mainly in summer, with intermittent flowers into fall. 'Stella de Oro' is another dwarf, with light yellow 2½-inch flowers with pale green throats and ruffled petals blooming on 12- to 18-inch stalks from late spring into fall. Species and hybrids vary in hardiness but there are daylilies suitable for each zone from 3 to 10.

Growing conditions. Daylilies thrive in full sun in any well-drained soil. They compete well with tree roots and will grow in light shade but may flower less. Propagate by dividing clumps every three to six years in fall or early spring. Space dwarf hybrids 1 to 1½ feet apart and the taller hybrids 2 to 3 feet apart. If small plantlets appear along the flower stalks, they can be removed and rooted as cuttings.

Landscape uses. Use daylilies as border plants; place them in the front, middle or back of the border according to their height. By selecting hybrids with different flowering times, it is possible to have daylilies in bloom continuously from spring to fall. Allow them to spread in an informal naturalistic garden. Planted in large groups, daylilies make an excellent ground cover under trees, in large sunny areas or on steep banks where their dense foliage will shade out weeds and their roots will slow

erosion. Plant special hybrids as specimen plants.

—

Heuchera (hew-KAIR-a)

Spikes of tiny white, pink or red bell-shaped flowers from spring to midsummer on wiry stems rising from low-growing clumps of marbled evergreen leaves with scalloped edges. Zones 3-10.

Selected species and varieties. *H. micrantha,* alumroot: loose clusters of white flowers on 2-foot stalks above gray-marbled leaves. Zones 4-10. *H. sanguinea,* coralbells: flowers in white or shades of pink and red on stems up to 2 feet tall. The variety 'Pluie de Feu' has bright red flowers on 18-inch stems; 'Queen of Hearts' has elongated red flowers; 'Snowflakes' bears white flowers on 2½-foot stems. Zones 3-9. *H. villosa,* hairy alumroot: airy spikes of white flowers on 3-foot stems above broad, bright green, toothed leaves. Zones 5-8.

Growing conditions. Plant coralbells and alumroots in full sun or light shade in a moist, well-drained soil enriched with organic matter. Once it is established, hairy alumroot can tolerate dry conditions. Coralbells tend to die out where summers are hot and dry. Space alumroots 1½ feet apart, and coralbells and hairy alumroots 1 foot apart. Crowns become woody after several years. Renew plants and propagate them by division every three years in spring or fall, setting divisions about a foot apart. Heucheras do not grow well in Zone 10 in the Southern states.

Landscape uses. Use coralbells and alumroots as edgings for sunny or shady borders where their attractive foliage will show to advantage even when plants are not in bloom. They are excellent plants for a lightly shaded area in a woodland garden and make good cut flowers.

—

× Heucherella (hew-ker-ELL-a)

Loose spikes of tiny flowers on 12-inch stalks above compact clumps of heart-shaped leaves from spring to midsummer and sometimes again in fall. Zones 4-8.

Selected species and varieties. × *H. tiarelloides* 'Bridget Bloom': clusters of ¼- to ½-inch flowers streaked with white and pink give an overall light pink effect.

Growing conditions. Heucherella thrives in full sun or light shade in

HEMEROCALLIS

HEUCHERA SANGUINEA

× HEUCHERELLA TIARELLOIDES 'BRIDGET BLOOM'

121

HIBISCUS

HOSTA UNDULATA 'ALBO-MARGINATA'

HOUTTUYNIA CORDATA 'CHAMELEON'

moist but not wet soil amply enriched with organic matter. Divide plants every three or four years in spring to propagate and to renew when the crowns have become woody, setting new plants 1½ feet apart.

Landscape uses. Plant heucherella in a moist woodland garden or use it at the front of a border where its foliage will remain attractive after its flowers are gone. Cut blossoms for arrangements.

Hibiscus (hy-BIS-kus)
Rose mallow

Large white, pink, rose or red flowers, each a flat whorl of overlapping satiny petals, on plants 4 to 12 feet in height in summer and fall. Zones 5-9.

Selected species and varieties. *H. coccineus*, scarlet rose mallow: deep red 5-inch blossoms on stems up to 12 feet long. Ferny leaves composed of narrow, pointed leaflets arranged like the fingers on a hand. Zones 6-9. *H.* × 'Lord Baltimore': 10-inch crimson flowers with ruffled petals. Plants 4 to 6 feet tall with dark green lobed leaves. Zones 5-9. *H. moscheutos*, rose mallow, giant rose mallow: typically white with purplish red throats on stems up to 7 feet tall lined with heart-shaped 8-inch leaves. There are numerous named hybrids in cream, pink or rose. Zones 5-9.

Growing conditions. Rose mallows require full sun and a very moist, even wet soil. Plants will tolerate drier soil and light shade but will not grow as tall. Set plants 2 to 3 feet apart. Mulch in winter in Zones 5-7. Propagate from seed or by transplanting the seedlings that appear around established plants. The cane-like stems need no support.

Landscape uses. Use rose mallows as a focal point in a wide border or large island bed or plant them in wet sites where they can seed themselves and establish large colonies.

Hollyhock see *Alcea*
Horse mint see *Monarda*

Hosta (HOS-ta)
Plantain lily

Broad, handsome clumps of leaves in a variety of colors, shapes and textures. Stalks of white, lavender or pale violet trumpet-shaped flowers above the foliage in summer or fall. Zones 3-9.

Selected species and varieties. *H. fortunei*, Fortune's hosta: clumps of gray-green 5-inch oval leaves with 1½-inch pale lilac flowers in midsummer. The variety 'Aureo-marginata' has leaves edged in creamy yellow. *H.* × 'Krossa Regal': vase-shaped 2-foot clumps of grayish blue leaves with 2- to 3-inch lavender flowers on 5-foot stalks in late summer. *H. lancifolia*, narrow plantain lily: narrow dark green glossy leaves 6 inches long in dense tufts up to 1½ feet tall with 2-inch white flowers tinged with violet on 2½-foot stalks from late summer to early fall. *H. sieboldiana*, Siebold's hosta: puckered blue-green leaves up to 10 inches across and 15 inches long in clumps up to 2 feet tall and twice as wide with white to pale lavender flowers on short stalks in summer. The variety 'Frances Williams' has yellow-edged leaves. *H. undulata*, wavy-leaved hosta: pointed 6-inch leaves striped in white or cream with curling edges in clumps up to 20 inches across with 2-inch lavender flowers on 3-foot stalks in midsummer. The leaves of the variety 'Albo-marginata' have broad white edges and 'Univittata' has a wide creamy stripe down the center of each leaf. *H. ventricosa*, blue hosta: glossy deep green 8-inch leaves with conspicuous veins and wavy edges in dense clumps with dark violet 2-inch flowers on 3-foot stalks in late summer. The variety 'Aureo-marginata' has leaves edged with yellow.

Growing conditions. Hostas do best in light to deep shade and a moist soil that is well drained summer and winter; they die out in a wet winter soil. They tolerate full sun if they are kept well watered during the growing season. Variegated types may not show as much color when grown in sun. Allow 1 foot between narrow plantain lilies and wavy-leaved hostas and 2 feet for the other hostas. Propagate by division in spring.

Landscape uses. Plant a single clump of hosta as a specimen. Use hostas to edge walks, in small groups in a border or in masses as a ground cover in a shaded garden.

Hound's tongue
see *Cynoglossum*

Houttuynia (hoo-too-IN-ee-a)

White flowers with prominent centers on spreading plants 12 to 15 inches tall with handsome heart-shaped leaves. Zones 5-9.

Selected species and varieties.
H. cordata 'Chameleon': flowers ½ inch across on reddish stalks above 3-inch dark green leaves with edges streaked yellow and pink.

Growing conditions. Plant houttuynia in full sun or shade in a constantly moist or even wet soil, spacing plants 1½ feet apart. Propagate by division. The creeping roots can be invasive.

Landscape uses. Use houttuynia as a ground cover for moist or boggy areas in a naturalistic garden.

Iberis (eye-BEER-is)
Candytuft

Spreading woody stems form low mounds of dark evergreen foliage that are covered with tiered clusters of white flowers in spring and sometimes again in fall. Zones 4-10.

Selected species and varieties.
I. sempervirens: wiry branching stems lined with narrow oblong 1½-inch leaves and tipped with white flower clusters. Plants up to 12 inches high and 2 feet across. The variety 'Autumn Snow' is a compact plant only 7 inches tall that blooms in both spring and fall. 'Purity' forms extremely neat 8-inch-high mats of foliage with spring blooms.

Growing conditions. Plant candytuft in full sun in moist, well-drained soil, spacing plants 12 to 15 inches apart. Dry conditions during the growing season will retard bloom. Shear after flowers fade to encourage bushy growth and prevent the centers of plants from dying out. Plants can be sheared formally. Propagate by seed sown the year before the plants are to bloom or by dividing mats in spring. Candytuft does not grow well in Zones 9 and 10 in the Southern states.

Landscape uses. Use candytuft in a rock garden, as an edging plant, sheared or unsheared, or as a filler at the front of a flower border. Allow its stems to tumble over the edge of a raised bed or a retaining wall.

Incarvillea (in-kar-VILL-ee-a)

Clusters of large trumpet-shaped flowers on sturdy stalks in late spring or early summer. Zones 6-10.

Selected species and varieties.
I. delavayi, hardy gloxinia: whorls of 3-inch rosy purple flowers with broad petals and yellow throats atop 1- to 2-foot stalks. Low-growing tufts of deeply divided 10-inch leaves are composed of narrow, pointed 2-inch leaflets.

Growing conditions. Plant hardy gloxinia in full sun in a moist, well-drained sandy soil enriched with organic matter. Space plants 1 foot apart. Provide ample water during the blooming season. Choose sites protected from winter winds and provide a deep mulch while plants are dormant. Incarvillea grows in Zone 10 only on the West Coast.

Landscape uses. Use hardy gloxinia as a specimen plant in a rock garden or tuck it into sheltered spots near terraces and walls.

Indigofera (in-dig-OFF-er-a)
Chinese indigo

Loose clusters of pealike summer flowers amid dark green ferny foliage in pairs of oval 2-inch leaflets. Zones 4-10.

Selected species and varieties.
I. incarnata, Chinese indigo: rosy ¾-inch flowers in slender 8-inch-long clusters on shrubby, sprawling plants up to 18 inches high.

Growing conditions. Chinese indigo does best in full sun in a well-drained sandy soil. Space plants 1½ feet apart. In Zones 9 and 10 Chinese indigo grows as a shrub and is not killed to the ground by frost as it is in Zones 4-8.

Landscape uses. Use Chinese indigo as a ground cover for slopes, where its dense roots slow erosion. Plant in front of shrubs or along the edge of a raised bed.

Inula (IN-yew-la)

Clumps of wiry stems 12 inches tall lined with narrow, pointed leaves and topped by daisy-like yellow summer flowers. Zones 4-9.

Selected species and varieties.
I. ensifolia, swordleaf inula: 1- to 1½-inch flowers with yellow centers surrounded by a fringe of narrow petals. Leaves up to 4 inches long are attractively curved.

Growing conditions. Plant swordleaf inula in full sun in a moist, well-drained soil, spacing plants 1 foot apart. Propagate from seed in spring or by division in spring or fall.

Landscape uses. Use swordleaf inula at the front of a sunny border or in a rock garden.

IBERIS SEMPERVIRENS

INCARVILLEA DELAVAYI

INDIGOFERA INCARNATA

INULA ENSIFOLIA

IRIS 'HALL OF FAME'

KNIPHOFIA UVARIA

Iris (EYE-ris)

Clumps of stiff, narrow, swordlike leaves and upright stalks of striking spring or summer blooms. Flowers are composed of erect petals called standards and drooping petals called falls. Petals may be ruffled, crested like a cockscomb down the centers of the falls or bearded, with colorful hairs at the base of the falls. The flowers are available in shades of almost every color except red, often with two or more colors in the same blossom. Zones 3-10.

Selected species and varieties. *I.* hybrids, bearded iris: a huge group of plants named for the small hairy patches, or beards, at the base of the falls. There is a color for every garden. Zones 3-10. Bearded irises are divided into dwarf, intermediate and tall classes based on plant size and are further subdivided according to flower size. Miniature dwarf bearded irises grow 8 inches tall with 1½- to 2½-inch midspring flowers; standard dwarf bearded irises grow up to 16 inches tall with 1½- to 2½-inch midspring flowers; intermediate bearded and border bearded irises grow to 28 inches, with 2- to 4-inch midspring to summer flowers. Miniature tall bearded irises grow from 18 to 26 inches, with 2-inch late-spring to summer flowers. The stately tall bearded irises are 28 inches or more in height, with late-spring to summer blooms up to 8 inches across. The variety 'Hall of Fame' is salmon pink. *I. cristata,* crested iris: 6 to 8 inches tall with 2½-inch lilac summer flowers marked with white or orange and white crests on the falls. Zones 4-8. The variety 'Abby's Violet' is an especially vivid violet with white and yellow crests. *I. ensata,* also called *I. kaempferi,* Japanese iris: clusters of beardless 4- to 10-inch midsummer flowers shaped like small orchids on 2- to 4-foot plants. There are hundreds of hybrids in white, blue, pink, violet and purple, often with yellow markings. Zones 5-9. The variety 'Haku Botan' bears huge white flowers. *I.* × 'Louisiana,' Louisiana iris: beardless summer flowers up to 4 inches across with narrow, ribbon-like standards and broad flat falls on 3- to 4-foot plants. Zones 5-10. *I.* Pacific Coast hybrids: plants 12 to 18 inches high with dark evergreen leaves and dainty beardless pastel flowers up to 3½ inches long. Zones 7-10. *I. pseudacorus,* yellow flag: delicate 2-inch yellow beardless flowers marked with brown on stalks up to 5 feet tall in summer. Zones 5-10. 'Variegata' has leaves streaked with yellow. *I. pumila,* dwarf bearded iris: tufts of 4- to 8-inch leaves with 2- to 3-inch bearded spring flowers. Zones 4-8. *I. sibirica,* Siberian iris: clusters of lavender to blue summer flowers up to 5 inches across on plants 1 to 4 feet high. Slender, grasslike foliage. Zones 3-9. The variety 'Flight of Butterflies' has blue-green leaves edged with white and 2-inch deep-blue flowers with conspicuously veined falls. 'Snow Queen' bears pure white flowers. *I. tectorum,* roof iris: plants to 12 inches tall with 2-inch lavender to purple-blue flowers with white crested falls in late spring. Zones 5-10. 'Alba' has white flowers.

Growing conditions. Irises do best in full sun although they will tolerate light shade. Plant bearded, crested, dwarf bearded, Pacific Coast, Siberian and roof irises in a moist, well-drained soil with their rhizomes level with the soil surface. Japanese irises, Louisiana irises and yellow flag prefer constantly moist soils. Pacific Coast hybrids tolerate drought and heat. Japanese, Louisiana, Pacific Coast, Siberian and roof irises do best when soil is slightly acid. Space the low-growing crested irises, dwarf bearded irises and roof irises 1 foot apart and the taller irises 1½ feet apart. Winter mulch is unnecessary except for Louisiana and roof irises. Propagate irises by dividing their rhizomes after the flowers fade. Bearded, Japanese, roof and yellow flag irises grow well in Zone 10 only on the West Coast.

Landscape uses. Use dwarf bearded, crested or roof irises at the front of a border or in a rock garden. Plant Japanese irises, yellow flag or Louisiana irises in moist soils at the edge of a stream, pool or moist woodland garden. Grow intermediate, border and tall bearded irises in a border or plant them along a wall or in front of evergreen shrubs.

—

Irish moss see *Arenaria*

Jack-in-the-pulpit see *Arisaema*

Jacob's-ladder see *Polemonium*

Japanese Solomon's-seal see *Polygonatum*

Joe-Pye weed see *Eupatorium*

Kangaroo-paw see *Anigozanthus*

—

Kniphofia (ny-FO-fee-a)
Red-hot poker, torch lily

Tall, leafless flower stalks tipped with long, densely packed clusters of drooping summer or fall flowers in vivid colors. Clumps of arching gray-green grassy leaves 1 inch wide and up to 3 feet long. Zones 6-10.

Selected species and varieties. *K. uvaria:* deep scarlet flowers up to 2 inches long that fade to yellow. Blossoms are crowded in dense 12-inch spikes on 3-foot stalks. There are numerous cultivars and hybrids in cream, yellow, orange, red or a combination of two colors that range in height from 2 to 6 feet and bloom at different times during the summer and fall.

Growing conditions. Plant red-hot poker in full sun in moist, well-drained sandy soil, choosing locations that are sheltered from wind. It does well in seaside garden conditions. Tie up the leaves and mulch the crowns to protect plants during winter in areas at the northern end of its range. Propagate red-hot poker by removing and planting the small offsets that grow at the edges of mature clumps, or by division every three to four years in the spring, setting new plants 1½ to 2 feet apart. Red-hot poker grows well in Zone 10 only on the West Coast.

Landscape uses. Use red-hot poker as a striking specimen at the middle or back of a border, where its foliage will also serve as a filler throughout the season. Cut the flower spikes for arrangements.

—

Ladybells see *Adenophora*
Lady's-mantle see *Alchemilla*
Lamb's-ears see *Stachys*

—

Lamiastrum (lay-mee-AS-trum)
Yellow archangel, golden dead nettle

Small yellow summer flowers in whorls amid 3-inch variegated heart-shaped leaves on spreading 1- to 2-foot plants. Zones 4-9.

Selected species and varieties. *L. galeobdolon:* hooded, hairy ¾-inch flowers in clusters of up to 15 blossoms.

Growing conditions. Plant yellow archangel in full sun or partial shade in any well-drained soil. Set plants 1½ to 2 feet apart. Yellow archangel spreads rapidly via creeping roots and can be invasive. Propagate by division in spring.

Landscape uses. Yellow archangel may be used as a ground cover in a naturalistic garden in sun or shade.

Lamium (LAY-me-um)
Dead nettle

Spreading plant with puckered leaves that are splotched or streaked with color. Hooded inch-long flowers in small clusters from spring through late summer. Zones 4-10.

Selected species and varieties. *L. maculatum,* spotted dead nettle: pink to purple flowers amid 3- to 4-inch toothed leaves with gray-green or cream streaks down their centers. The variety 'Aureum' has yellow-tinted leaves, 'Beacon Silver' has pink flowers with silvery, green-bordered leaves, and 'White Nancy' has white flowers with silver and green leaves.

Growing conditions. Plant spotted dead nettle in partial to deep shade in any well-drained soil. Space plants 1½ to 2 feet apart. Spotted dead nettle is invasive. Propagate from seed or by division in spring.

Landscape uses. Use spotted dead nettle to fill in spaces left by spring bulbs or as a ground cover under trees and shrubs in a woodland garden. It can be used as a foliage plant by pruning it back to prevent bloom.

—

Larkspur see *Delphinium*

—

Lavandula (lav-AN-dew-la)
Lavender

Spikes of tiny fragrant late-spring and summer flowers at the tips of erect stems lined with narrow gray-green woolly leaves that are evergreen in warm climates. Zones 5-10.

Selected species and varieties. *L. angustifolia,* English lavender: whorled clusters of blue-violet flowers stacked in 3-inch spikes atop 3-foot stems. The leaves are aromatic. The variety 'Hidcote' has dense spires of purple flowers on compact 18-inch plants. 'Munstead Dwarf' grows to 1 foot tall.

Growing conditions. English lavender needs full sun and a moist, well-drained soil enriched with organic matter such as peat moss, compost or leaf mold. Space plants 1 to 1½ feet apart. Shear plants annually in early spring to keep clumps neat. Propagate by dividing plants in spring. English lavender grows in Zone 10 only on the West Coast.

Landscape uses. Use English lavender in an ornamental herb or rock garden or near the front of a border. Plants can also be trimmed into a low

LAMIASTRUM GALEOBDOLON

LAMIUM MACULATUM 'BEACON SILVER'

LAVANDULA ANGUSTIFOLIA 'HIDCOTE'

LEONTOPODIUM ALPINUM

LIATRIS 'KOBOLD'

LIGULARIA PRZEWALSKII 'THE ROCKET'

hedge. Dry the flowers for sachets that remain fragrant for years.

—

Lavender see *Lavandula*
Lavender cotton see *Santolina*
Leadwort see *Ceratostigma*
Lenten rose see *Helleborus*

—

Leontopodium
(le-on-to-PO-dee-um)

Starry white summer flowers on creeping stems forming mats 6 to 12 inches high. Zones 5-10.

Selected species and varieties. *L. alpinum,* common edelweiss: clusters of tiny yellow ¼-inch flowers encircled by pointed petal-like white or gray woolly bracts in a star-shaped arrangement to 1½ inches across. Handsome narrow gray woolly leaves.

Growing conditions. Plant common edelweiss in full sun in a well-drained sandy, alkaline soil, spacing plants a foot apart. Propagate from seed or by division in spring. It grows well in Zones 9 and 10 only on the West Coast.

Landscape uses. Use common edelweiss singly or massed in a sunny rock garden or plant it in the crevices of a wall.

—

Leopard plant see *Ligularia*
Leopard's-bane see *Doronicum*

—

Liatris (ly-AY-tris)
Blazing star, gay-feather

Long wands of late-summer or fall flowers crowded at the top of upright stems above narrow swordlike foliage. Translucent green balloon-shaped buds open to purple or white flowers. The flowers have threadlike projections that give them a fuzzy appearance. The blooms open from top to bottom. Zones 3-10.

Selected species and varieties. *L. aspera:* 3-foot stems tipped with as many as 40 pale purple inch-wide flowers. Zones 4-8. *L. pyncnostachya,* Kansas gay-feather, tall gay-feather: stems up to 5 feet tall tipped with foot-long spikes of ½-inch rosy purple flowers. Leaves up to 16 inches long at the bases of stems, decreasing in size toward the top. Zones 3-8. *L. spicata,* spiked gay-feather: stems 3 to 6 feet tall tipped with foot-long spikes of ½-inch purple or white flowers. Zones 3-10. 'Kobold' is a compact form growing only 18 inches tall with deep purple flowers.

Growing conditions. Plant gay-feathers in full sun or light shade in a moist, well-drained sandy soil, spacing plants 1 foot apart. Propagate from seed or by division in spring. Gay-feathers grow well in Zones 9 and 10 only on the West Coast.

Landscape uses. Use the taller varieties of gay-feather near the back of a border. The shorter *L. spicata* 'Kobold' is suitable for the front of a border. Gay-feathers make excellent cut flowers and can be dried for winter bouquets.

—

Ligularia (lig-yew-LAY-ree-a)

Large, rounded heart- or kidney-shaped leaves, sometimes toothed or splotched with color, forming graceful clumps of foliage 2 to 4 feet tall. Bright yellow or orange flowers in summer. Zones 4-10.

Selected species and varieties. *L. dentata,* bigleaf goldenray: toothed, heart-shaped leaves up to a foot long. Small clusters of 2½- to 5-inch summer flowers with brown centers surrounded by a fringe of orange petals on stalks 3 to 4 feet tall. Zones 4-8. The variety 'Desdemona' has leaves with deep purple undersides on purple leafstalks; 'Gregynog Gold' has 3-inch yellow-orange flowers on 6-foot stems, and 'Othello' has leaves with purple undersides. *L. przewalskii* 'The Rocket': prominently toothed dark green triangular to round leaves in 4-foot mounds. Six-foot flower stalks with 12- to 18-inch spires of yellow ½-inch summer flowers. Zones 4-8. *L. tussilaginea:* leathery evergreen kidney-shaped leaves 6 inches long and a foot wide in low clumps topped with fuzzy, branched 2-foot flower stalks that bear 2-inch yellow summer flowers. Zones 6-10. The variety 'Argentea' has edges touched with cream; the leaves of 'Aureo-maculata,' or leopard plant, are irregularly splotched with round yellow freckles.

Growing conditions. Plant ligularias in full sun in a constantly moist but not wet soil amply enriched with organic matter. Ligularias grow in light shade but the flower stalks will lean toward the sun. The leaves may wilt on hot sunny summer afternoons, but they recover quickly. Allow 3 feet of space for *L. przewalskii* and 2 feet for the other species.

Propagate by division in spring, setting new plants 2 feet apart. *L. tussilaginea* grows in Zone 10 only on the West Coast.

Landscape uses. Use ligularia singly as a specimen plant or as a bold feature in a perennial border. Use the leaves of the leopard plant in floral arrangements.

—

Lilyturf see *Liriope*

—

Limonium (ly-MO-nee-um)
Sea lavender, statice

Wiry, sharply angled stalks with tiny lavender summer flowers in a cloud of blooms up to 3 feet across. Leathery, oblong leaves form a rosette. Zones 4-10.

Selected species and varieties. *L. latifolium:* stalks 1 to 2½ feet tall with many widely angled branches bear clusters of ⅛-inch flowers. Dark green leaves up to 8 inches long are evergreen. 'Violetta' has deep blue-violet flowers.

Growing conditions. Sea lavender requires full sun and a moist well-drained soil. It tolerates seashore conditions. Space plants 1½ feet apart. Propagate from seed or by division in spring. Seedlings or divisions take two or three years to reach blossoming size and may need staking. Sea lavender grows well in Zone 10 only on the West Coast.

Landscape uses. Plant sea lavender at the front of a border, where its neat foliage can be seen, or use it in the middle of a border as a lacy filler. Sea lavender blooms for many weeks. The flowers can be used fresh or dried in arrangements.

—

Linum (LY-num)
Flax

Yellow or blue saucer-shaped 1-inch blossoms. Flowers last only a day but are succeeded by new crops for continuous bloom over a long period in spring and summer. Zones 5-10.

Selected species and varieties. *L. flavum,* golden flax: bright yellow flowers in loose clusters on wiry 1- to 1½-foot stems from late spring to early summer. The variety 'Compactum' grows only 6 inches tall. *L. perenne,* perennial flax: 1- to 2-foot-long stems lined with narrow blue-green leaves bear clusters of sky blue flowers from midspring to midsummer.

Growing conditions. Flax requires full sun and a well-drained soil. Flowers will not open in shade. Space plants 1 to 1½ feet apart. Although flax plants can be divided, they live only a few years and are best propagated from seed sown in spring or by transplanting the many seedlings that spring up around mature plants. Golden and perennial flaxes grow in Zone 10 only on the West Coast.

Landscape uses. Use flax in a rock garden or at the front of a border.

—

Liriope (li-RY-o-pee)
Lilyturf

Spreading mounds of arching leaves. Evergreen or nearly so, depending on the climate. Flower spikes amid foliage from midsummer to fall. Zones 6-9.

Selected species and varieties. *L. muscari,* big blue lilyturf: tiny ¼-inch purple flowers clustered in spikes on stems 1 to 2 feet tall. The variety 'Majestic' has very dark green leaves and dense, compact flower spikes. 'Monroe's White' has white flowers. 'Variegata' has leaves streaked with white or yellow.

Growing conditions. Big blue lilyturf grows in full sun to deep shade in any well-drained soil. 'Monroe's White' and 'Variegata' do best in shade. Tolerates heat, poor or dry soil, and seaside conditions. Sometimes dies to the ground in fall in Zones 6 and 7. Space new plants 12 inches apart. Established plants can be cut to the ground in spring to renew straggly foliage.

Landscape uses. Plant big blue lilyturf singly or in groups at the front of a bed or border or use it as an edging. It also makes an excellent ground cover under large trees or shrubs or on steep slopes.

—

Lobelia (lo-BEE-lee-a)
Cardinal flower

Stiff stems up to 3 feet tall tipped with spires of bright red or blue tubular flowers with drooping lower lips from summer through fall. Zones 3-8.

Selected species and varieties. *L. cardinalis,* cardinal flower: red flowers 1½ inches long on leafy stems from early summer through fall. Zones 3-8. *L. siphilitica,* great blue lobelia, blue cardinal flower: 1-inch-long blue flowers on stems with hairy leaves from midsummer through fall. Zones 4-8.

LIMONIUM LATIFOLIUM

LINUM PERENNE

LIRIOPE MUSCARI 'MONROE'S WHITE'

LOBELIA CARDINALIS

LUPINUS RUSSELL HYBRIDS

LYCHNIS CORONARIA 'ALBA'

LYSIMACHIA PUNCTATA

Growing conditions. Lobelias grow best in partial shade in a moist or wet soil. Both species tolerate full sun, and great blue lobelia will tolerate dry conditions. Space plants 1 foot apart. Plants may need staking. Lobelias live only a few years. Propagate by removing and replanting the offsets that develop each year or by sowing seed. Lobelias often seed themselves.

Landscape uses. Use cardinal flower or great blue lobelia in a moist meadow garden, beside a stream or in a bog garden. Great blue lobelia can also be planted in a border.

———

Loosestrife see *Lysimachia;* see *Lythrum*

Lungwort see *Pulmonaria*

Lupine see *Lupinus*

———

Lupinus (loo-PY-nus)
Lupine

Heavy spikes of pealike summer flowers in blue, pink, cream, red, yellow or white. Deeply cut foliage resembling a hand with widespread fingers is attractive throughout the season. Zones 3-9.

Selected species and varieties. *L. perennis,* wild lupine: downy foliage on 2-foot-high plants. Flowers usually blue, sometimes white or pink. Zones 3-9. Russell hybrid lupines are vigorous plants 4 feet or more tall. Clear, lovely colors on long spikes of blooms. Zones 4-8.

Growing conditions. Grow wild lupine in an acid, well-drained sandy soil in full sun or light shade. It will tolerate poor, dry soil. Russell hybrids do well in moist soil rich in organic matter. Space wild lupines 1½ feet apart and Russell hybrid lupines 2 feet apart. Remove flower spikes after blooming. Propagate from seed. Because of its deep roots, lupine is difficult to divide or transplant. Russell hybrids do well in Zones 7 and 8 only where summer nights are cool.

Landscape uses. Wild lupine is a fine plant for a naturalistic garden and may also be grown in a formal border. Russell hybrids are suited to the middle or rear of a border or can be grown in large groups in a bed of their own.

———

Lychnis (LIK-nis)

Summer flowers in white or bright shades of pink, red or purple, borne singly or in clusters. Zones 4-10.

Selected species and varieties. *L. arkwrightii,* Arkwright campion: clusters of 1½-inch brilliant red flowers on stems a foot tall. Zones 7-9. *L. chalcedonica,* Maltese cross: heavy clusters of scarlet flowers an inch across with deeply indented petals on plants 2 to 3 feet high. Zones 4-8. *L. coronaria,* mullein pink: flat, brilliant cerise blossoms atop 2½-foot stems that rise from tufts of woolly gray foliage. Zones 4-10. The variety 'Alba' has white flowers. *L. viscaria,* German catchfly: small bright pinkish purple or reddish purple flowers in loose clusters atop sticky stems a foot high. Zones 4-10. The variety 'Flore Pleno' has thick, frilly double flowers. 'Zulu' has hot red flowers.

Growing conditions. Arkwright campion and Maltese cross do best in moist, rich soil in full sun or light shade. Mullein pink does best in a light soil in full sun, where it will self-sow prolifically. Plant German catchfly in a well-drained sandy soil in full sun. Space plants 1 to 1½ feet apart. Propagate by seed.

Landscape uses. Use lychnis in the front or middle of a border, according to height, or allow the plants to seed themselves in a meadow garden. Their brilliant colors are enhanced by a background of dark green foliage.

———

Lysimachia (ly-si-MAK-ee-a)
Loosestrife

Vigorous, easy-to-grow plant with spikes of small white flowers or cup-shaped yellow flowers on erect stems in spring or summer. The genus *Lythrum* has the same common name. Zones 4-8.

Selected species and varieties. *L. clethroides,* gooseneck loosestrife: dense, gracefully curved spikes of ½-inch white flowers atop 3-foot stems from midsummer to late summer. Neat, tapering dark green leaves. Zones 4-8. *L. punctata,* yellow loosestrife: deep yellow flowers marked inside with a brown circle on stems 2 to 3 feet tall. Large, deeply veined, pointed oval leaves crowd the stems. Zones 5-7.

Growing conditions. Loosestrifes thrive in moist soil in full sun or light shade. Space plants 2 feet apart. They can spread quickly and overcrowd neighboring plants. Propagate by dividing the thick mat of roots in early spring.

Landscape uses. Loosestrifes may be planted in a border if their spread is kept in check with frequent division.

They require less attention in a naturalistic garden where they can spread freely into wide clumps.

Lythrum (LY-thrum)
Loosestrife

Dense cylindrical spikes of pink to purple blossoms in summer on bushy upright plants with 4-inch willow-like leaves. The genus *Lysimachia* has the same common name. Zones 3-9.

Selected species and varieties. *L. salicaria,* purple loosestrife: 3 to 4 feet tall with pinkish purple flowers in spikes a foot or more long. Cultivars include 'Happy,' 1½ feet high with clear pink blossoms; 'Morden's Pink,' 3 feet tall with rose pink blossoms and dark green foliage; and 'Robert,' a 2-foot plant with bright rose red flowers and foliage that turns red in fall.

Growing conditions. Loosestrifes thrive in wet meadowlands and along river edges but also do well in moist, well-drained soil. Full sun is best but loosestrifes will grow in light shade. Space plants 1½ feet apart. They may be left alone for years to develop into large clumps, and the taller ones rarely need staking. They can be increased by division, but this can be difficult because the roots are tough and woody. Remove fading flower heads to prevent a large crop of seedlings. The cultivars seem to be sterile, but the species, which is a European import, is crowding out native plants in many American wetlands.

Landscape uses. Use loosestrifes in the middle or at the back of a border for many weeks of color. They are also effective planted in drifts in a large naturalistic garden. Place the cultivar 'Robert' where its bright fall foliage will show to advantage.

Macleaya (mak-LAY-a)
Plume poppy

Fluffy foot-long clusters of small flowers tip 6- to 8-foot stems in middle to late summer. Attractive rounded leaves with large lobes. Zones 3-9.

Selected species and varieties. *M. cordata,* plume poppy: numerous ½-inch ivory blossoms appear in clusters on the upper half of the stems. Gray-green leaves up to a foot across with undulating edges and silvery undersides stand out from the main stems on short stalks. Attractive seedpods.

Growing conditions. Grow plume poppy in ordinary well-drained soil in full sun. If young plants are set in rich soil they will grow quickly to blooming size. Space plants 3 to 4 feet apart. Plants will self-sow or may be increased by digging up rooted sections from the perimeter of the plant and resetting them.

Landscape uses. Plant plume poppy singly as a specimen in front of a hedge, fence or building. It may also be used at the back of a wide border, though its handsome foliage will be less visible.

Mallow see *Malva*
Maltese cross see *Lychnis*

Malva (MAL-va)
Mallow

Flowers 2 inches across with five satiny, notched pink or white petals from summer to early fall on plants 2 to 4 feet tall with finely cut foliage. Zones 4-9.

Selected species and varieties. *M. alcea,* hollyhock mallow: 2-foot plants with loose spikes of deep pink or white flowers resembling hollyhocks, though more delicate in texture. *M. alcea* 'Fastigiata' is 3 to 4 feet tall and narrower in form with pink flowers. *M. moschata,* musk mallow: rose or white blossoms and dark green finely cut, lobed foliage on symmetrical, bushy 3-foot plants. *M. moschata* 'Alba' has white flowers.

Growing conditions. Plant mallows in ordinary garden soil that is on the dry side and in full sun or light shade. In hot climates they need deeper, moister soil enriched with organic matter. Space plants 2 feet apart. Though not long-lived, they are easy to grow from seed and will self-sow. Mature clumps can be divided in spring or fall.

Landscape uses. Use mallows in a border according to height. They may also be allowed to self-sow in a large naturalistic garden. Musk mallow's flowers, neat form and pretty foliage make it an especially desirable plant.

Marguerite see *Anthemis;*
see *Felicia*
Marjoram see *Origanum*
Marsh marigold see *Caltha*
Matilija poppy see *Romneya*
Meadow beauty see *Rhexia*

LYTHRUM SALICARIA 'MORDEN'S PINK'

MACLEAYA CORDATA

MALVA MOSCHATA

MECONOPSIS CAMBRICA

MERTENSIA VIRGINICA

MIMULUS LEWISII

MISCANTHUS SINENSIS 'ZEBRINUS'

Meadow rue see *Thalictrum*

Meadowsweet see *Filipendula*

Mealy-cup sage see *Salvia*

■

Meconopsis (me-con-OP-sis)

Poppy-like yellow or orange flowers above mounds of ferny foliage in summer. Zones 6-9.

Selected species and varieties. *M. cambrica,* Welsh poppy: yellow or orange blossoms 2 to 3 inches across on 1½-foot stems. Finely cut 6-inch leaves are silvery on the undersides.

Growing conditions. Welsh poppy needs a lightly shaded location and moist, well-drained soil rich in organic matter. Space plants 1 foot apart. It does well along the Pacific coast, where summers are relatively cool, but is difficult to grow where summers are hot.

Landscape uses. Welsh poppy is well suited to a shady woodland garden, a rock garden or a perennial bed. It looks pretty in drifts beneath deciduous trees.

■

Merrybells see *Uvularia*

■

Mertensia (mer-TEN-see-a)
Bluebells

Pink buds open to fragrant trumpet-shaped blue flowers in spring. Zones 4-8.

Selected species and varieties. *M. virginica,* Virginia bluebells: loose nodding clusters of 1-inch flowers on plants from 1 to 2 feet high. Flowers may be various shades of blue and are occasionally pink or white. A plant often has buds and open flowers at the same time. Long, oval blue-green leaves.

Growing conditions. Virginia bluebells grow best in partial shade where the soil is acid, moist, well drained and rich in organic matter. They can tolerate full sun. Space them 1 foot apart. The plants go dormant in summer and need drier soil then. They can be propagated by seed or by division after they go dormant. They may self-sow.

Landscape uses. Virginia bluebells can be used in a woodland garden or a shady perennial bed and are attractive in drifts under trees at the edge of a lawn. Because they are dormant in summer, they should be interplanted with plants that fill up the spaces they

leave, such as hostas, fringed bleeding hearts or ferns.

■

Michaelmas daisy see *Aster*

Milkweed see *Asclepias*

■

Mimulus (MIM-yew-lus)
Monkey flower

Oddly shaped tubular flowers in pink, red or yellow that somewhat resemble the face of a monkey. Summer-blooming. Zones 4-10.

Selected species and varieties. *M. cardinalis:* 2-inch scarlet flowers on plants 3 feet high with 4-inch oblong hairy leaves. Zones 4-10. *M. guttatus,* common monkey flower: 2½-inch yellow flowers, usually with red or brown spots in their throats, on plants up to 2 feet high. Zones 4-6. *M. lewisii,* Lewis' monkey flower: 2-inch pink or rose red flowers on plants up to 2½ feet tall. Zones 4-6.

Growing conditions. All three species of monkey flower can flourish in a moist, moderately fertile soil. *M. cardinalis* and *M. lewisii* do best in semishade. *M. lewisii* may be grown in drier soil than the others, and common monkey flower does well in a damp or even wet soil. Common monkey flower will grow in light shade or full sun. Space new plants 1½ to 2 feet apart. Common monkey flower may be propagated by seed or by division. Propagate other monkey flowers by seed sown where the plants are to remain permanently. If they are in a good spot, the plants will self-sow.

Landscape uses. Grow monkey flowers in a naturalistic garden or a border. Common monkey flower may be grown in a wet meadow or by the banks of a stream.

■

Miscanthus (mis-KAN-thus)

Tall, fine-textured grass with long, narrow, gracefully arching leaves and feathery flower clusters on erect stems in late summer or early fall. Clump turns golden tan in winter. Zones 5-9.

Selected species and varieties. *M. sinensis,* eulalia grass, Japanese silver grass: 6 to 8 feet tall; width of clump 3 feet or more. Fawn-colored flower clusters up to 8 inches long, followed by seed heads that persist through winter if the clump is left standing. Zones 5-9. *M. sinensis*

'Gracillimus,' maiden grass: 4 to 5 feet tall with silvery green leaves ¼ inch wide. Silvery white flowers. Zones 5-9. *M. sinensis condensatus:* 6 to 8 feet tall with purplish flowers. Zones 6-9. *M. sinensis* 'Purpurascens': 3 to 4 feet tall. Foliage turns purplish red in late summer. Reddish flowers. Zones 5-9. *M. sinensis strictus,* porcupine grass: 6 to 8 feet tall with pale yellow bands across the leaves. Zones 6-9. *M. sinensis* 'Zebrinus,' zebra grass: 5 to 6 feet tall with yellow stripes across the leaves. Pinkish brown flower clusters. Zones 6-9.

Growing conditions. Plant these grasses in well-drained soil, spacing plants 3 feet apart. They all grow best in full sun but will tolerate light shade. Cut clumps to within 2 to 6 inches of the ground before new spring growth appears. Propagate by division in early spring.

Landscape uses. These grasses are good additions to the rear of a border, where they form a fine-textured green backdrop for the flowers of lower-growing perennials as well as providing late-season bloom and winter interest if left standing after frost. They can be grouped with contrasting coarse-leaved foliage plants or, in the case of the taller varieties, used as specimens or screens.

—

Mist flower see *Eupatorium*

—

Monarda (mo-NARD-a)

Small, tubular red, pink, lavender or yellow flowers blooming from summer to early fall in dense 2- to 3-inch clusters surrounded by aromatic leaves on square stems. Monarda belongs to the mint family. Zones 4-9.

Selected species and varieties. *M. didyma,* bee balm: red flowers on 3-foot plants. The variety 'Cambridge Scarlet' has flowers in a clearer, more brilliant red; 'Croftway Pink' bears rose pink flowers; and 'Mahogany' has deep purplish red flowers. *M. fistulosa,* wild bergamot, horse mint: lavender blossoms on plants that may grow 5 feet tall. *F. punctata,* horse mint: grows 3 feet high with showy curved pink bracts and small yellow flowers with purple spots.

Growing conditions. Monardas do best in moist, rich soil in full sun or light shade. They grow rapidly in these conditions and may in fact become invasive. In drier soil they are

shorter and less invasive. Space plants 1½ to 2 feet apart. Divide plants in spring.

Landscape uses. Monardas are well suited to naturalizing in a meadow or woodland garden. *M. didyma* and its varieties are also attractive in small groups in a border. Do not plant monardas where they may crowd out smaller or less vigorous plants. Monardas of all sorts attract bees and hummingbirds.

—

Monkey flower see *Mimulus*
Monkshood see *Aconitum*
Montbretia see *Crocosmia*
Moss campion see *Silene*
Mullein see *Verbascum*
Mullein pink see *Lychnis*

—

Myosotis (my-o-SO-tis)
Forget-me-not

Clusters of small blue flowers, each with a yellow, pink or white eye, on plants 8 inches to 1½ feet high, from spring to summer. Zones 3-10.

Selected species and varieties. *M. scorpioides,* forget-me-not: loose clusters of ¼-inch china blue flowers on stems that rise from a mat of tapering oval leaves. Occasionally a pink blossom appears among the blue ones.

Growing conditions. Plant forget-me-nots in partial shade in moist but not wet soil. They will also tolerate full sun as long as they receive ample moisture. Set plants 9 to 12 inches apart. Propagate in spring by division or from seed. In Zones 9 and 10 forget-me-nots grow only on the West Coast.

Landscape uses. Use forget-me-nots among wildflowers in a naturalistic woodland garden, plant them in drifts along a stream or in a damp meadow or use them at the front of a shady border.

—

Nepeta (ne-PEE-ta)
Catmint

Tiny blue flowers in spikes on a low-growing plant with gray-green triangular or heart-shaped aromatic foliage loved by cats. Blooms spring to midsummer. Zones 4-8.

Selected species and varieties. *N. mussinii,* catmint: soft blue or lavender-blue flowers on 1-foot

MONARDA DIDYMA 'CROFTWAY PINK'

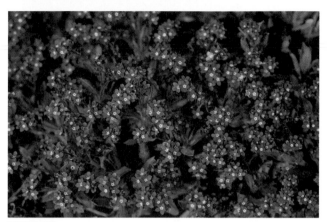
MYOSOTIS

NEPETA MUSSINII

OENOTHERA FRUTICOSA

ORIGANUM VULGARE 'AUREUM'

PAEONIA 'KANSAS'

stems. The plant spreads to 1½ feet in width.

Growing conditions. Grow catmint in full sun in sandy, well-drained soil. Poor soil keeps it compact and attractive; in rich soil it is likely to sprawl. Space plants 1 to 1½ feet apart. Stems may be cut back by half after flowering to encourage a second blooming. Increase by division or by seed.

Landscape uses. Catmint is a fine ground cover. It may also be used in the front of a border, in a rock garden or in an herb garden. Its subtle blues and lavenders combine well with soft pinks, yellows and other blues.

—

New Zealand flax see *Phormium*

Nippon daisy see *Chrysanthemum*

Obedient plant see *Dracocephalum*

October daphne see *Sedum*

—

Oenothera (ee-no-THEE-ra)

Showy four-petaled summer flowers in yellow, white or pink. Zones 4-9.

Selected species and varieties. *O. fruticosa,* common sundrops: 1- to 2-inch yellow flowers in clusters at the tops of 1- to 2-foot stems. Zones 4-8. *O. missouriensis,* Ozark sundrops: thin-textured yellow blossoms 4 to 5 inches across on trailing stems. Zones 4-9. *O. speciosa,* showy evening primrose: white or pink blossoms on plants 6 inches to 1½ feet tall. Zones 5-8. *O. tetragona,* common sundrops: lemon yellow flowers on a plant about 3 feet high; may be perennial or biennial. Zones 4-8. *O. tetragona* and *O. fruticosa* are often confused with each other.

Growing conditions. Grow evening primroses and sundrops in full sun and well-drained soil. They do well even in poor and dry soils and can become invasive, especially showy evening primrose. Allow 2 feet between Ozark sundrops and 1 to 1½ feet for the other species. Grow Ozark sundrops from seed. Propagate other species by seed or by division in spring.

Landscape uses. Use showy evening primrose in a naturalistic garden where it will not crowd out less robust plants. Both common sundrops and Ozark sundrops are fine border plants; their bright yellow flowers contrast well with other colors.

Origanum (o-RIG-an-um)
Marjoram

Low, neat mat of aromatic, oval 1½-inch leaves and wiry, branching flower stalks bearing small spikes of rose to purple flowers in late summer. Zones 4-10.

Selected species and varieties. *O. vulgare* 'Aureum,' variegated pot marjoram: a cultivar valued mainly for its foliage, which is golden yellow until midsummer and then turns green. Flower stalks are 1½ to 2 feet tall.

Growing conditions. Pot marjoram needs full sun and moist, well-drained soil. Space plants 1½ feet apart. Propagate in spring by division or from seed.

Landscape uses. Use variegated pot marjoram as a colorful, aromatic edging for a border. Pick the leaves for use as a culinary herb.

—

Oxeye see *Heliopsis*

Oxeye daisy see *Chrysanthemum*

—

Paeonia (pee-O-nee-a)
Peony

Showy spring and early-summer blossoms on bushy plants that grow up to 4 feet in height and may thrive for decades. Blossoms range from white and creamy yellow through pinks and dark purple-red and may have single, double or semidouble rows of petals. Shoots emerge red and ferny in spring, then develop into lush, deeply divided foliage. Zones 3-10.

Selected species and varieties. *P. mlokosewitschii,* Caucasian peony: earliest flowering peony, with 2-inch single yellow blossoms on plants 2 feet high with blue-green foliage. Zones 6-8. *P. officinalis,* common peony: a 2- to 4-foot-high plant with 3- to 6-inch-wide blooms in red, pink, light yellow or white. Zones 3-10. Its hybrids have different blooming times, from spring to early summer, and come in five forms: single, with one row of petals and prominent yellow stamens; Japanese and anemone, with a single row of petals and large, conspicuous stamens that look like finely cut petals; semidouble, with several rows of petals and visible stamens; and double, with full heads of petals and no stamens readily visible. *P. tenuifolia,* fernleaf peony: the smallest and most delicate of the peonies, growing about 1 foot high, with finely divided foliage and single red-purple flowers in early summer. Zones 6-8. The variety 'Plena' is a double form. 'Laciniata' is taller with broader leaves. 'Rosea' has single pink blossoms. 'Kansas' has bright red blossoms on very strong stems in midseason.

Growing conditions. Peonies need well-drained soil enriched with organic matter. They thrive in sun and grow in light shade but become leggy and weak in heavy shade. Plant container-grown peonies whenever the ground is not frozen, any time from late August until the ground freezes. Space plants 3 feet apart. Set crowns an inch below the soil surface; planting too deep results in failure to bloom. Divide in fall; cut roots apart with a knife and leave at least three eyes to each piece. Common peony and its hybrids do well in Zones 9 and 10 only on the West Coast.

Landscape uses. Use peonies in a border or in front of shrubs, as specimens, as hedges, or along a wall or a fence. Their foliage is an asset after the flowers have faded. Use fernleaf peony in a rock garden. Peonies are excellent cut flowers.

—

Panicum (PA-ni-cum)

Tall, upright grass with narrow leaves and long, feathery clusters of small buff-colored flowers from midsummer to early fall. Zones 5-9.

Selected species and varieties. *P. virgatum,* switch grass: 5 to 7 feet tall, spreading by underground stems to form dense clumps. Leaves ½ inch wide and up to 2 feet long turn golden in fall. Flowers bloom above the foliage in clusters up to 20 inches long. *P. virgatum* 'Rotstrahlbusch,' red switch grass: grows 3 to 4 feet tall and has red foliage in fall.

Growing conditions. Plant switch grass in full sun in moist, well-drained soil, spacing plants 2 to 3 feet apart. Divide clumps in early spring.

Landscape uses. Switch grass is well suited to a naturalistic meadow garden where it can spread without overcrowding other plants. It is also attractive as a specimen or in small groups in a border or an island bed. Where it is desirable to control its spread, remove the bottom of a large plastic flower pot, sink the pot in the ground and plant the switch grass in it.

—

Pansy see *Viola*

Papaver (pap-AY-ver)
Poppy

Large late-spring to early-summer blossoms with silky crinkled petals in white and shades of red, pink or orange ranging from the delicate to the flamboyant. Finely cut downy gray-green foliage. Zones 3-9.

Selected species and varieties. *P. orientale,* Oriental poppy: numerous varieties with showy blossoms up to 8 inches or more across, with conspicuous black stamens and petals that often have dark blotches at their bases. Plants grow 3 to 4 feet tall. The variety 'Brilliant' is clear scarlet. 'Princess Louise' is salmon-colored.

Growing conditions. Grow Oriental poppies in full sun in any well-drained soil. Foliage dies down after flowering. New leaves appear in late summer or early fall. Propagate from root cuttings.

Landscape uses. Site Oriental poppies in a border next to plants that will fill in the bare spots left when the poppies' foliage dies down.

—

Pasque flower see *Anemone*
Pearly everlasting see *Anaphalis*

—

Pennisetum (pen-i-SEE-tum)

Graceful clumps of narrow, arching foliage and bristly flower clusters on long, slender stems in summer and fall. Clumps turn tan in fall and can be left standing through winter. Zones 6-9.

Selected species and varieties. *P. alopecuroides,* Chinese pennisetum, fountain grass: 3 to 4 feet tall. Small silvery rose flowers in cylindrical clusters up to 6 inches long, followed by seed heads that persist into winter if the clump is left standing. The variety 'Hameln,' dwarf fountain grass, grows 2 to 3 feet tall. *P. caudatum,* white-flowering fountain grass. Four to 5 feet tall. It is similar to Chinese pennisetum, but its flowers are white.

Growing conditions. Plant fountain grass in a well-drained soil in full sun, setting plants 2 feet apart. Cut plants to within 6 inches of the ground before new growth appears in spring. Propagate by seed or by division in early spring.

Landscape uses. Use fountain grass as a dense, fine-textured backdrop for lower-growing perennials in

PANICUM VIRGATUM

PAPAVER ORIENTALE 'GLOWING EMBERS'

PENNISETUM

PENSTEMON SMALLII

PEROVSKIA ATRIPLICIFOLIA

PHLOX BIFIDA

a border or group it with plants with contrasting coarse-textured foliage. Fountain grass is especially effective in winter when it is planted in masses.

—

Penstemon (pen-STEE-mon)
Penstemon, beard-tongue

Loose spikes of pink, red, lavender or purple tubular two-lipped flowers with fine hairs inside in spring and summer. Zones 4-10.

Selected species and varieties. *P. barbatus,* beardlip penstemon: a 3- to 6-foot plant with narrow oval leaves and spikes of red flowers in early summer. Zones 4-9. Varieties include 'Bashful': 1-foot-high plant with salmon-colored blossoms; 'Prairie Fire': 2 feet tall with scarlet blossoms; and 'Rose Elf': 1½ to 2½ feet tall with rosy blooms. *B. × gloxinioides,* gloxinia penstemon: 2-foot-tall plant with 2-inch flowers in shades of red in early summer. Zones 6-10. *P. grandiflorus:* 3- to 4-foot plant with bluish leaves and lavender blossoms in late spring. Zones 3-7. *P. hirsutus,* hairy beard-tongue: heavily bearded lavender flowers held above a mound of leaves on 1½-foot stems in late spring and early summer. Zones 6-8. *P. hirsutus* 'Pygmaeus': lavender flowers on 8-inch stems. *P. pinifolius:* narrow scarlet flowers in summer on 1-foot-tall plant with needle-like evergreen foliage. Zones 5-9. *P. smallii:* 2-foot-tall clumps of glossy foliage and pinkish purple flowers striped inside with white in spring. Zones 4-8.

Growing conditions. Grow penstemons in moist, well-drained soil in full sun or light shade. Space low-growing species and cultivars 1 foot apart and taller ones 1½ to 2 feet apart. All tend to be short-lived and suffer in extremes of heat and cold. Propagate by seed or by division.

Landscape uses. The smaller penstemons make fine rock garden plants and good edging for a border or a walk. Plant taller species and cultivars in the middle of a border or at the back. Daisy-like flowers such as erigerons make an interesting contrast with the foxglove shape of penstemon flowers.

—

Peony see *Paeonia*

—

Perovskia (per-OV-skee-a)

Three- to 5-foot-high shrubby plant with aromatic silvery leaves and small blue blossoms that appear in late summer. Zones 5-8.

Selected species and varieties. *P. atriplicifolia,* azure sage, Russian sage: flowers densely packed at the ends of stems, clustered more loosely below. Silvery foliage and small blossoms give a lacy effect. The leaves and stems smell like sage when crushed. The plant spreads to about 3 feet across.

Growing conditions. Azure sage grows best in well-drained soil in full sun. Space plants 2 to 3 feet apart. Propagate by seed. Cutting the plant to the ground in early spring promotes good bloom.

Landscape uses. Plant azure sage in a border or island bed, where it combines well with ornamental grasses. It can also be used as any airy hedge or screen.

—

Peruvian lily see *Alstroemeria*

—

Phlox (flox)

Clusters of five-petaled flat-faced flowers in orange, red, pink, lavender, purple, blue or white on stems that trail or grow erect to 4 feet. Some phlox bloom in spring, others in summer or early fall. Zones 3-10.

Selected species and varieties. *P. bifida,* prairie phlox: grows to 10 inches with spring flowers that have white to light blue deeply cut petals. Zones 5-8. *P. carolina,* Carolina phlox: white to pinkish purple flowers on plants 3 to 4 feet tall. Blooms in late spring. Zones 4-9. *P. divaricata,* wild blue phlox: a creeping plant up to 1 foot tall with pale lavender-blue flowers. Spring-blooming. Zones 3-8. *P. divaricata* 'Fuller's White' has white blossoms. *P. maculata,* wild sweet William: 3-foot plant with glossy leaves and pink, purple or white flowers in loose clusters from spring through summer. Zones 4-9. The variety 'Alpha' has pink blossoms, and 'Omega' has white flowers with a lavender eye. *P. paniculata,* border phlox: the common phlox of the summer garden. Grows to 4 feet high with white, pink, red, orange, lavender or purple flowers in heavy clusters. Zones 4-9. The variety 'Mt. Fujiyama' has large heads of white flowers; 'Orange Perfection' has orange flowers, and 'Starfire' has early blooms of intense red. *P. stolonifera,* creeping phlox: 6- to 12-inch-high plant with early-spring blossoms of lavender-blue. Zones 5-8. 'Blue

Ridge' has clear blue flowers, and 'Bruce's White' has white flowers. *P. subulata,* moss pink: low-growing mat of stiff needle-like evergreen leaves smothered in spring with blooms of white, pink, blue, lavender or red flowers, depending on the variety. Zones 4-10.

Growing conditions. Phlox species have varied cultural needs. Moss pink and prairie phlox do best in full sun and sandy soil. The other species require moist, well-drained soil rich in organic matter. Wild blue phlox and creeping phlox require light shade. Border phlox, wild sweet William and Carolina phlox do best in full sun and need plenty of water in the summer. Remove about half of the young shoots from border phlox in spring for best blossoming. Border phlox needs good air circulation to prevent powdery mildew, so space plants at least 2 feet apart. Divide them every three to four years to keep them robust. Space the other tall-growing phlox 1½ to 2 feet apart and the lower-growing phlox 1 to 1½ feet apart. Propagate by division.

Landscape uses. Border phlox is a mainstay of perennial borders for summer color, and Carolina phlox and wild sweet William are also well suited to borders. Use creeping phlox and wild blue phlox as ground covers under trees and shrubs or interplant them with bulbs in a shaded garden. Prairie phlox and moss pink can be used as rock garden plants, as ground covers or at the front of a border.

—

Phormium (FORM-ee-um)

Bold fan-shaped plant with leathery swordlike leaves and red flowers on tall stalks up to 15 feet in height. Zones 8-10.

Selected species and varieties. *P. tenax* 'Variegatum,' New Zealand flax: stiff gray-green leaves up to 9 feet long striped with yellow. Plum red flowers appear in clusters on stalks that rise several feet above the foliage.

Growing conditions. New Zealand flax grows best in moist soil in full sun or light shade. It tolerates windy sites and does well in seaside gardens. In Zone 8 plant it in a warm, sheltered spot. Space plants 3 to 5 feet apart. Propagate New Zealand flax by seed or by division.

Landscape uses. Use New Zealand flax alone as a specimen plant, combine it with shrubs or plant it in a perennial border for a spiky accent.

Physalis (FISS-a-lis)

Brightly colored inflated papery pods up to 2 inches across resembling tiny Oriental lanterns in fall. Zones 4-10.

Selected species and varieties. *P. alkekengi,* Chinese lantern: 1- to 2-foot plant with creamy white star-shaped midsummer flowers largely hidden by 3-inch oval leaves. Deep red to orange seedpods containing edible fruits develop in fall.

Growing conditions. Plant Chinese lantern in full sun or partial shade in any well-drained soil, spacing plants 2 feet apart. The creeping roots can be invasive. Propagate in spring by division or from seed.

Landscape uses. Use Chinese lantern alone or as a filler in an informal border where its invasive tendency can be kept under control. To use the pods in winter bouquets, cut stems just as the leaves begin to fade and hang them upside down until dry.

—

Physostegia see *Dracocephalum*
Pincushion flower see *Scabiosa*
Pink see *Dianthus*
Plantain lily see *Hosta*

—

Platycodon (plat-i-KO-don)
Balloon flower

Fat, balloon-like buds open into cup-shaped blue, pink or white flowers that bloom all summer. Zones 3-9.

Selected species and varieties. *P. grandiflorus:* deep blue flowers 2 to 3 inches across on 2- to 3-foot plants with oval blue-green leaves. The variety 'Album' has white flowers; 'Shell Pink' has pink flowers. *P. grandiflorus mariesii,* Maries' balloon flower: 1½-foot plant with either blue or white flowers.

Growing conditions. Plant balloon flowers in a light, moist, well-drained acid soil enriched with organic matter such as peat moss, compost and leaf mold. They grow best in full sun, although light shade helps the pink flowers to retain their color. Space plants 1½ feet apart. Propagate by division in spring or by seed. Plants started from seed will bloom their second year. New growth is late to appear in spring.

Landscape uses. Balloon flower is a good plant for dependable color all summer long in a perennial border. The smaller Maries' balloon flower is suitable for a rock garden.

PHORMIUM TENAX 'VARIEGATUM'

PHYSALIS ALKEKENGI

PLATYCODON GRANDIFLORUS MARIESII

POLEMONIUM CAERULEUM

POLYGONATUM ODORATUM THUNBERGII 'VARIEGATUM'

POLYGONUM AFFINE

PORTERANTHUS TRIFOLIATUS

Plumbago see *Ceratostigma*

Plume poppy see *Macleaya*

Pocketbook plant
see *Calceolaria*

—

Polemonium
(po-lee-MO-nee-um)
Jacob's-ladder

Clusters of small nodding flowers in white or shades of blue and purple. Small apple green oval leaves arranged in neat pairs climb up the stems in a ladder-like effect. Blooms from spring into summer. Zones 4-9.

Selected species and varieties. *P. caeruleum:* grows to 3 feet with 1-inch blue to purple flowers from midspring to early summer. There is also a white variety. *P. reptans,* creeping Jacob's-ladder: grows 1 foot tall with ¾-inch light blue to lavender-blue flowers in loose drooping clusters in spring.

Growing conditions. Plant Jacob's-ladder in moist, well-drained soil with plenty of organic matter in partial shade. Space plants 1½ to 2 feet apart. Propagate Jacob's-ladder by division or by seed. Creeping Jacob's-ladder will self-sow.

Landscape uses. Use *P. caeruleum* in a shaded border. Plant creeping Jacob's-ladder in a woodland garden or a shaded rock garden.

—

Polygonatum (po-lig-o-NAY-tum)
Solomon's-seal

Handsome green oval leaves are held horizontally along graceful arching stems. Dangling creamy white bell-shaped flowers in late spring. Zones 4-9.

Selected species and varieties. *P. odoratum thunbergii* 'Variegatum,' variegated Japanese Solomon's-seal: 4-inch leaves edged and tipped in white on plants that grow 2 to 3 feet high. The flowers are fragrant and tinged with green.

Growing conditions. Variegated Solomon's-seal grows best in moist, acid soil rich in organic matter, and in shade. Set plants 1 foot apart. Propagate by seed or by division in spring or autumn.

Landscape uses. Plant Japanese Solomon's-seal with spring bulbs and woodland perennials such as Virginia bluebells, or among azaleas and other shade-loving shrubs. The foliage of Japanese Solomon's-seal is suitable for use in flower arrangements.

Polygonum (po-LIG-o-num)

Tiny pink, red or white flowers borne in spikes on erect stems held above mounds of tongue-shaped leaves in summer or fall. Zones 4-7.

Selected species and varieties. *P. affine,* Himalayan fleece flower: a 6- to 9-inch spike of rosy flowers in summer above a spreading mat of dark green 4-inch leaves that turn bronze in fall. *P. bistorta,* snakeweed: a clump-forming plant with pink or white flowers in dense spikes on 1½-foot stems in summer. *P. bistorta* 'Superbum': 2- to 3-foot-high plant with bottle-brush spikes of pink flowers in late summer and early fall.

Growing conditions. Grow Himalayan fleece flower in any well-drained soil in full sun. Space plants 1 foot apart. Mulch lightly in winter. Snakeweed prefers a moist soil or even wet soil, and requires some shade where summers are hot. Space plants 1½ to 2 feet apart. Propagate by seed or by division in early spring.

Landscape uses. Use Himalayan fleece flower in a rock garden or as a ground cover. Snakeweed provides a strong vertical accent in a border.

—

Poor robin's plantain
see *Erigeron*

Poppy see *Papaver;* see *Romneya*

Poppy mallow see *Callirhoe*

Porcupine grass see *Miscanthus*

—

Porteranthus (por-ter-AN-thus)

Bushy plant up to 3 feet tall with clusters of dainty starry flowers in early summer. Zones 5-8.

Selected species and varieties. *P. trifoliatus* (also called *Gillenia trifoliata*), bowman's-root: inch-wide white or pale pink flowers on long reddish stalks. Stems lined with pointed oval compound leaves that have serrated edges.

Growing conditions. Plant bowman's-root in open shade in a moist, well-drained acid soil enriched with organic matter such as peat moss, compost or leaf mold. It will grow in full sun where summers are not excessively hot and dry. Space new plants 1½ to 2 feet apart. Propagate bowman's-root by dividing plants in spring.

Landscape uses. Use bowman's-root in a woodland garden under deciduous trees or plant it as an airy filler in the middle of a sunny border.

Potentilla (po-ten-TILL-a)
Cinquefoil, five-finger

Spring or summer blossoms resembling small roses in white, yellow, pink or shades of red. Leaves are composed of three or five leaflets arranged like the fingers on a hand. Zones 4-9.

Selected species and varieties. *P. atrosanguinea*, Himalayan cinquefoil: inch-wide deep red late-spring and summer flowers on plants 1½ feet tall. Zones 5-8. The variety 'Gibson's Scarlet' has scarlet blossoms. *P. nepalensis*, Nepal cinquefoil: clusters of inch-wide rose red summer flowers on 1½-foot plants with large leaves up to 1 foot across. Zone 5. The cultivar 'Roxana' has rosy salmon blossoms. *P. recta*, sulfur cinquefoil: pale yellow inch-wide summer flowers on 2½-foot plants with hairy gray leaves. Zones 4-7. The variety 'Warrenii' has bright yellow flowers on bushy 2-foot plants. *P. tridentata*, wineleaf cinquefoil: clusters of tiny ¼-inch white flowers from spring through summer above neat foot-high mats of leaves with three shiny dark green leaflets that turn brilliant wine red in fall and are sometimes evergreen. Zones 4-8.

Growing conditions. Plant cinquefoils in sun or light shade in well-drained sandy soil. Sulfur cinquefoil does best in hot, dry spots and can be invasive. The leaves of wineleaf cinquefoil show their best fall color in an acid soil. Allow 2 feet between Himalayan and Nepal cinquefoils and 1 foot for sulfur and wineleaf cinquefoils.

Landscape uses. Use cinquefoils in a border or in a rock garden. Allow sulfur cinquefoil to spread in a naturalistic garden. Plant wineleaf cinquefoil in a rock garden, use it as a ground cover or underplant it with small spring bulbs.

—

Primrose see *Oenothera*;
see *Primula*

—

Primula (PRIM-yew-la)
Primrose

Clusters of flat five-petaled spring flowers of nearly every color, often with lobed, ruffled or fringed edges, borne on leafless stalks above rosettes of oval leaves. Zones 4-10.

Selected species and varieties. *P. helodoxa*, amber primrose: soft yellow inch-wide flowers on stalks up to 3 feet tall. Zones 6-9. *P. japonica*, Japanese primrose: whorls of white, rose or deep lavender inch-wide flowers at intervals on 2-foot stalks. The variety 'Miller's Crimson' has deep red blossoms; 'Postford White' is white. Zones 5-8. *P. × polyantha* hybrids, polyantha primrose: 9-inch stalks with abundant clusters of 1½-inch flowers in white, pastels, deep blue or blood red. Zones 5-10. *P. sieboldii*, Japanese star primrose: stalks up to 1 foot tall with nodding heads of pink, rose, white or purple 2-inch flowers with nearly heart-shaped petals above crinkly oval leaves that disappear in summer. Zones 5-9. *P. vulgaris*, English primrose: single 1½-inch pale yellow spring flowers on stalks 6 inches tall. Zones 4-9.

Growing conditions. Most primroses do best in light shade in constantly moist, well-drained soil enriched with organic matter. Amber primrose and Japanese primrose need boggy soil. Japanese star primrose, which dies down in summer, tolerates both full sun and deep shade. Space plants 1 foot apart. Polyanthus primroses tend to be short-lived and are often treated as annuals. In Zones 9 and 10 they grow well as perennials on the West Coast only. Propagate primroses from seed or by division every three to four years in spring.

Landscape uses. Use Japanese and amber primroses at the edges of ponds and streams or in a bog garden. Use other primroses in a border, a rock garden or a woodland garden with plants such as astilbe and fern.

—

Prunella (pru-NELL-a)
Self-heal

Erect spikes of 1-inch hooded summer blossoms in shades of blue, violet or pink on foot-high stems rising from broad mats of oval leaves. Zones 5-9.

Selected species and varieties. *P. grandiflora*: blue or violet flowers in heavy 12-inch spikes. The creeping stems have inch-long leaves. The variety 'Pink Loveliness' has profuse pink blossoms on 10-inch stalks; 'Rosea' has rosy pink flowers, and 'Rotkappchen' has deep rose flowers.

Growing conditions. Self-heal thrives in full sun or light shade in any well-drained soil. In a warm climate it does better in a moist, shaded spot. Space plants 1 foot apart. Propagate from seed or by division.

Landscape uses. Plant self-heal as a ground cover, or use it in small

POTENTILLA RECTA 'WARRENII'

PRIMULA SIEBOLDII

PRUNELLA GRANDIFLORA 'ROTKAPPCHEN'

PULMONARIA ANGUSTIFOLIA

RANUNCULUS

RHEXIA MARIANA

RODGERSIA PODOPHYLLA

groups at the front of a border or in a woodland garden.

—

Pulmonaria (pul-mo-NAY-ree-a)
Lungwort

Pink, blue or white spring blossoms shaped like small bells, and oval leaves that may be solid dark green or marked with gray. Zones 4-8.

Selected species and varieties. *P. angustifolia,* blue lungwort: dense clusters of pink buds opening to ½-inch flowers that change to bright blue above narrow dark green leaves on 1-foot plants. *P. saccharata,* Bethlehem sage: 1-inch blue or white flowers above gray-spotted leaves on 1- to 1½-foot plants. Foliage is often evergreen. The variety 'Mrs. Moon' has large pink buds and bright blue flowers.

Growing conditions. Blue lungwort and Bethlehem sage flourish in light shade in a rich, moist soil. Space plants 1 to 1½ feet apart. They may wilt in dry weather but rain revives them. Divide plants in fall or grow them from seed.

Landscape uses. Use blue lungwort and Bethlehem sage in groups of three or more at the front of a shady border, as an edging for a path or in drifts among shrubs. The foliage of Bethlehem sage remains handsome until frost or even longer.

—

Purple rock cress see *Aubrieta*
Pussy-toes see *Antennaria*
Queen-of-the-prairie
see *Filipendula*

—

Ranunculus (ra-NUN-kew-lus)
Buttercup

Spring or summer flowers with single or double rows of waxy white, yellow orange, red or pink petals. Foliage is deeply lobed and scalloped. Zones 5-10.

Selected species and varieties. *R. asiaticus* 'Superbissima,' Persian buttercup: 1- to 4-inch semidouble white, yellow, orange, red or pink flowers on stems 1 foot tall in summer. Zones 7-10. *R. repens,* creeping buttercup: single yellow flowers up to an inch wide on 1½- to 2-foot stems above 6-inch mats of foliage in spring. The variety 'Flore Pleno' has profuse double-petaled flowers. Zones 5-8.

Growing conditions. Plant buttercups in sun or light shade. Persian

buttercup needs a well-drained soil; creeping buttercup does best in a moist soil. Allow 1 foot between Persian buttercups and 1½ feet between creeping buttercups. Grow Persian buttercup as an annual north of Zone 7. Divide in spring or fall.

Landscape uses. Use Persian buttercup in a border or in a raised bed that will provide good drainage. Creeping buttercup spreads by runners and makes a good ground cover. It can also be planted in a border if its runners are periodically removed to limit its spread.

—

Red-hot poker see *Kniphofia*
Red valerian see *Centranthus*
Reed grass see *Calamagrostis*

—

Rhexia (REX-ee-a)
Meadow beauty

Clumps of stems lined with pairs of narrow oval pointed leaves and tipped with branching clusters of purple flowers with four broad, squarish petals in summer and fall. Zones 4-9.

Selected species and varieties. *R. mariana,* Maryland meadow beauty: pale purple flowers up to 1½ inches across on stems 1 to 2 feet tall in summer and fall. Zones 5-9. *R. virginica,* deer grass, common meadow beauty: rosy purple flowers 1½ inches across on square stems up to 1½ feet tall in summer. Zones 4-9.

Growing conditions. Maryland meadow beauty and deer grass need full sun and constantly moist or wet acid soil. Space plants 1½ feet apart. Propagate by dividing well-established clumps in spring or fall.

Landscape uses. Use Maryland meadow beauty and deer grass in a boggy or marshy site, in a naturalistic garden or on the sunny bank of a pool or a stream.

—

Rock cress see *Arabis*
Rockfoil see *Saxifraga*

—

Rodgersia (ro-JER-see-a)

Bold leaves, 1 foot or more across, composed of five deeply veined leaflets with jagged edges. Plumy clusters of cream, white or pink flowers in summer. Zones 5-8.

Selected species and varieties. *R. aesculifolia,* fingerleaf rodgersia:

3 to 4 feet tall with crinkly bronze-tinted leaves on long, hairy stalks. Zones 6-8. Tiny creamy white to pink flowers in 1½-foot plumes. *R. podophylla,* bronzeleaf rodgersia: 3 feet tall or more with 1-foot cream-colored plumes and leaves that are bronze in spring and fall, green in summer. Zones 5-8.

Growing conditions. Plant rodgersia in full sun or light shade in constantly moist, even boggy soil, spacing plants 3 feet apart. Without constant moisture, the leaf edges turn brown. Protect from wind, which will tatter leaves. Propagate by division in spring.

Landscape uses. Use rodgersia beside a stream or a pond or in a bog garden, or plant it in a border where it can be kept constantly moist.

Romneya (ROM-ney-a)
California tree poppy, matilija poppy

Late-summer white flowers up to 6 inches across with crinkled satiny petals on branching stems up to 8 feet tall. Zones 7-10.

Selected species and varieties. *R. coulteri:* sweetly fragrant white flowers with a center of prominent yellow stamens. Gray-green foliage deeply divided into several toothed segments.

Growing conditions. California tree poppy blooms best in full sun in a dry, infertile soil, but it can be grown in well-drained soil. Space new plants 3 feet apart. Cut stems back to 6 inches in fall. In Zone 7 California tree poppy must have fast-draining soil and a winter mulch. Propagate from seed.

Landscape uses. Give California tree poppy a sunny site where there is plenty of room for its invasive roots. Use in arrangements, first searing the cut stems over a flame.

Roscoea (ros-KO-ee-a)

Orchid-like hooded summer flowers in a sheath of foot-high lance-shaped leaves. Zones 7-10.

Selected species and varieties. *R. humeana,* Hume roscoea: clusters of two to eight deep violet 4-inch blossoms.

Growing conditions. Plant roscoea in full sun or light shade in a sandy soil enriched with organic matter such as peat moss. Space plants 6 inches apart. Propagate by division.

Landscape uses. Use roscoea in small groups at the front of a border or plant it in a rock garden.

Rose mallow see *Hibiscus*

Rudbeckia (rood-BEK-ee-a)
Coneflower

Masses of large daisy-like yellow flowers with a raised dark cone at the center from midsummer into fall on vigorous, easy-to-grow plants. Zones 4-9.

Selected species and varieties. *R. fulgida,* orange coneflower, black-eyed Susan: flowers 1 to 1½ inches across with orange-yellow petals surrounding a brownish black central cone that is decorative after the petals fall. Height 2 to 3 feet. The variety 'Goldsturm' bears masses of 3- to 4-inch golden yellow flowers on compact 2-foot plants.

Growing conditions. Plant coneflowers in full sun or light shade in almost any moist, well-drained fertile soil. Space plants 1½ to 2 feet apart. They tend to spread quickly and may need to be divided every two years. Propagate by division in early spring or from seed.

Landscape uses. Use coneflowers in the front or middle of a border or plant them in large drifts in a naturalistic meadow garden. Their dark cones provide interest in the garden in late fall and winter.

Rue see *Ruta*
Russian sage see *Perovskia*

Ruta (ROO-ta)
Rue

Shrubby plant grown primarily for its mounds of lacy blue-green foliage. Small yellow flowers in 2-inch clusters in summer. Zones 4-10.

Selected species and varieties. *R. graveolens,* common rue: grows up to 3 feet tall with aromatic ever-green or semi-evergreen leaves finely divided into oval lobes. Foliage causes skin irritation in some people.

Growing conditions. Common rue prefers full sun and a moist, well-drained soil. Space plants 1½ to 2 feet apart. Cut stems back by half every two years in early spring to increase bushiness. To encourage vigorous foliage growth, shear off flower

ROMNEYA COULTERI

ROSCOEA HUMEANA

RUDBECKIA FULGIDA

RUTA GRAVEOLENS

SALVIA FARINACEA

SANGUISORBA CANADENSIS

SANTOLINA CHAMAECYPARISSUS

buds as they appear. Propagate by division in spring. At the northern end of its range, common rue requires a site sheltered from winter winds and winter mulching of its roots.

Landscape uses. Use common rue as a foliage plant in a sunny border. In mild climates, it makes an attractive low evergreen hedge.

—

Sage see *Artemisia;* see *Perovskia;* see *Pulmonaria;* see *Salvia*

St. John's camomile
see *Anthemis*

—

Salvia (SAL-vee-a)
Sage

Spikes of white, blue or purple flowers on plants with hairy or woolly foliage. Zones 4-10.

Selected species and varieties. *S. argentea,* silver salvia: white summer flowers tinged with yellow or pink on branching stems up to 4 feet tall above low mounds of handsome woolly 6-inch gray leaves. Zones 5-8. *S. azurea grandiflora,* Pitcher's salvia: whorls of inch-long deep blue flowers in branched sprays from late summer into fall at the tips of 5-foot hairy stems with narrow gray-green leaves. Zones 6-10. *S. farinacea,* mealy-cup sage: lavender-blue flowers on 4-foot stems with silvery evergreen foliage from late spring to fall. Zones 8-10. The variety 'Blue Bedder' has blue blossoms spotted with white in 8-inch spikes. *S. officinalis,* garden sage: short spikes of white or bluish purple flowers on 2-foot plants with aromatic gray-green hairy, wrinkled leaves. Zones 4-10. *S. × superba* 'East Friesland': intense purple summer blossoms in slender 18-inch spikes on plants 2 feet tall. Zones 5-9.

Growing conditions. Plant salvias in full sun in well-drained to dry average soil, spacing plants 1½ to 2 feet apart. Grow salvias from seed sown in spring or fall. Pitcher's salvia, mealy-cup sage and East Friesland salvia can also be propagated by division in fall or early spring.

Landscape uses. Plant sages in a border, rock garden or herb garden, placing silver salvia and garden sage where their attractive leaves will be an asset after the flowers fade. Use the leaves of garden sage as a flavoring in cooking.

—

Sandwort see *Arenaria*

Sanguisorba (san-gwi-SOR-ba)
Burnet

Creamy white or rose pink summer or fall flowers in dense spikes like bottle brushes, and lacy foliage composed of several paired leaflets. Zones 4-9.

Selected species and varieties. *S. canadensis,* American burnet, great burnet: creamy flowers in dense, stiff spikes up to 8 inches long above bright green leaves in late summer or fall. Plants grow to 3 feet in a garden, up to 6 feet in boggy ground. Zones 4-8. *S. obtusa,* Japanese burnet: 3 to 4 feet tall with 2- to 4-inch arching rose pink flower spikes above gray-green leaves in summer. Zones 6-9.

Growing conditions. Burnets do best in full sun or light shade in moist, well-drained soil enriched with peat moss. Space plants 2 feet apart. Propagate by division in early spring or fall, or from seed.

Landscape uses. Use burnets toward the back of the border, where American burnet is especially valuable for its late-season bloom and Japanese burnet for its pretty combination of rose pink and gray-green. American burnet grows well in wet soil and can be used beside streams or in a bog garden.

—

Santolina (san-to-LEE-na)
Lavender cotton

Low shrubby mounds of aromatic, finely cut evergreen leaves and yellow flower buttons in early summer. Zones 6-10.

Selected species and varieties. *S. chamaecyparissus,* lavender cotton: mounds of silvery foliage up to 2 feet tall and 2 feet wide; ¾-inch flowers on slender 6-inch stalks. Zones 6-9. *S. virens,* green lavender cotton: spreading plants 18 inches tall with narrow toothed green leaves 2 inches long and creamy yellow ½-inch flowers on 10-inch stalks. Zones 7-10.

Growing conditions. Plant lavender cotton in full sun in any well-drained garden soil. It tolerates seaside conditions. Space plants 1½ to 2 feet apart. Cut them back heavily in spring or after flowering to keep them bushy and compact. Provide winter mulch at the northern end of the range. Propagate from seed or by rooting cuttings in spring.

Landscape uses. Use lavender cotton as an edging plant for paths and beds or as a foliage plant in a border or rock garden. It responds well to pruning and can be sheared into formal shapes.

Saponaria (sap-o-NAR-ee-a)

Clusters of pink flowers with five fringed or notched petals in late spring and summer. Zones 4-9.

Selected species and varieties. *S. ocymoides,* rock soapwort: trailing plants 6 to 12 inches high with loose sprays of ½-inch bright pink blossoms in late spring and summer. Small downy semi-evergreen leaves. Zones 4-9. *S. officinalis,* bouncing bet: clusters of pale pink inch-wide blossoms in midsummer on jointed stems up to 3 feet tall. Blossoms open mainly at night. Zones 4-8.

Growing conditions. Plant rock soapwort and bouncing bet in full sun in any well-drained garden soil. Space rock soapworts 1 foot apart and bouncing bets 3 feet apart. Bouncing bet needs staking and can be invasive in moist, fertile soils. Propagate by division in spring or fall, or from seed sown in spring.

Landscape uses. Plant rock soapwort in a rock garden or at the front of an informal border, allow it to spill over the edge of a retaining wall or use it as a ground cover. Use bouncing bet at the middle of a border or in a naturalistic garden.

Saxifraga (sax-IF-ra-ga)
Saxifrage, rockfoil

Loose, airy clusters of pink or white blossoms atop branching stalks up to 2 feet tall rising from rosettes of evergreen leaves in spring and early summer. Zones 6-9.

Selected species and varieties. *S. stolonifera,* strawberry geranium, strawberry saxifrage: ¾-inch white blossoms and round scalloped leaves veined in white with reddish undersides. The variety 'Tricolor' has leaves edged in pink and cream. *S. × urbium,* London Pride saxifrage: ½-inch pink flowers on red stalks and bright green spoon-shaped, toothed leaves.

Growing conditions. Saxifrages do best in light shade and a moist well-drained gravelly soil. Space plants 6 to 9 inches apart. Propagate by division in spring or summer. Strawberry geranium can also be propagated by removing and planting the little offsets that grow at the ends of its numerous runners.

Landscape uses. Use saxifrages in a rock garden, around a shady pool or as a dense evergreen ground cover along the edges of a border.

Scabiosa (skab-i-O-sa)
Pincushion flower

Blue, lavender or white summer flowers up to 3 inches across with centers like tiny pincushions surrounded by ruffly petals. Flower stalks 2½ feet long rising from tufts of narrow light green leaves. Zones 4-10.

Selected species and varieties. *S. caucasica,* pincushion flower: flat blue or white frilled blossoms. The variety 'Clive Greaves' has blue-lavender flowers; 'Miss Willmott' has creamy white blossoms.

Growing conditions. Plant pincushion flower in full sun in a light, moist, well-drained neutral to alkaline soil. In hot areas it does better in light shade; it grows well in Zones 9 and 10 only on the West Coast. Space plants 1½ to 2 feet apart. Remove faded blossoms to encourage flower production. Propagate from seed or by division in spring.

Landscape uses. Since individual plants produce only a few flowers each, group pincushion flowers for more impact in a bed or border. The blossoms make good cut flowers.

Scottish bluebells
see *Campanula*
Sea holly see *Eryngium*
Sea lavender see *Limonium*
Sea pink see *Armeria*

Sedum (SEE-dum)
Stonecrop

Drought-tolerant plant with clusters of tiny star-shaped flowers in yellow, white or pink and plump, fleshy overlapping leaves. Zones 3-10.

Selected species and varieties. *S. aizoon,* Aizoon stonecrop: flat clusters of small yellow spring flowers atop 1½-foot stems with fleshy toothed leaves. The variety 'Auranticum' has flowers of a richer yellow and deeper green leaves on reddish stems. Zones 4-10. *S. ×* 'Autumn Joy': 2-foot plant with toothed gray-green leaves and flat clusters of pink fall flowers that turn rusty red and remain colorful throughout winter. *S. maximum*

SAPONARIA OCYMOIDES

SAXIFRAGA STOLONIFERA

SCABIOSA CAUCASICA 'MISS WILLMOTT'

SEDUM × 'AUTUMN JOY'

141

SILENE VIRGINICA

SISYRINCHIUM STRIATUM

SMILACINA RACEMOSA

'Great Stonecrop': greenish white late-summer flowers on 1- to 2-foot plants with fat oval gray-green leaves. Zones 4-10. *S. maximum* 'Atropurpureum' bears flat reddish flower heads and has maroon-purple leaves. *S.* × 'Ruby Glow': bright pink fall flowers and gray-blue leaves on compact 8-inch plants. Zones 4-10. *S. sieboldii,* Siebold stonecrop, October daphne: small dense heads of bright pink flowers from late summer through fall on low, arching 9-inch stems with blue-gray, nearly triangular leaves. Zones 3-10. *S. spectabile,* showy stonecrop: large dense heads of bright pink fall flowers on 1½-foot stems with 3-inch gray-green leaves. Zones 3-10. The variety 'Brilliant' has bright raspberry pink flowers.

Growing conditions. Sedums flourish in full sun or light shade in any well-drained garden soil. They will grow in poor, dry soils. Space Siebold stonecrops 1 foot apart and the other species and cultivars 1½ to 2 feet apart. Sedums are easily increased by division or by rooting leaf or stem cuttings.

Landscape uses. Use sedums in a rock garden or border, where they are valuable for both flowers and foliage. The maroon leaves of *S. maximum* 'Atropurpureum' make an interesting accent among green-leaved perennials, and the dried flower heads and stems of 'Autumn Joy' sedum are handsome additions to a winter garden. Butterflies flock to sedum flowers.

Self-heal see *Prunella*
Shasta daisy see *Chrysanthemum*
Shooting-star see *Dodecatheon*
Siberian bugloss see *Brunnera*

Silene (sy-LEE-ne)

Low-growing cushions of foliage topped by white, pink or red flowers with five wedge-shaped, lobed petals in summer and fall. Zones 4-9.

Selected species and varieties. *S.* × 'Robin's White Breast': cushiony mounds of silver-gray foliage 8 inches high covered with small bell-shaped white flowers. Zones 6-9. *S. schafta,* moss campion: branched flower stalks up to a foot high bearing pink or rosy purple 1-inch flowers singly or in pairs above a dense 6-inch-high rosette of light green leaves from midsummer through fall. Zones 4-9. *S. virginica,* fire-pink catchfly:

sticky 2-foot branched flower stalks with clusters of inch-wide pink to red flowers rising from flat rosettes of narrow 4-inch evergreen leaves throughout summer. Zones 4-8.

Growing conditions. Plant silenes in full sun or light shade in a light, moist, well-drained soil enriched with compost or leaf mold. Space plants 1 foot apart. Propagate by sowing seed or dividing in spring.

Landscape uses. Use silenes at the front of a sunny border, in a rock garden or at the margins of a woodland garden.

Sisyrinchium (sis-i-RINK-ee-um)
Blue-eyed grass

Dainty blue or yellow flowers, each lasting one day, on stalks up to 2 feet high above clumps of narrow grayish or blue-green leaves. Zones 7-10.

Selected species and varieties. *S. bellum,* California blue-eyed grass: grassy foliage and stalks up to 20 inches tall bearing ¾-inch blue or pale violet flowers with purple veining in spring. Zones 7-10. *S. striatum,* Argentine blue-eyed grass: ¾-inch pale yellow flowers veined with purplish brown on the reverse on 15- to 24-inch stalks in summer. Foot-high clumps of evergreen iris-like foliage. Zones 8-10.

Growing conditions. Plant blue-eyed grasses in full sun in moist, well-drained soil, spacing plants 1 foot apart. Propagate by division in fall or from seed.

Landscape uses. Use blue-eyed grasses in a border or rock garden or plant them at the edge of a walk or terrace. Their vertical flower stalks and foliage combine well with airy, fine-textured perennials such as threadleaf coreopsis or rounded bushy forms like that of peonies.

Slipperwort see *Calceolaria*

Smilacina (smy-la-SY-na)
False Solomon's-seal

Feathery plumes of small, creamy, fragrant late-spring flowers at the tips of arching 3-foot stems with bright green foliage. Zones 4-9.

Selected species and varieties. *S. racemosa:* abundant flowers in 4- to 6-inch branched clusters followed by red fall berries. Broad, pointed oval leaves up to 6 inches long with prominent ribs.

Growing conditions. Plant false Solomon's-seal in partial shade in a moist acid soil enriched with organic matter. Space plants 1 to 1½ feet apart. Propagate by division in spring or from seed sown in fall.

Landscape uses. Combine false Solomon's-seal with spring bulbs and ferns in a shady border or plant it in front of shade-loving shrubs such as rhododendrons.

Snakeroot see *Cimicifuga*
Snakeweed see *Polygonum*
Sneezeweed see *Helenium*
Soapweed see *Yucca*
Soapwort see *Saponaria*

Solidago (sol-i-DAY-go)
Goldenrod

Plumy clusters of tiny flowers in shades of yellow from middle or late summer into fall. Zones 3-10.

Selected species and varieties. *S. canadensis,* Canada goldenrod: branching plumes of shaggy yellow flowers on 5-foot stems with narrow, pointed 6-inch leaves. The variety 'Peter Pan' has canary yellow blossoms on compact plants only 2½ feet tall. Zones 3-10. *S. nemoralis,* gray goldenrod: golden yellow flowers in plumes with curved tips on 2- to 3½-foot plants with gray-green stems and foliage. Zones 4-9. *S. sempervirens,* seaside goldenrod: clusters of yellow flowers on 2- to 5-foot plants with leaves up to 16 inches long. Zones 5-8.

Growing conditions. Plant goldenrods in full sun in any well-drained soil that is not too rich. They also tolerate light shade and considerable dryness. Seaside goldenrod will grow under seashore conditions. Space plants 1½ to 2 feet apart. Propagate by division or from seed. Goldenrods self-sow prolifically and may be invasive, especially in very fertile soil.

Landscape uses. Use goldenrods in a naturalistic meadow garden or group them in a border with other late-season perennials such as asters, Pitcher's salvia or sneezeweed.

Solomon's-seal
see *Polygonatum*
Speedwell see *Veronica*
Spiderwort see *Tradescantia*
Spurge see *Euphorbia*

Stachys (STA-kis)
Betony

Tubular lavender to purple inch-long summer flowers in loose whorls at the tips of stems to 1½ feet tall. Attractive silvery gray oval or green heart-shaped leaves. Zones 4-10.

Selected species and varieties. *S. byzantina,* lamb's-ears, woolly betony: grown primarily for its dense, often evergreen 8-inch-high mats of woolly silver-gray oval leaves 4 to 6 inches long. Inconspicuous pinkish purple blossoms. 'Silver Carpet' is a nonflowering variety. *S. macrantha,* big betony: showy purple flower clusters and dark green wrinkled heart-shaped leaves with scalloped edges. The variety 'Robusta' has deep rosy pink flowers.

Growing conditions. Lamb's-ears requires full sun and a well-drained to dry soil that is not too fertile. Space plants 1 to 1½ feet apart. Big betony grows best in full sun but will tolerate light shade. Grow it in average garden soil that is well-drained, spacing plants 9 to 12 inches apart. Propagate by division or from seed. Betonies grow well in Zones 9 and 10 only on the West Coast.

Landscape uses. Use lamb's-ears as an edging for a perennial border or a rose bed, in clumps in a rock garden, or let it spread to form a silvery ground cover. Plant big betony near the front of a border. Its flowers are good for cutting.

Statice see *Limonium*
Stokes' aster see *Stokesia*

Stokesia (STOKES-ee-a)
Stokes' aster

Flowers up to 5 inches across with lacy fringed petals in white or shades of blue from summer into fall on 1- to 2-foot stalks that rise from a rosette of strap-shaped leathery leaves. Zones 5-10.

Selected species and varieties. *S. laevis:* lavender-blue blossoms with white centers. The rosette of smooth glossy leaves up to 12 inches long is evergreen in most zones. The variety 'Blue Danube' has clear blue flowers, 'Blue Moon' has pale purplish blue flowers, and 'Silver Moon' has white blossoms.

Growing conditions. Stokes' aster should be planted 1½ feet apart in full sun or light shade in a well-drained sandy soil that is not too fer-

SOLIDAGO CANADENSIS 'PETER PAN'

STACHYS BYZANTINA 'SILVER CARPET'

STOKESIA LAEVIS

STYLOPHORUM DIPHYLLUM

TANACETUM VULGARE

THALICTRUM AQUILEGIFOLIUM

tile. Space plants 1½ feet apart. Provide a winter mulch in cold areas. Remove dead flowers to prolong bloom. Propagate by division in early spring or from seed.

Landscape uses. Use Stokes' asters in groups of three or more near the front of a border. The blue-flowered varieties are especially effective with perennials that have gray foliage, such as *Achillea* 'Moonshine' or lavender cotton. Stokes' asters are excellent cut flowers.

Stonecrop see *Sedum*
Strawberry geranium
see *Saxifraga*

Stylophorum (sty-LOFF-or-um)
Celandine poppy

Clusters of two to five deep yellow flowers that last for several weeks in spring. Gray-green deeply lobed leaves. Zones 5-9.

Selected species and varieties. *S. diphyllum:* flowers up to 2 inches across on stalks 1½ feet high are followed by silvery seedpods.

Growing conditions. Plant celandine poppy in light shade in a moist soil rich in organic matter such as leaf mold, peat moss or compost. Space new plants 1 foot apart. Celandine poppy self-sows readily and can also be propagated by division in fall.

Landscape uses. Use celandine poppy in a shaded border with hostas and astilbes. It may also be planted in drifts under deciduous trees in a woodland garden or in small clumps in a rock garden.

Sundrops see *Oenothera*
Sunflower see *Helianthus*
Sweet William see *Dianthus;*
see *Phlox*
Switch grass see *Panicum*

Tanacetum (tan-a-SEE-tum)
Tansy

Clusters of ¼-inch button-like yellow flowers from late summer to early fall above strongly scented ferny foliage. Zones 4-10.

Selected species and varieties. *T. vulgare,* tansy: 2- to 3-foot plant with finely divided leaves. The variety *crispum,* fernleaf tansy, has more

finely cut leaves. Flowers are long-lasting. Leaves can be safely used as a flavoring only in very small quantities; larger amounts are poisonous.

Growing conditions. Tansy thrives in full sun or partial shade in well-drained average soil. In moist, fertile soil it can become invasive. Space plants 1½ to 2 feet apart. Propagate by division or from seed. Tansy does not do well in Zone 10 in Florida.

Landscape uses. Use fernleaf tansy in a perennial border for both its foliage and its flowers or plant it in an ornamental herb garden.

Tansy see *Tanacetum*
Tartarian daisy see *Aster*

Thalictrum (thal-IK-trum)
Meadow rue

Graceful branched clusters of small flowers with tassel-like stamens and petal-like lavender, yellow or pink sepals. Attractive lacy foliage. Zones 4-10.

Selected species and varieties. *T. aquilegifolium,* columbine meadow rue: double lavender blossoms like spiky little balls in late spring and early summer and gray-green lobed foliage on plants up to 3 feet tall. Zones 6-10. *T. delavayi:* airy 1-foot clusters of lavender-pink blossoms with yellow stamens in summer on plants up to 7 feet tall. Zones 4-10. *T. dioicum,* early meadow rue: greenish yellow flowers in spring or early summer on 2-foot plants with ferny foliage. Zones 4-7. *T. rochebrunianum,* lavender mist meadow rue: abundant lavender blossoms from middle or late summer into early fall on 5-foot plants. Zones 6-9. *T. speciosissimum,* dusty meadow rue: fluffy lemon yellow midsummer flowers and feathery blue-green foliage on 5-foot plants. Zones 5-9.

Growing conditions. Plant meadow rues in full sun or light shade in a rich, moist, well-drained soil. Space columbine and early meadow rues 1 to 1½ feet apart and the taller species 1½ to 2 feet apart. The taller kinds may need staking. Propagate by division in spring or from seed. Meadow rues grow well in Zones 9 and 10 on the West Coast only.

Landscape uses. Meadow rues can be used in the front, middle or back of a border, depending on their height. A dark evergreen hedge provides a good backdrop for their finely cut foliage and helps to keep the tall species erect.

Thermopsis (ther-MOP-sis)

Spikes of pealike bright yellow blossoms in late spring or early summer. Zones 4-9.

Selected species and varieties. *T. villosa (T. caroliniana),* Carolina bush pea, Carolina false lupine: 1-inch flowers open from the bottom to the top of dense 12-inch spikes. Grows 3 to 5 feet tall with blue-green leaves composed of three pointed oval leaflets that have smooth upper surfaces and downy undersides.

Growing conditions. Carolina bush pea grows best in full sun and a light, moist, well-drained soil. It can also tolerate light shade, infertile soil and drought. Space plants 3 feet apart. Propagate from cuttings taken in late spring or from seed sown in fall to bloom the following spring.

Landscape uses. Plant Carolina bush pea at the back of a border. It is a good choice for a naturalistic meadow garden or for poor, dry locations where few perennials will grow. Cut spikes for arrangements when the first flowers open.

Thrift see *Armeria*
Tickseed see *Coreopsis*
Toad lily see *Tricyrtis*
Torch lily see *Kniphofia*

Tradescantia
(trad-es-KANT-ee-a)
Spiderwort

Clusters of white, pink, red, blue or purple three-petaled flowers on 2-foot stems rising from clumps of long, narrow straplike leaves. Individual flowers last only a day but open in succession for continuous late-spring or early-summer bloom. Zones 4-9.

Selected species and varieties. *T. × andersoniana:* hybrids 2 feet tall with inch-wide flowers in various shades of white, blue, red and purple. Zones 4-9. 'Zwaanenberg Blue' has large blue blossoms; 'Snowcap' has pure white flowers. *T. hirsuticaulis:* bluish purple flowers on foot-high plants. Dies back in midsummer, then sends up new foliage in fall. Zones 6-9. *T. ohiensis,* Ohio spiderwort: rose or blue flowers on plants 2 to 2½ feet tall. Zones 5-9.

Growing conditions. These spiderworts grow well in light shade and a moist, well-drained soil enriched with organic matter. *T. × andersoniana* and *T. ohiensis* also do well in boggy spots, and *T. hirsuticaulis* tolerates drier soils. All three species can also tolerate full sun. Allow 1 foot of space for *T. hirsuticaulis* and 1½ to 2 feet for the other spiderworts. If their foliage becomes messy and is cut to the ground after flowering, the plants will send up fresh foliage. Propagate by division in spring.

Landscape uses. Spiderworts are well suited to a border beneath deciduous trees, a naturalistic woodland garden or a sunny border. Use *T. × andersoniana* hybrids and *T. ohiensis* in big gardens.

Transvaal daisy see *Gerbera*

Tricyrtis (try-SER-tis)
Toad lily

Spotted, intricately shaped flowers with fuzzy, forked stamens bloom on arching or upright stems 2 to 3 feet tall in fall. Zones 4-8.

Selected species and varieties. *T. formosana stolonifera:* arching stems with shiny dark green leaves. Branching clusters of 1-inch flowers with many purple spots on a pale mauve or whitish background. *T. hirta,* hairy toad lily: clusters of creamy white inch-wide flowers heavily spotted with purple bloom in the joints between the 6-inch hairy leaves and the stems and at the stem tips.

Growing conditions. Toad lilies do best in light shade in a rich, moist, well-drained acid soil. Space plants 1½ to 2 feet apart. Propagate by division.

Landscape uses. Use toad lilies in a border or rock garden for late-season color along with other fall-blooming perennials such as Japanese anemones, choosing sites where its small flowers can be appreciated close up.

Trillium (TRILL-ee-um)

White spring flowers with three petals on 6- to 18-inch stems above a whorl of three broad, oval pointed leaves. Zones 3-8.

Selected species and varieties. *T. grandiflorum,* snow trillium: pure white flowers 3 to 6 inches across turn slowly to pink as they age. The

THERMOPSIS VILLOSA

TRADESCANTIA HIRSUTICAULIS

TRICYRTIS HIRTA

TRILLIUM GRANDIFLORUM

TROLLIUS × CULTORUM

UVULARIA GRANDIFLORA

VALERIANA OFFICINALIS

VERATRUM VIRIDE

deep green leaves are up to 6 inches long and have conspicuous veins and wavy edges.

Growing conditions. Plant trillium in light to deep shade in a moist, well-drained, slightly acid soil enriched with organic matter, spacing plants 1 foot apart. Propagate by division or from seed.

Landscape uses. Plant snow trillium in groups for luminous patches of white in a naturalistic woodland garden or a shady border.

Trollius (TROL-ee-us)
Globeflower

Waxy orange or yellow flowers with curving, overlapping petals in spring and occasionally in summer or fall. Low clumps of deeply cut dark green leaves. Zones 5-10.

Selected species and varieties. *T. europaeus,* common globeflower: lemon yellow 2-inch globe-shaped flowers on stems 2 feet long. The variety 'Superbus' has light yellow flowers and often blooms a second time in late summer and early autumn. *T. ledebourii,* Ledebour globeflower: stems up to 3 feet tall with orange 2½-inch flowers with long petal-like orange stamens filling their centers. The variety 'Golden Queen' has deep orange flowers on 2-foot-long stems. *T. × cultorum:* globe-shaped yellow or orange flowers on 3-foot stems.

Growing conditions. Plant globeflower in partial shade in a constantly moist, even wet soil enriched with organic matter such as peat moss or compost. They can take full sun if the soil is not allowed to dry out. Globeflowers grow naturally in swampy places and will not tolerate dryness. Space plants 1½ feet apart. Propagate by division in fall or from seed. Remove fading flowers to prolong the blooming season. Globeflowers grow well in Zones 9 and 10 on the West Coast only.

Landscape uses. Use globeflowers at the edges of ponds, streams or boggy meadows or in moist, shady wildflower gardens. The yellow of the common globeflower makes a pretty foil for blue or violet flowers, and both globeflowers go well with yellow flowers. The foliage of both species remains attractive all season long. Both species' flowers and foliage are suitable for use in arrangements.

Turtlehead see *Chelone*

Uvularia (yew-vew-LAY-ree-a)
Merrybells

Dainty yellow lily-like flowers dangle from arching leafy stems up to 2 feet tall in spring. Zones 4-9.

Selected species and varieties. *U. grandiflora,* great merrybells: lemon yellow 2-inch flowers. Bright green lance-shaped leaves up to 5 inches long with downy undersides. The leaf bases encircle the stem.

Growing conditions. Great merrybells require partial shade and a moist, well-drained, slightly acid soil enriched with organic matter. Space plants 9 inches apart. Propagate by division in fall.

Landscape uses. Plant big merrybells in large drifts in a woodland garden or in groups in the shaded foreground of a rock garden or border. They can also be used as a ground cover.

Valerian see *Centranthus;* see *Valeriana*

Valeriana (val-ee-ri-AY-na)

Rounded clusters of fragrant white, pink or lavender flowers in summer on stems 3 to 4 feet tall with attractive ferny leaves. Zones 4-10.

Selected species and varieties. *V. officinalis,* common valerian, garden heliotrope: tiny ³⁄₁₆-inch flowers in airy heads above foliage composed of paired pointed leaflets.

Growing conditions. Common valerian thrives in full sun or light shade in almost any soil. Space plants 1½ to 2 feet apart. Propagate from seed or by division in spring or fall.

Landscape uses. Use common valerian in the middle or back of a border for both its flowers and its fragrance. Common valerian's flowers are good for cutting.

Veratrum (vee-RAY-trum)
False hellebore

Clusters of small yellow-green flowers in summer on stout stems 4 to 6 feet tall. Large bright green boldly textured leaves. Zones 3-7.

Selected species and varieties. *V. viride,* American false hellebore: inch-wide flowers in clusters up to 2 feet long. The deeply veined broad, oval leaves are up to a foot long. Plants become dormant and disappear in summer.

Growing conditions. Plant American false hellebore in light shade in a moist, well-drained fertile soil. Space plants 2 feet apart. Division is seldom necessary. Propagate from seed or by division in fall. The plant's leaves, seeds and roots are poisonous.

Landscape uses. Use American false hellebore singly or in small groups as a bold leafy accent in a woodland garden, or plant it at the back of a shady border. Both the flowers and the seed heads that follow can be used in arrangements.

Verbascum (ver-BAS-cum)
Mullein

Branched spikes with densely packed yellow or white blossoms on stems 3 feet tall in summer. Zones 5-9.

Selected species and varieties. *V. chaixii,* Chaix mullein: inch-wide yellow flowers with woolly purple centers. Woolly silvery green leaves up to 6 inches long grow in a mound at the base of plants and become smaller and sparser toward the top of the stem. The cultivar 'Album' has white flowers with purple centers.

Growing conditions. Choose a site in full sun in well-drained sandy soil and space plants 1½ to 2 feet apart. Propagate from seed or root cuttings, or by division.

Landscape uses. Use Chaix mullein as a stately vertical feature in a sunny border. The attractive woolly leaves are semi-evergreen.

Verbena (ver-BEE-na)

Clusters of tiny white, red, blue, pink or lavender flowers all summer long. Zones 6-10.

Selected species and varieties. *V. bonariensis:* tufts of fragrant lilac to purple flowers on wiry 3- to 5-foot stems above dark green wrinkled leaves. Summer into fall. Zones 8-10. *V. canadensis,* rose verbena: balls of ⅝-inch deep-rose blossoms on creeping stems that form dense mats 6 inches tall. Zones 6-10. *V. peruviana,* Peruvian verbena: crimson flowers on 3- to 4-inch-high trailing plants. Zones 8-10. *V. rigida,* vervain: blue to purplish flowers in 3-inch spikes on 1- to 2-foot plants in summer and fall. Zones 8-10. *V. tenuisecta,* moss verbena: purple or violet flowers in 2-inch heads on foot-high plants. Zones 8-10.

Growing conditions. Plant verbenas in full sun in any moist but well-drained soil. *V. bonariensis* will also grow well in poor, dry soils. Space the low-growing verbenas 1 foot apart and allow 2 feet of space for *V. bonariensis.* Propagate from seed sown in spring.

Landscape uses. Plant the low-growing verbenas in a rock garden or as an edging for a sunny border. *V. bonariensis* is most effective in groups of three or more and makes a pretty show with blue-flowered plants or with pale yellow flowers.

Veronica (ver-ON-i-ka)

Small blue, pink or white flowers clustered in 6-inch spikes at the tips of erect stems in summer. Zones 4-10.

Selected species and varieties. *V. grandis holophylla:* blue flowers on 2- to 3-foot plants with thick, shiny dark green leaves. Zones 4-10. The cultivar 'Lavender Charm' has blue-lavender blossoms. *V. spicata,* spike speedwell: pink or blue ¼-inch flowers on 1½-foot plants. Zones 4-8. The variety 'Blue Spires' has blue blossoms on 2-foot plants. 'Icicle' has pure white flowers on 15-inch stems with glossy leaves; 'Minuette' has spikes of clear pink blossoms.

Growing conditions. Veronicas grow well in full sun or light shade in a moist, well-drained soil. Allow 1½ to 2 feet of space for *V. grandis holophylla* and 1 to 1½ feet for spike speedwell. Remove fading spikes to prolong flowering. Propagate by division in fall. *V. grandis holophylla* grows well in Zone 10 only on the West Coast.

Landscape uses. Plant veronicas in a border for a long period of color. Their strong spiky forms make an interesting contrast with airy, fine-textured plants such as Russian sage.

Veronicastrum
(ver-on-i-CAS-trum)
Culver's root

Small white or pink tubular flowers in branching clusters from summer into fall on 4- to 6-foot plants. Zones 3-9.

Selected species and varieties. *V. virginicum:* white flowers in 9-inch spikes that dip gracefully at their tips, and lance-shaped 6-inch leaves arranged in whorls. The variety 'Roseum' has soft pink blossoms.

Growing conditions. Plant Culver's root in full sun or light shade in a moist, well-drained acid soil,

VERBASCUM CHAIXII 'ALBUM'

VERBENA RIGIDA

VERONICA SPICATA

VERONICASTRUM VIRGINICUM

VIOLA ODORATA

YUCCA FILAMENTOSA

spacing plants 1½ to 2 feet apart. Propagate by division in spring or from seed sown in spring or fall.

Landscape uses. Use Culver's root in a wildflower garden or at the back of a border.

—

Vervain see *Verbena*

—

Viola (VY-o-la)
Violet

Flat five-petaled spring flowers in a rainbow of colors. Tufts of heart-shaped toothed leaves on long stems. Zones 3-10.

Selected species and varieties. *V. canadensis,* Canada violet: fragrant white blossoms with yellow centers; the edges and backs of the petals are tinged with lavender. Grows to 1 foot. Zones 4-8. *V. cornuta,* horned violet, tufted pansy: blossoms like small pansy faces in a range of colors from white through apricot, yellow, orange and purple. Grows 8 to 12 inches tall. Zones 5-10. *V. odorata,* sweet violet: fragrant blossoms up to an inch wide in white or violet on 8-inch plants with large heart-shaped leaves. Zones 5-10. The variety 'Alba' has white blossoms; 'Royal Robe' has dark purple flowers. *V. pensylvanica,* smooth yellow violet: yellow blossoms on 6-inch plants. Zones 3-8. *V. striata,* striped violet: white flowers with purplish stripes on plants from 6 to 18 inches tall. Zones 5-7.

Growing conditions. Violets do best in light shade in a moist, well-drained fertile soil. In these conditions they will self-sow and spread. Space horned violets 1½ feet apart and the other species and varieties 8 to 12 inches apart. Propagate from seed or by division. Propagate sweet violet by removing and transplanting the small offsets that grow at the tips of its long runners. Horned and sweet violets grow in Zones 9 and 10 on the West Coast only.

Landscape uses. Use violets in a shaded wildflower garden or as the edging for a border in the shade of taller perennials. Violets also make a pretty ground cover or underplanting for shrubs.

Violet see *Viola*
Virginia bluebells see *Mertensia*
Welsh poppy see *Meconopsis*
Western sage see *Artemisia*
Wild ginger see *Asarum*
Wild indigo see *Baptisia*
Windflower see *Anemone*
Wine-cups see *Callirhoe*
Wormwood see *Artemisia*
Yarrow see *Achillea*
Yellow archangel see *Lamiastrum*

—

Yucca (YUK-ka)

Spikes of fragrant, waxy white bell-shaped flowers in summer over a stiff rosette of sword-shaped evergreen foliage between 2 and 3 feet tall. Yuccas are actually shrubs, but they are used as perennials. Zones 3-10.

Selected species and varieties. *Y. filamentosa,* Adam's-needle: white or cream blossoms 2 inches in diameter in branched 1- to 3-foot spikes on stalks that range up to 10 feet in height. One-inch-wide gray-green leaves with curly white threads along the edges. Zones 5-10. *Y. glauca,* soapweed: greenish white 2-inch flowers in slender spikes above grayish green ½-inch-wide leaves edged in white or pale gray with curly threads. Zones 3-10.

Growing conditions. Yuccas do best in full sun and a fast-draining, sandy soil, but they can also be planted in light shade or in a heavier soil. Space new plants 2 to 3 feet apart. Propagate by digging up and replanting the suckers that spring up around the base.

Landscape uses. The bold form of its leaves makes yucca a dramatic focus year-round and its tall flower spikes stand out in summer. Plant yucca as a specimen, at the corner or end of a bed or border, or next to an architectural feature such as a gate or flight of steps. Yuccas are mainstays of desert gardens.

—

Zebra grass see *Miscanthus*

FURTHER READING

Better Homes and Gardens, Step-by-Step Successful Gardening. Des Moines: Meredith, 1987.

Bloom, Alan, *Perennials for Your Garden.* Chicago: Floraprint U.S.A., 1981.

Bloom, Alan, *Perennials in Island Beds.* London: Faber & Faber, 1977.

Brookes, John, *The Garden Book.* New York: Crown, 1984.

Brooklyn Botanic Garden, *Beds and Borders.* New York: Brooklyn Botanic Garden, 1986.

Brooklyn Botanic Garden, *Perennials and Their Uses.* New York: Brooklyn Botanic Garden, 1985.

Burke, Ken, ed., *All about Perennials.* San Francisco: Ortho Books/Chevron Chemical Company, 1981.

Crockett, James Underwood, *Crockett's Flower Garden.* Boston: Little, Brown, 1981.

Cumming, Roderick W., and Robert E. Lee, *Contemporary Perennials.* New York: Macmillan, 1960.

Douglas, William Lake, et al., *Garden Design.* New York: Simon and Schuster, 1984.

Harper, Pamela, and Fred McGourty, *Perennials: How to Select, Grow & Enjoy.* Tucson, Arizona: HP Books, 1985.

Hay, Roy, ed., *Practical Gardening Encyclopedia.* New York: Van Nostrand Reinhold, 1977.

Hobhouse, Penelope, *Color in Your Garden.* Boston: Little, Brown, 1985.

Hudak, Joseph, *Gardening with Perennials.* Portland, Oregon: Timber Press, 1985.

Jekyll, Gertrude, *A Gardener's Testament.* Woodbridge, Suffolk: Antique Collectors' Club, 1982.

Nehrling, Arno, and Irene Nehrling, *The Picture Book of Perennials.* New York: Hearthside Press, 1964.

Reader's Digest Editors, *Illustrated Guide to Gardening.* Pleasantville, New York: Reader's Digest Association, 1978.

Roper, Lanning, *Hardy Herbaceous Plants.* Harmondsworth, Middlesex: Penguin, 1960.

Rose, Graham, *The Low Maintenance Garden.* New York: Viking Press, 1983.

Schenk, George, *The Complete Shade Gardener.* Boston: Houghton Mifflin, 1984.

Taylor, Norman, *Taylor's Guide to Perennials.* Boston: Houghton Mifflin, 1986.

Thomas, Graham Stuart, *Perennial Garden Plants.* London: J.M. Dent & Sons, 1982.

Wilson, Helen Van Pelt, *Successful Gardening with Perennials.* New York: Doubleday, 1976.

PICTURE CREDITS

The sources for the illustrations in this book are listed below. Cover photograph by Grant Heilman Photography. Watercolor paintings by Nicholas Fasciano except pages 84, 85, 86, 87, 88, 89: Lorraine Moseley Epstein. Maps on pages 78, 79, 81, 83: digitized by Richard Furno, inked by John Drummond.

Frontispiece paintings listed by page number: 6: *Daubigny's Garden* by Vincent van Gogh, courtesy Hiroshima Museum of Art, Hiroshima, Japan. 36: *Poppy* by Georgia O'Keeffe, courtesy Museum of Fine Arts, St. Petersburg, FL. 52: detail from screen *Iris and Bridge* by Ogata Korin, courtesy Metropolitan Museum of Art, New York, NY. Louisa E. McBurney Gift Fund, 1953 (53.7.1).

Photographs in Chapters 1 through 4 from the following sources, listed by page number: 8, 10, 12, 14: Derek Fell. 18: Joanne Pavia. 20: Eric L. Heyer, Grant Heilman Photography. 22: Pamela Harper. 26: Pamela Zilly. 28: Felice Frankel. 30: Bob Grant. 34: Ken Druse, courtesy Oehme, van Sweden & Associates Inc. 38: Andy Alonso. 40: Saxon Holt. 42: Thomas Eltzroth. 44: Margaret Hensel. 46: Walter Chandoha. 48: Felice Frankel. 50: Bob Grant. 54: Saxon Holt. 56: Walter Chandoha. 58: Thomas Eltzroth. 62: Bethany Eden Jacobson. 64: Ann Reilly. 68: Pamela Harper. 70: Derek Fell. 72: Wayne Ambler.

Photographs in the Dictionary of Perennials by Pamela Harper, except where listed by page and numbered from top to bottom. Page 94, 1, 95, 1, 96, 2: Saxon Holt. 98, 3: Derek Fell. 99, 1: Ann Reilly. 102, 3: Paul Kingsley. 103, 3: Bob Grant. 106, 2: Cole Burrell. 107, 1: Robert Lyons. 107, 3: Derek Fell. 109, 3: Steven Still. 109, 4, 110, 1: Horticultural Photography, Corvallis, OR. 111, 3: Cole Burrell. 113, 3: Steven Still. 114, 3: Ann Reilly. 115, 2, 117, 1: Cole Burrell. 120, 1: James van Sweden. 121, 1: Grant Heilman Photography. 122, 1: Horticultural Photography, Corvallis, OR.. 123, 4: Cole Burrell. 124, 2: Saxon Holt. 125, 3: Derek Fell. 126, 2: Robert Lyons/Color Advantage. 127, 1, 4, 129, 2, : Derek Fell. 130, 3: Joanne Pavia. 131, 2: Horticultural Photography, Corvallis, OR. 132, 2: Steven Still. 133, 1: Robert Lyons/Color Advantage. 133, 3: Steven Still. 134, 2: Derek Fell. 135, 2: Saxon Holt. 136, 1: Ann Reilly. 136, 3: Saxon Holt. 138, 2: Horticultural Photography, Corvallis, OR. 138, 4: Steven Still. 139, 1: Derek Fell. 139, 4: Grant Heilman Photography. 140, 1: Derek Fell. 142, 1: Cole Burrell. 143, 1: Steven Still. 144, 1: Cole Burrell. 144, 2, 145, 3: Saxon Holt. 146, 3: Steven Still. 146, 4: Cole Burrell. 147, 4: Steven Still.

ACKNOWLEDGMENTS

The index for this book was prepared by Lynne R. Hobbs. The editors also wish to thank: Wayne S. Ambler, Ambler's Flower Farm, Ashland, Virginia; Lynn Batdorf, U.S. National Arboretum, Washington, D.C.; Alison Bell, Washington, D.C.; Kurt Bluemel, Kurt Bluemel, Inc., Baldwin, Maryland; Jeffrey Burns, Robbinsdale Farm & Garden, Robbinsdale Minnesota; Allen Bush, Holbrook Farm and Nursery, Fletcher, North Carolina; Chris Tucker Haggerty, Alexandria, Virginia; Kenneth E. Hancock, Annandale, Virginia; Peggy Hedgpeth, Mrs. McGregor's Garden Shop, Arlington, Virginia; Ginny Hunt, Western Hill Nursery, Occidental, California; Diane Letourneau, Mrs. McGregor's Garden Shop, Arlington, Virginia; James A. McKenney, Potomac Nursery and Flower Center, Potomac, Maryland; Ramah Overton, U.S. Botanical Garden, Washington, D.C.; Jayne E. Rohrich, Alexandria, Virginia; Muchtar Salzmann, University of California Cooperative Extension, Santa Rosa, California; Nancy Schuhmann, Mrs. McGregor's Garden Shop, Arlington, Virginia; Brooke Stoddard, Alexandria, Virginia; Jo Thomson, Alexandria, Virginia; Rebecca Zastrow, Brookside Gardens, Wheaton, Maryland.

INDEX

Numerals in italics indicate an illustration of the subject mentioned.

Ground pink, in scree gardens, 29
Growth buds, 20. *See also* Eyes
Gypsophila, 111. See also Baby's-breath

H

Hardy ageratum. *See Eupatorium*
Hardy gloxinia. *See Incarvillea*
Hedychium, 118-119
Helenium, 119. See also Sneezeweed
Helianthus, 119. See also Sunflower
Helichrysum, 119
Helictotrichon, 120
Heliopsis, 120. See also False sunflower
Heliotrope. *See Valeriana*
Hellebore. *See Helleborus; Veratrum*
Helleborus, 120. See also Lenten rose
Hemerocallis, 121. See also Daylily
Heuchera, 121. See also Coralbells
Heucherella, 121-122
Hibiscus, 122
Hickory, and shade-tolerant plants, 26
Hollyhock, staking of, 37. *See also Alcea*
Horse mint. *See Monarda*
Hosta, 122; adaptability to shade, 10, *26;* for fragrance, 88; for low-maintenance garden, 88; from mail-order nurseries, *42*
Hound's tongue. *See Cynoglossum*
Houttuynia, 122-123; adaptability to shade, 10
Humus, 12, 27; use in transplanting, 11, 41

I

Iberis, 123. See also Candytuft
Incarvillea, 123
Indigofera, 123
Inula, 123
Iris, 124; for cut flowers, 89; for fragrance, 88; in island beds, *20;* longevity of, 64; for orange or white monochromatic garden, 89. *See also* Bearded iris
Irish moss. *See Arenaria*
Island beds, 7, *20*-21
Italian bugloss, for blue and lavender monochromatic garden, 89. *See also Anchusa*

J

Jack-in-the-pulpit. *See Arisaema*
Jacob's-ladder. *See Polemonium*
Japanese Solomon's-seal. *See Polygonatum*
Joe-Pye weed. *See Eupatorium*

K

Kangaroo-paw. *See Anigozanthus*
Kniphofia, 124-125. *See also* Red-hot poker

L

Lady's-mantle. *See Alchemilla*
Ladybells. *See Adenophora*
Lamb's-ears, in borders, 14. *See also Stachys*
Lamiastrum, 125
Lamium, 125
Larkspur. *See Delphinium*
Lavandula, 125-126. *See also* Lavender
Lavender: to attract butterflies, 89; for blue and lavender monochromatic garden, 89; for cut flowers, 89; for fragrance, 88. *See also La-vandula*
Lavender cotton. *See Santolina*
Leadwort. *See Ceratostigma*
Leaf-shredding machine, *45. See also* Mulch; Shredded leaves
Lenten rose, adaptability to shade, 10, 26. *See also Helleborus*
Leontopodium, 126
Leopard's-bane, for gold and yellow monochromatic garden, 89. *See also Doronicum*
Leopard plant. *See Ligularia*
Liatris, 126. See also Gay-feather
Light shade, plants adaptable to, 10-11. *See also* Shade
Ligularia, 126-127
Lily of the Nile. *See Agapanthus*
Lilyturf. *See Liriope*
Lime, to correct pH level of soil, 39
Limestone: to correct pH level of soil, 12; in scree gardens, 28
Limonium, 127. See also Statice
Linum, 127
Liriope, 127
Lobelia, 127-128. *See also* Cardinal flower
Loosestrife, in borders, *18. See also Lysimachia; Lythrum*
Low-maintenance plants, 88
Lungwort. *See Pulmonaria*
Lupine, for cut flowers, 89; in island beds, *20;* staking of, 48. *See also Lupinus*
Lupinus, 128. See also Lupine
Lychnis, 128; for orange monochromatic garden, 89
Lysimachia, 128-129. *See also* Loosestrife
Lythrum, 129; for low-maintenance garden, 88. *See also* Loosestrife

M

Macleaya, 129
Mail-order nurseries, 42-43
Maintenance calendar, by zones and months, *80*-83
Mallow. *See Malva*
Maltese cross. *See Lychnis*
Malva, 129

Maple leaves, alkalinity of, 51
Marguerite. *See Anthemis; Felicia*
Marjoram. *See Origanum*
Marsh marigold. *See Caltha*
Matilija poppy. *See Romneya*
Meadow beauty. *See Rhexia*
Meadow rue. *See Thalictrum*
Meadowsweet. *See Filipendula*
Mealy-cup sage. *See Salvia*
Meconopsis, 130
Medium shade, plants adaptable to, 10-11. *See also* Shade
Merrybells. *See Uvularia*
Mertensia, 130
Metal planters, 30
Michaelmas daisy. *See Aster*
Microclimate, 78
Milkweed. *See Asclepias*
Mimulus, 130
Miscanthus, 130-131
Missouri primrose, in scree gardens, 29. *See also Oenothera*
Mist flower, for blue and lavender monochromatic garden, 89. *See also Eupatorium*
Monarda, 131. See also Bee balm
Monkey flower. *See Mimulus*
Monkshood: for blue and lavender monochromatic garden, 89; for low-maintenance garden, 88. *See also Aconitum*
Monochromatic garden, 89
Montbretia. *See Crocosmia*
Moss campion. *See Silene*
Mulching, 44, *45;* for winter protection, 50
Mullein. *See Verbascum*
Mullein pink. *See Lychnis*
Myosotis, 131. See also Forget-me-not

N

Nepeta, 131-132. *See also* Catmint
New Zealand flax. *See Phormium*
Nippon daisy. *See Chrysanthemum*
Nitrogen, percentage of in fertilizer, 44

O

Oak, and shade-tolerant plants, 26
Oak leaves, acidity of, 51
Obedient plant. *See Dracocephalum*
October daphne. *See Sedum*
Odd-number grouping of plants, 18
Oenothera, 132. See also Evening primrose; Missouri primrose; Primrose
Organic compost, to correct pH level of soil, 12
Oriental poppy, and root cuttings, *70. See also Papaver*
Origanum, 132

REDEFINITION

Senior Editors	Anne Horan, Robert G. Mason
Design Director	Robert Barkin
Designer	Edwina Smith
Illustration	Nicholas Fasciano
Design Assistant	Sue Pratt
Pictures	Deborah Thornton
Production Editor	Anthony K. Pordes
Research	Gail Prensky, Susan Stuck, Mary Yee
Text Editors	Sarah Brash, Sharon Cygan
Writers	Gerald Jonas, Bonnie Kreitler, Ann Reilly, David S. Thomson
Business Manager	Catherine M. Chase
PRESIDENT	Edward Brash

THE CONSULTANTS

C. Colston Burrell is Curator of Plant Collections at the Minnesota Landscape Arboretum, part of the University of Minnesota, where he oversees the arboretum's collections and develops regional interest in the horticulture of the upper Midwest. He was formerly Curator of Native Plant Collections at the National Arboretum in Washington, D.C. He is the author of publications about ferns and wildflowers.

Sarah E. Broley is a landscape designer in Washington, D.C. She has redesigned the grounds for a number of public and private historic properties in Virginia and Kentucky. She has taught garden design at George Washington University.

Time-Life Books Inc.
is a wholly owned subsidiary of

TIME INCORPORATED

FOUNDER	Henry R. Luce 1898-1967
Editor-in-Chief	Jason McManus
Chairman and Chief Executive Officer	J. Richard Munro
President and Chief Operating Officer	N. J. Nicholas Jr.
Editorial Director	Ray Cave
Executive Vice President, Books	Kelso F. Sutton
Vice President, Books	George Artandi

TIME-LIFE BOOKS INC.

EDITOR	George Constable
Executive Editor	Ellen Phillips
Director of Design	Louis Klein
Director of Editorial Resources	Phyllis K. Wise
Editorial Board	Russell B. Adams Jr., Dale M. Brown, Roberta Conlan, Thomas H. Flaherty, Lee Hassig, Donia Ann Steele, Rosalind Stubenberg, Kit van Tulleken, Henry Woodhead
Director of Photography and Research	John Conrad Weiser
PRESIDENT	Christopher T. Linen
Chief Operating Officer	John M. Fahey Jr.
Senior Vice President	James L. Mercer
Vice Presidents	Stephen L. Bair, Ralph J. Cuomo, Neal Goff, Stephen L. Goldstein, Juanita T. James, Hallett Johnson III, Carol Kaplan, Susan J. Maruyama, Robert H. Smith, Paul R. Stewart, Joseph J. Ward
Director of Production Services	Robert J. Passantino
	Editorial Operations
Copy Chief	Diane Ullius
Production	Celia Beattie
Library	Louise D. Forstall
Correspondents	Elisabeth Kraemer-Singh (Bonn), Maria Vincenza Aloisi (Paris), Ann Natanson (Rome)

Library of Congress Cataloging-in-Publication Data
Perennials.
   (The Time-Life gardener's guide)
   Bibliography: p.
   Includes index.
   1. Perennials.
I. Time-Life Books. II. Series.
SB434.P473 1988   635.9'32   87-26700
ISBN 0-8094-6604-X
ISBN 0-8094-6605-8 (lsb)

Time-Life Books Inc. offers a wide range of fine recordings, including a *Rock 'n' Roll Era* series. For subscription information, call 1-800-621-7026, or write Time-Life Music, P.O. Box C-32068, Richmond, Virginia 23261-2068.